PRAISE FOR GAMBIT

For anyone curious about the intersection of critical thought and artistic feeling in contemporary writing from Africa, *Gambit* offers an opening. Gathered here are nine disparate voices, talking fact and weaving fiction. A gambit, as the title announces, that pays.

A. Igoni Barrett,
Love Is Power, or Something Like That

A brilliant collection. The interviews are thoughtful and show the commitment of these writers to their craft. The stories educate and entertain. Another generation of African writers announces itself boldly.

Helon Habila,
Oil on Water; ed. of *The Granta Book of the African Short Story*

Gambit takes what we think we know of "African" writing and spins it on its head. Welcome to some of the boldest new talent from the vast, complex, and layered continent that is Africa. Expect provocation, delight, and pure reading pleasure.

Maaza Mengiste,
Beneath the Lion's Gaze

This is a generous book. It is impressive in the diversity and range of its conversations; the stories are some of the best discoveries in contemporary African writing I have made this year. The writers are to be congratulated on so eloquently chronicling our stories.

Chika Unigwe,
Night Dancer

GAMBIT

NEWER AFRICAN WRITING

edited by

Emmanuel Iduma

Shaun Randol

Many Many thanks Anthony e onebs
05. 03. 2014

Anthony,
Thanks so much
for your support. I am
humbled.

S

THE MANTLE

New York

Printed in the United States of America at McNally Jackson Books, 52 Prince Street, New York, NY 10012.

First Edition

ISBN 978-1-938022-88-3

ACKNOWLEDGMENTS

The journey toward *Gambit* would have been rougher without the editorial, logistical, and emotional support of many. For your contributions, we are humble and grateful. We would like to extend a special thanks to Kyawswar Thant (a.k.a. KST), who designed our cover.

We also want to thank everyone who helped make the *Gambit* fundraiser on Indiegogo a success. This book would not be possible without the valuable contributions of so many, including El Anatsui, Anonymous, Anthony Campusano, Wil Carter, Lucinda Duddy, George Garland, Eric Garrison, Lisa Guaqueta, Krista Looper, Sebastian Milardo, Jake Perry, Kalpana Raina, Kavitha Rajagopalan, Anne V. Smith, David Levi Strauss, Chaw Ei Thein, Andy Thornton, Aung Zaw Tun, and many more.

All the contributors to this book were committed to this project from the start. We are grateful for their cooperation, patience, and vision.

With gratitude,
Emmanuel and Shaun

TABLE OF CONTENTS

GAMBIT

NEWER AFRICAN WRITING

A NECESSARY PROJECT

Shaun Randol

Pairing interviews with some of Africa's emerging writers alongside their original short stories makes *Gambit: Newer African Writing* unique among so-called "world literature." Literature's ability to bridge cultural divides is without question, but great fiction doesn't emerge in a vacuum. Knowing the writers and the cultures from where that fiction arises deepens our appreciation of the text and enriches our understanding of the social and political context surrounding the creation of that story. With short stories, *Gambit* introduces new fiction from Africa's next generation of writers. With interviews, the people, histories, and environments behind those tales are brought to life.

Gambit features nine writers from across the African continent. Each writer is interviewed in-depth about their background, writing process, literary inspirations and aspirations, and ideas about the global literary scene. Each interview is followed by an original short story. If you count the novelist, *Gambit* co-editor and interviewer Emmanuel Iduma—and I most certainly do— that's ten new African voices represented in these pages. The writers—three women and seven men—hail from Botswana, Malawi, Nigeria, Somalia, and Zimbabwe and represent a cross-section of continental experiences.

"I noticed the blatant silence when it came to our own voices— African voices—on issues, and felt it was necessary to contribute," said *Gambit* contributor Dango Mkandawire in an interview for Malawi's *Nyasa Times* newspaper. He continues:

There are different styles and focuses in the pieces and just to be a part of something that broad and involving is very exciting for me personally. Also, I would hope that because I have somehow filtered through, there is some Malawian somewhere, gifted and imaginative, our own slumbering Balzac, so to speak, who will dare to dream and start writing; to begin documenting history through fiction; to show us the face of the zeitgeist.

The very title of this anthology speaks to its possibilities. In rhetoric, a gambit is a remark intended to open a conversation. In chess, a gambit is an opening move, one that takes risks and accepts initial setbacks to establish a long-term winning strategy. Both of these definitions apply to this book. *Gambit* aims to open up the conversation about what is (or is not) African writing, who or what African writers are and represent, and how this conversation can broaden the reader's understanding of places and people so foreign to their own experiences. Further, *Gambit* seeks to challenge the publishing industry's assumptions of quality African and world literature and to encourage similar publishing efforts elsewhere.

What a gambit is not—and therefore what *Gambit* is not—is a wager. This is not a gamble. We are not rolling the dice hoping for an uncertain outcome. We are sure our goals are worthy. The book's very existence encourages us—and hopefully the reader—to expand concepts of and relationships with the fluctuating landscapes of literary minds near and far.

From the beginning, *Gambit* has been a shoestring project, financed more with can-do attitude than money. A sense that we were participating in a cause greater than the book itself kept the effort moving, inch by inch, toward realization. To pull it off, we required the belief of the participating writers, the dedication of voluntary guides, the assistance of close friends, and crowd-sourced financing of a modest sum. We could not have done it otherwise.

Gambit is published by *The Mantle* (www.mantlethought.org), an online forum where the next generation of critics, artists, and essayists worldwide participate in critical discourse on politics, culture, and philosophy. The website initially published the interviews found in this book. From there the series evolved to this unique nonfiction-fiction anthology. *Gambit* fulfills the mission of *The Mantle,* insomuch that voices not typically given the chance to be heard are elevated.

Emmanuel and I had similar and different reasons for seeing this project through. (I won't speak for him; you can read his ideas in the next essay.) Common between us is the desire to disrupt the current publishing landscape, especially the Western-centric model of recognizing literary talent. Coming from the Midwest, where a rich literary tradition ekes out a living in derided "flyover country," I am fully aware of and frustrated by the New York literati's elite provincialism, judgments, and aesthetics. (The irony is not lost on me that I am currently based in Queens.) Much has been said about this topic, so I will not rehash the arguments here.

Our peripheral positions in the global literary landscape embolden our determination to disrupt a publishing status quo, and those positions also encourage our socio-political aspirations. For me, the project has always been about expanding Western comprehensions of worlds outside our own and to invite new voices into long-running conversations on arts, politics, and society. In this Information Age, when cultural multitudes are available literally at our fingertips, mutual understanding and respect has never been more imperative. If we are to live together in peace, we must first understand who and what makes up our earthly neighborhood.

Technology and innovations in transportation have made the world smaller, for better and for worse. When the American government launches a drone attack in Pakistan, a half a world away, the repercussions are soon felt in the United States. No longer can acts of aggression be perpetuated without some sort of blowback. On the side of beauty, though, are those happy moments when the world can share in the insane fun of a Korean pop singer's parody of life in a wealthy district of Seoul. This anthology was made possible by the same technology that allows news, information, and entertainment—good and bad—to be shared by a global audience. The results represent the beautiful side of globalization. *Gambit*, then, is a humble gesture toward betterment of our world made through informing and storytelling. If we can better understand "them," then perhaps we'll be more inclined toward cultural—not military—engagement.

Though my co-editor and I had somewhat different reasons for embarking on this ambitious project, the effort succeeded because the paths led to the same literary destination. That's a unique process, even rare. The results speak for themselves because, ultimately, we encourage the writers to speak for themselves.

March 23, 2014
Queens, New York City

WHAT IS NEWER AFRICAN WRITING?

Emmanuel Iduma

In late 2011, after being commissioned to blog about "African Letters" on *The Mantle,* I was drawn to the idea that there would be no other way to present the thoughts of emerging African writers than by engaging them in conversations about their writing, their craft, and what I considered the politics of visibility. As the conversations progressed in 2012, I realized that in almost every case the writers had developed a firm sense of purpose, a commitment to craft, and a willingness to engage with the increasingly problematic questions surrounding contemporary writing in Africa.

At the time much had already been said about the dangers of a single African story, and it did not interest me to perpetuate the argument. I hoped that the conversations would account for what it meant to work as largely invisible writers within the continent, without book contracts, but edging toward renown. I reached out to writers I knew in person, and sometimes our previous relationship formed the basis for the ensuing conversations. In the time since the conversations appeared online and now that they have been collected in this book, a number of changes have occurred in the fledgling careers of these writers. Some of the writers have published their first books, some have been nominated for awards, and there are others who have recently signed publishing contracts. The intervening time has caused me to reflect deeply, as the title of this book suggests, on what could be "newer" about African writing.

By formulating "newer" I affirm that the new is still being unraveled. I play into the notion that there was a renewed interest in African writing sometime in the early 2000s, the founding of the Caine Prize in 2001 possibly instigating this resurgent curiosity. As African writers began to receive acclaim from Western literary institutions, and given the authority of these institutions, territories were delineated—on one side were writers established by virtue of the acclaim they received and on the other were writers yet unrecognized. This second group I termed "emerging."

"Emerging" is problematic because it suggests there is a standard of success that writers tagged as such aim to attain. It's almost predictable what manner of success the writer could have: to be shortlisted for the Caine Prize and then to sign a contract with a reputable London or New York-based agency, then another contract with a publisher who would buy the rights for everywhere except Africa. When the book is released it is praised by acclaimed critics. Then perhaps another major award: the Man Booker Prize or the Orange Prize. Nothing, of course, is wrong with recognition in this manner, and drawing attention to how this is a potential stereotype for success does not begrudge the writers of their achievements. Regardless, I speculate that there are alternative ways to draw attention to and affirm the visibility of writers who are based in their home countries—this is the central impulse of my work with *Gambit*.

That most of the writers whose work receives international acclaim live and teach outside the continent is indicative of how visibility in the literary world works. (Certainly, this quandary is not particular to contemporary African writing. In his polemic

MFA vs NYC (n+1, 2014), editor Chad Harbach derides New York City's centrality in the American literary landscape.)

What is the politics of visibility in relation to "home-based" African writing? In general, this inquiry has something to do with how books are distributed and the socioeconomic character of an African country's readership. It is hardly questionable, from a market point of view, that to be published while based at home is to operate from the fringes of the literary world's acclaim.

Gambit becomes a way to identify with writing that is happening mostly within the continent. To write at home appears not only possible, but timely, if a "newer" order is to be affirmed. How timely? Well, timely to the extent that the idea of the West as a center, or as a site for guaranteed success, can be debunked. Sure, the publishing structure works better in New York and London, but the agents and publishers in those cities cannot be the definitive arbiters of excellent African writing.

In thinking about "arbiters," it is essential to point out how, if publishers outside the continent determine visibility, it would not be long before writers pander to mimetic templates. Gilles Deleuze forewarned against this. In a conversation with Antoine Dulaure and Charles Parnet in October 1985 (*L'Autre Journal*: 8), the philosopher warned: "We may congratulate ourselves on the quantitative increase in books, and larger print runs—but young writers will end up molded in a literary space that leaves them no possibility of creating anything." He goes on to speak about the "monstrosity of a standard novel," the kind of novels that set out to imitate:

What gets imitated is always itself a copy. Imitators imitate one another, and that's how they proliferated and give the impression that they're improving on their model, because they know how it's done, they know the answers.

It is arguably the same impulse that necessitated Helon Habila's invective, in a review of NoViolet Bulawayo's *We Need New Names* published on the Guardian UK website, leveled against a "Caine-Prize aesthetic:"

> ...that has emerged in a vacuum created by the judges and the publishers and agents over the years, and which has begun to perpetuate itself. Writing is an incestuous business: style feeds on style, especially if that particular style has proven itself capable of winning prizes and book deals and celebrity.

It is necessary to remain wary of declamations against style, or the choice of subject matter, yet a dialogue between Delueze and Habila is set up to emphasize the need to pay attention to writing on the African continent that happens outside the margin of the Western marketing schema. In this specific context, I refuse to believe we have found exhaustive answers to what successful literature from Africa is, or can be. Unless we imagine a kind of success that is inclusive of a writing practice that becomes fecund in a writer's home country, literature will merely become a game show, a "product" and not a project, as the editors of *n+1* write in their state-of-global-literature essay "World Lite."

Already we know that this game show can be thwarted. As an exemplar, recall what *Kwani?* achieved in 2013 with its one-off manuscript prize. Receiving almost 200 entries from around the continent, a long list of 30 was selected, then a shortlist of 7, and then 3 winners. The sentiment *Gambit* shares with *Kwani?* is one of a publishing project that prefigures a schema of recognition, one that operates within the periphery (the outside boundary) and makes a gesture not informed by renown.

The writers we present here were considered for something other than market metrics. The game show we attempt to contravene is one that thrives on the immediacy of acclaim, one that judges a writer's impact by the fervor on social media.

Book publishing in Africa is admittedly a tough sector. A glaring evidence of this is the nature of how this book was published—by an independent publisher in New York, crowd-funded by supporters mostly based in America. This fact confirms my earlier worry that home-based writers are being molded in a literary space that leaves them no possibility of creating anything. Regardless, I dare to insist that we can carry on with Delueze's insight: "A creator who isn't grabbed around the throat by a set of impossibilities is no creator." This book, as immodest as this might sound, results from being grabbed around the throat, by a number of impossibilities. It is a kind of pushing-through that negates the standard procedure of publishing books out of, or in relation to, Africa. ("Africa" as a parenthetical term, and not a closed-off box, as the word for a continent, and a word invoked to qualify all our diversities.)

Gambit is pushing-through in another sense: the interviews function as the gestalt of the writers' sensibilities. We are reminded that one's critical outlook is a toolbox that helps shape what is created (isn't writing making?), and how that is done. In these interviews we are confronted with virtues, central to the writing impulse, but peculiar to the individual writer. The writers invite us to agree to a tacit understanding of the world they create, the world they are creating in, and the guideposts they have appropriated for themselves in the process. The writer Guy Davenport refers to this as "the writer's code of manners."

When Chinua Achebe visited the University of Texas in 1969, he was asked if he was doing any form of writing given the responsibilities that came with his involvement with the Biafran secessionist movement. His response:

> I started a novel just before the war which seemed to me at the time terribly important – I already had the idea for it as far back as '66 – but I finally gave it up because it later seemed to me completely unimportant.

And so if *Gambit* is a gesture, a "code of manners," it functions equally as a gift system. It receives the tradition instituted by Achebe and his generation of writers, a tradition of critical thought, one that spent time with things (such as identity and political engagement) in order to name them; a tradition that did not attend to the unimportant.

Again Delueze, in that 1985 conversation, says:

> What's really terrible isn't having to cross a desert once you're old and patient enough, but for young writers to be born in a desert, because they're then in danger of seeing their efforts come to nothing before they even get going. And yet, and yet, it's impossible for the new race of writers, already preparing their work and their styles, not to be born.

The question that arises from Delueze's prescient metaphor of young writers being born in a desert is: how are writers born? Or, how are newer writers born? The starting point is always to recognize that without the current system of validation for African writers, the alternative scheme I propose would be baseless. I cannot purport to know the answers to the these questions, and it is delusional to think that there is a perfect model waiting to be conjured into reality; it should not be presumptuous to hope there's a way to imagine ourselves out of a system of validation that rarely presents alternatives, a system that says the efforts of writers would come to nothing if their work is not appropriated at the center of global publishing. *Gambit* is certainly not a well-formed alternative (of the nine writers featured, five are Nigerian, four are based in the diaspora, none is from North Africa, etc.) Yet, if modesty will permit, I present this as one step on a long, narrow road.

March 23, 2014
Manhattan, New York City

ABDUL ADAN

EMMANUEL IDUMA: Do we say that there is a hyphen between the words "home" and "identity"? And that writers such as yourself walk within that hyphen trying to understand what is home, how home shifts, how home never remains the same, perhaps how no place is home? I ask this to understand how your "Somalification," to use your word, might *not* have been interrupted by schooling and living elsewhere.

ABDUL ADAN: I have been struggling with this for a while, this intersection between "home" and "identity," especially since I started to write. I have pondered many a night on how to introduce myself to readers. It isn't that I didn't or don't have a home. It's my identity that, as you speculated, has continued to shift and still does. I am from the Gedo region, a large piece of land that lies in western Somalia and extends into parts of north eastern Kenya. But the people who were on the Kenyan side weren't as Somali by manners as those in Somalia. They were Kenyanized Somalis. So, in a way, my Somali-ness has always had interferences one way or another. I am used to these interferences. Sometimes when I think of how much non-Somaliness comes through me, I feel I could use some Somalification myself.

EI: I am drawn, infinitely, even obsessively, to making words "free" and "rhythmic." Is this a necessity? For instance, I have read of postcolonial attempts to wrest the colonial language, divest it of all its imperial configurations. What do you seek to do with the English language?

AA: I intend to use the English language in the way that suits my craft best. If that means creating a word out of nowhere, so be it. But, at all times, I take clarity into account. The average intelligent reader must be able to understand the word without external reference. I do not think of the English language as belonging to the imperialists anymore; I think of it as mine, a tool among many tools for me. In twisting and corrupting it to suit my needs, I am in no way motivated by its history as a colonial language. I yearn to make it more of mine each day. It resists me without doubt. It's a jealous language. It's aware of the other languages that are desperately competing for my attention. My role is to coax it, strip it of its defenses, assure it, so I can use it better each time, with minimum effort.

EI: Yet, I should point out that, to use a certain analogy, you can shake the tree but the roots still remain planted. In this sense, you might wish to "corrupt" and twist the English language, but the words—the letters that are your tools—cannot be taken apart from their colonial history. For even if we dare to define the language as what it *is* for us, we cannot escape what it *was*, and how that past implicates itself in present usage. You get my drift?

AA: I understand what you mean. True, it came to us from elsewhere. But to me, its history means little when it comes to its usage in my art. The owners brought it to me. My role is to assimilate it into my work, and, like I said before, make it more of mine. I aim to use it with a degree of authority at some point. The more twisting that goes into it, the more my authority over it. Where I find myself is where I work from. The past has done its work, shaping me into who I am. I feel no need to prod the history of the English language in Africa, or how that affects the African usage of it presently.

EI: You know, when Khalid in your story "The Somalification of James Karangi" says that James ought to understand whether he was for and against his brother, I easily recall Scott Peterson's book, *Me Against My Brother*, in which as an epigraph he lists a hierarchy of priorities ordered by a Somali proverb: "Me and my clan against the world; Me and my family against my clan; Me and my brother against my family; Me against my brother." How can we think of the proverb without reading selfishness into it?

AA: I think you should go ahead and read selfishness into it, keeping in mind it isn't any selfishness that's specific to Somalis. One is protective of his space naturally, and protects more and more as he gets closer to himself, then finally himself most.

EI: While reading "The Somalification..." I recalled what Kwasi Wiredu calls a "malleability of mind," which makes intercultural dialogue possible. Perhaps, like James, we are being inducted to a new way of seeing, that we can have malleable minds?

AA: I am flattered that you inferred from my story such grand concepts as "malleability of mind." Yes, I believe we can have malleable minds, but I did not intend it in the story. In the case of James, I think he changed more in the way of being than in the way of seeing, so that any alteration to his "way of seeing" only resulted from his new way of being. I'd prefer to think that his inner self changed, so that everything could follow thereafter. His attitude, humor, and temperament were merely results of that altered core.

3

If in real life, for instance, I move to some distant place and assimilate into a new culture—as is probably happening to me now, albeit gradually—my way of seeing won't necessarily change into that of my new culture. On the contrary, it would merge with what I had before, and form a new culture. Sometimes this mix of one thing and another doesn't necessarily result in something better than either. So if James were to live his new Somali life, it would be likely that he would be far more enterprising than the original Somalis, and could display such an inclination for rage as would make them seem like a bunch of Gandhis.

EI: There's the possibility that literature is concerned with the perpetual struggle to understand what it means to be human. For instance, Siyad in your story "A Bag of Oranges" says, "You will define that happiness." Do you find yourself, like your characters, attempting to define those essential "intangibles" that make up our existence?

AA: Yes, but I try to break it up into its concrete parts as opposed to just defining. Though not so much in the way of the tortured Siyad. Perhaps, in attempting to understand elusive themes in life, I am more like Khalid. Self-questioning is (and has been) a daily exercise for me. Themes like "happiness" and "sorrow" aren't exactly what concern me. My questions regularly involve matters that are essential to me, such as, "What do I really need to have in life to make it what I would consider successful?" Lately the answer to that has been to impress my father, have an income and a loving family, and enough days off to visit libraries and attend readings. I keep wondering if these pleasures would be as enjoyable as they are once I wrinkle up and slow down in my gait.

EI: Is there any reason why the Kenyan-Somali hybrid features in your stories?

AA: It's simple really. I haven't learned to write about the Somali-Somalis. And I fear that I might learn to write about Somali-Americans next. Perhaps it's worth understanding that when I mention the word "Somali," it's not so much a nationality as it is an ethnicity. Especially now, given that Somalia is a broken nation, Somalis exist wherever they are as an ethnic group above all else. The name "Somali" as an ethnicity is way older than "Somalia." The tribal identity is the better thing to identify with. It distances one from the failures of Somalia and merges one with all other Somalis: Djibouti, north eastern Kenya, southern Ethiopia, and the diaspora.

EI: Perhaps a glimpse into your childhood might help us understand the kind of writer you have become, the sensibilities that you have acquired. What was most exciting about growing up?

AA: The greatest excitement of my life, growing up and even as an adult, has always been my father. My childhood files are buried very deep in my head, but I can recall a few things. In primary school, I was that child who was very quiet in class and took minimal risks. I hated crowds and still do. When I walked home at the lunch hour, I looked down at the ground and lost myself in the arrangement of the stones, the sand particles, etc. Often I forgot about whichever boy I was walking with and wouldn't notice when we separated. My teachers and classmates knew me as the "absentminded boy." If my father noticed the same, he didn't mention it. Many a time, resting under a shade in our compound, he'd send me to get him a pillow from the bedroom and I would return with a thermos, a flashlight, or a radio. Sometimes it would be the radio he sent me for, and I would be back with a pillow.

A more unfavorable episode resulting from this "absentmindedness" was when a teacher sent me to his office to grab him some chalk. I had gone to the office, stood at the door, not knowing how I got there, and reluctantly had gone back to ask him again. He grabbed me by my pants and gave me a thrashing. "Where was your mind, boy?" This involuntary, mental detachment from my immediate surroundings has stuck with me ever since, and in that, I was lonely going into young adulthood.

My father's stories were what excited me most as a child. We took trips, too. My father owned about 200 camels and in the rainy season, we loaded everything onto a Land Rover and left for the encampments. On the way, my father would be pointing out every hill and tree by its name, explaining each, its significance to the people and to history.

Often his stories would feature the Shifta War between Somali separatists and the Kenyan government in the early 1960s. On most evenings, I would be seated by his side on the mat, and ask questions about his childhood. Sometimes, our conversations veered off into ancient Arabic poetry and our clan's history. It was as though he was attempting to keep it alive and by instinct, knowing one doesn't live forever, I was amassing as much information as possible, to the point of memorizing every poem he recited to me, even in passing. Of course, he did not know I would eventually try to make myself into a storyteller in a different, broader tradition. He was talking for the pleasure of it.

EI: And what kind of writer have you *become*?

AA: I do not know if I have got to the point where I can accurately refer to myself as "a writer." In my writing so far, I see a confusion I haven't intended upon myself. I guess I am the artist who creates out of inner impulses, and who, hopefully, is devoid of ideology.

EI: While reading your story "The Deaths of Old Graham," I was thinking of how a transcendent reality seems even more evident than we dare to admit. Indeed, Old Graham's story is not entirely new; my Mum tells me of a similar experience with my paternal grandfather, who "died" more than once. Why does the metaphysical fascinate you?

AA: I like the freedom found in metaphysical narratives. In this sort of a story, I could put characters in improbable situations and aim for diverse effects. It can hardly fail in getting the effect through, precisely because I could do what I want with it. Before writing it, metaphysical realities did not come to my mind. All I wanted was to create an unusual situation and take it to an unthinkable resolution.

EI: Old Graham's story equally justifies what has been said about a short story: that it is a glimpse of a slice of life. Do you agree with this? That stories do not "end"? That the last word only triggers a chain of reactions in the reader's mind?

AA: Yes, I agree. Stories do not necessarily end, but they need resolutions. In some stories, many of the events happen in the so-called "negative space," the unwritten part. In others, the main conflict is brought to a conclusion, but naturally, the characters—

7

as beings with names—do not have to end there. Rather it's the situation that ended. I believe with Old Graham I achieved what I wanted. If it does raise a question in the reader's mind, then fine. That was also intended. Some readers like to conclude it by themselves, though. The narrative was controlled by the idea of a man being led by the hand to some place people are usually carried to. Everything else was meant to make that possible. And after Old Graham's event, whichever way it ends, his son is still alive.

EI: I have recently been playing with the thought that stories can be written without the need for resolutions. To keep the "situation" as though it keeps happening—maybe this way you can keep the reader thinking about the story as one that unfolds in endless layers. Ah, permit me, I hope this is not tangential.

AA: I think Nabokov ended some of his stories like that. Still, upon careful reading, one finds he has provided enough clues for the reader to end the story. Basically, the story's main conflict has to either conclude, leaving a few open ends for the sub-conflicts, and if not concluded, then at least enough hints have to be found throughout the story for a reader to end it, whichever way. In some Chekhov stories you would see a single sentence at the end that hints at a continuation of the events already depicted. I saw this simply as an attempt on the writer's part to bring things as close to life as possible.

EI: In writing fiction, do you consider the possibility of multi-layered perspectives? For instance, in the first paragraph of "We Can See You" we get the perspective of Mahmud Yare as well as jobless youths and shoe shiners.

AA: I always do. Thanks for noticing. I feel, however, that this comes out more in some stories than others. With "We Can See You" I wasn't fully conscious of doing that. But in others, as in "The Somalification of James Karangi," I was aware of what I was doing. It was the only way I knew how to write, especially at the time that I wrote those two stories. I am evolving every day and quite young in my craft. I have yet to try most of what I am thinking about. I am generally happier when I succeed in getting vague perspectives through, as opposed to such laid-bare scenes as the first parts of "We Can See You."

EI: For Mahmud Yare, I figure it isn't home that changed or makes him late for prayers when he returns. It is a condition similar to what is experienced by Ibou, in Melissa Myambo's "La Salle de Départ." As such, I come away with the conclusion that what we call "home" is an assemblage of our collective viewpoints. Does this resonate with you?

AA: Not at all. I see "home" in very simple terms. Home is where one makes a living and lives. For Mahmud, his home hasn't been changed by his movement, but again, that's his personality. He is the inflexible type.

EI: In considering the nuance of religion, do you assume it is a "character" embodied with all the fluidity of a person? Or do you consider it a motif that is inevitable, which must be written about?

AA: It's a bit of both really. It has enough life to be a character of its own, and a very mysterious and profound one at that. I am experimenting with different voices now, looking for my particular flair. So you might find a few more of my stories in which religion plays one role or another. But I hope I can minimize this over time. I think in "dialoguing" religion you are alluding to a scene in "We Can See You," in which external worries interfere with Mahmud Yare's concentration in prayer. I was seeking a particular effect in that instance, an effect easily recognizable to Muslim readers. But generally, I have little interest in capturing religion in art, unless it infringes on the character's emotions in some way. Although, since religion abounds in irony—something really attractive to me—I might explore it in writing. But I am not very sure. I am still thinking about it.

EI: What is the most important thing that has happened to you as a writer?

AA: It was an e-mail I received from *African Writing*, informing me that they accepted my story. My first acceptance, yes. I can't forget it.

EI: Is there any success you are afraid of?

AA: I am afraid of being acclaimed and failing to keep up the reputation.

EI: Do you feel obliged to anyone as a writer? For when we contemplate "reputation," I'm worried that too much attention is accorded others.

AA: I feel most obliged to myself, but I think this changes when one accumulates readership. Written work is for reading. I do not wish to write some interesting stuff and then follow through with boring stuff. Often I can tell when I am writing something boring. I am the first it bores.

EI: Most of your stories have been published on the continent. Does this say anything about the growing need to, as they say, "tell our own stories"? And perhaps it speaks of an equally essential need to take a swipe at illiteracy and ineffective educational systems.

AA: Possibly, but more from the publisher's viewpoint I would imagine. I am not sure what "our own" stories are. I avoid thinking in such collective terms. I just want to communicate my artistic whims to whoever will pay attention.

I am afraid the "illiteracy" you speak of eludes me. I grew up among people who can read but hardly do. I would say there is a greater need to get people more interested in reading, as opposed eliminating illiteracy. My hope is that "our people" would understand better the need for written stories, insofar as it attempts to give some order to the otherwise disorderly web of their lives. I am not referring to the order of resting under a shade and reading a book. I am talking about the order that art forms like fiction give to life.

EI: What other matters preoccupy your thoughts, aside from an unfinished story?

AA: Finances, family, and education. I really want to be done with this degree as soon as possible. I want to settle down as a family man real soon.

EI: Are there writers whose writing stimulates your work?

AA: There are writers who taught me much through their work. Among them are Bessie Head, Chinua Achebe, Anton Chekhov, Guy de Maupassant, and H. H. Munro. I have learned different things from each of these writers. I am trying to fight off an overwhelming influence of V. S. Naipaul, who wrote the best novel I have ever read: *A House for Mr. Biswas.* I am a very slow reader. Big books intimidate me. Even longer short stories do. I don't mind though. In a way, I would like to minimize external influences, except ones that comes without my noticing.

EI: What does being outside Somalia mean to you? Does it, as someone suggested of all immigrant writers, make you feel *more* given that you're living in an "advanced society"? Or does such transplanting suggest that you're constantly a hybrid person, navigating between the part of you that is Somalian and another that is being educated in America?

AA: It's the latter. I navigate between the two. When the mood calls for it, I am a raging, Somali nationalist. At other times, I argue from a Kenyan viewpoint. And at others, I speak like the Republican Congressman of my district here in the state of Missouri. Each time, my arguments are clear and substantiated. Being away from my land of origin has given me multiple personalities. This isn't so bad for my craft.

June 11, 2012

THE SOMALIFICATION

OF JAMES KARANGI

Abdul Adan

One afternoon, three young people were sitting around a table at Khalfan's restaurant in downtown Mombasa. Their gestures and murmurs were like those of disloyal soldiers plotting a mutiny. The trio was comprised of Khalid Bawazir, his cousin Ayaan, and her forbidden fiancé James Karangi, a.k.a. Mohamed.

"I told you from the beginning," Khalid was lamenting, "there's little hope along the line of religion. You could be the Imam and lead all of the late-night prayers in the month of Ramadan, but the Somali guy who steals shoes from the same mosque would stand a higher chance of taking her hand."

"This is tribalism! It's un-Islamic. You should have told her mother that," protested James.

"I have told her everything I could, upon Ayaan's request, knowing that it won't work," said Khalid. "But you better understand that what we are dealing with here is way beyond tribalism. She is talking of differences in appearance, hair-types and such nonsense." He looked at Ayaan and she nodded, saying, "You've certainly done your best, my beloved cousin."

"That isn't my best," corrected Khalid. "I haven't exhausted all of my resources yet. Like I promised before all this began, I am committed to your happiness, my dear." He tenderly squeezed Ayaan's shoulder and continued, "You have every right to marry the man of your choice. If he happens to be a Kikuyu, a Luo, or a Meru, I will always have your back." He smiled upon saying Meru, reached into his pocket and produced a small plastic bag

13

filled with *khat*. "This is a half-kilo; it's my fix for the day. Were it not for the Merus," he shook his head, "would I have this here today?"

James, who was a new Muslim, looked away and laughed modestly. Ayaan held her veil to her lips to suppress her laughter.

"Well, I called you here today," announced Khalid, "because I believe I have the solution to this mess once and for all." He spoke in a low pitch, like an ailing old man delivering a farewell speech to his sons.

"I am tired," he went on. "I can no longer watch our young people being oppressed by unreasonable traditions. All humans are one. So long as their internal components are the same, there's no point in some assuming superiority over others. It's ridiculous. I mean seriously, which of the world's races or tribes are immune to tuberculosis, pneumonia, cholera, or the need for water and sleep? I have tried convincing my people, both on my father's side and my mother's, that all humans are the same and that our differences are mostly man-made. I have even asked my mother to divorce my Yemeni father and take back all of the experiences they have had together if indeed she is an honest Somali. But, unfortunately, I am a result of their marriage, and they've named me 'Khalid the immortal.'" He paused, faced Ayaan and added, sounding furious, "If James can't marry you, then my father ought not to have married my mother."

His voice rose to a frenzy which seemed to boil from his throat, and he stood from his chair shaking his head and biting his lips. "I can't take this anymore! Can't you see this ignorance undermining our humanity?" he said, bending forward over the table toward his overwhelmed listeners.

"Can't you see?" he repeated, louder this time.

"Khalid!" said Ayaan, trying to calm him.

14

"I'm tired!" he shouted, and then quickly looked about him as if embarrassed.

"Khalid!"

He put his hands in his pockets and walked over to the restaurant window. Then he went to the bathroom, washed his face, dried it, and came back to the table, apparently composed.

"Anyway," he said grimly, "you're being mistreated because you're not Somali. What my aunt and Sharmake don't know is that we can change that."

Sharmake was Ayaan's elder brother. A young man of fiery temper who'd sworn to kill James if he ever found him in his sister's presence.

"How is that possible?" asked James.

"I can see to your Somalification. It's just a matter of time. All I need is your full cooperation."

"I have embraced Islam. What more is needed?"

"You still don't understand, do you? Listen to me. Do you love my cousin?"

Ayaan's eyes lit up and she looked eagerly at James, as though this had been the question she'd anticipated all afternoon. James, for his part, turned his gaze away from Khalid and stared at the table, his hands shaking.

"Do you doubt my feelings for her?" he said.

Khalid brought his fist down hard on the table, nearly knocking over his glass of water. "Give me a yes or no before I declare this over, and side with my aunt and Sharmake."

James started sweating and his face quivered. Khalid was a key person in his quest to marry the girl of his dreams. The mere thought that he could lose Khalid's support set his nerves going. He leaned forward trying to say something, but words failed him.

"C'mon, give me an answer," insisted Khalid. When James didn't reply at once, Khalid crossed his arms and looked away, through the restaurant door. "If you ever thought," he said, "that you can sneak your way into my cousin's heart without loving her truly, then you're fooling yourself and only yourself because I am here for her. My interest in this is for her to be happy. I don't care whether she's fallen for a lion in the bush. If I have to ensnare him and remove all his teeth and claws to ensure her comfort I would. Break her heart, and you have yourself an adversary in me. If you don't love her, tell me now and we shall close this chapter. But once it goes beyond this point, then you're in it for good. And I will Somalify you for her. Her mother will have no case against you. If she tries anything to jeopardize an eligible Somali man's marriage to her daughter, then she will have to answer to the elders. Just be clear and honest with me and I will help you."

"Somalify me?" asked James uncertainly.

"That's beside the point! Do you love her?"

"Of course I do!" said James. His voice was loud, firm and impatient.

"Now we are talking," said Khalid pleasantly. "You will be Somalified *Inshallah*. I will call HassanZuu right away. He's had the entire house to himself since his parents moved to Zanzibar. That's where most of your Somalification will take place."

*

The Somalification of James Karangi was to begin, according to Khalid, with a demonstration of loyalty. James must use his physical resources to help a member of the community in a special project. If he dared question his role it would indicate disloyalty, and so he agreed to help a Somali, in this case Khalid, retrieve some money from a *khat* dealer. Khalid claimed that he had overpaid the man earlier that morning. The two young men walked into the *khat* store at sunset. It was Khalid who addressed the shopkeeper.

"I'm here for my money," he said.

"What money?" asked the *khat* seller, a middle-aged man with a round belly and a red cap on his head.

"I overpaid you this morning. You owe me 150 shillings. Let's not waste time. C'mon, hand it over."

"You are crazy!"

"Okay, James," said Khalid. "Use your Kikuyu muscles; you won't be having them for long."

James jumped over the counter that separated the seller and his customers. He took hold of the man's right arm and twisted it behind his back. Khalid grabbed the man's head and pushed it down against the *khat* leaves on the counter. As it was a humid evening and as the man was sweating, some of the *khat* leaves attached themselves to his face, making it look like a collage. He gave little resistance, only shouting repeatedly, "Are you crazy?!" It had never occurred to him that one of his trusted customers would turn on him.

Khalid reached into the cash-drawer and retrieved 200 shillings. He searched for smaller bills but there were none, just coins. Then he reached into the man's back pocket and found a number of 20-shilling bills. He replaced the 200 and counted the smaller bills until he had 140, before putting the rest back in the man's pocket. He opened the drawer again and added a 10-shilling coin. When he had 150 shillings he showed it to James and ordered him to release the man.

"A Somali man must take only what's his. You understand?"

They left the shop and headed for HassanZuu's home. He was waiting for them when they arrived. Khalid asked James to

17

sit down and took HassanZuu aside for what he called "a brief high-level consultation."

"This is the project I have been waiting for, Brother," he whispered to HassanZuu. "We now have a chance to help someone get married to his love. There's isn't a more noble undertaking. I will need your full support. It shouldn't take more than two weeks."

"Anything you say, my brother," said HassanZuu. Of all of Khalid's friends, he was the most loyal and practical. "I have the rope and all other things ready for you. I have also secured the door. Everything is as you've requested."

Khalid hugged HassanZuu and returned to the backroom where James was waiting. HassanZuu followed him a short while later, carrying a small, narrow bed. James sat crouched in a corner. Khalid tapped his shoulders and smiled at him, tight-lipped.

"Do you trust me?"

*

James spent the night in HassanZuu's backroom by himself. The rules were that he should have as little human contact as possible for a week, and that he should not leave his room except for the calls of nature, and then under the strictest supervision. The next morning HassanZuu brought him black tea for breakfast. For lunch he received no food. When he asked HassanZuu later in the afternoon, he was met with a short, cold answer: "It's the rules." HassanZuu didn't even look at him directly. He wasn't a Somali and therefore was to keep himself as distant as possible from James, by Khalid's direction.

That evening Khalid came to see James in his room, carrying a tightly-folded plastic bag. James could see the opening of the bag, from which green and reddish *khat* leaves stuck out.

"Ever tried these blessed twigs?" Khalid asked. James shook his head. Khalid called aloud to HassanZuu to bring in the dinner of rice, mixed with spaghetti. James took to his meal. Khalid ate little, saying, "I am only helping you along."

A white carpet was spread before them and Khalid brought out the contents of the plastic bag. He handed a bunch of the twigs tied together by a small string to James, and they began the chewing session. James chewed reluctantly and was amused by Khalid's creativity in the first minutes of chewing. He spoke continuously, with focus, energy, and an analytical ability James had never thought he possessed. Khalid's left cheek protruded gradually till it stretched to the full and shone as though carefully polished. Meanwhile, James was undergoing an ordeal. His jaws ached and his inner cheeks were getting bruised, but he kept chewing; he had agreed to the Somalification, he reminded himself.

The first practical lessons began an hour into the chewing. Khalid had ordered a bottle of Coca-Cola to be brought in from outside. He drilled a small hole in the top. There wasn't a need for a bottle-opener. All one needed to do, he said, was suck at the hole and swallow whatever came through. That way the drink would last two people through the entire chewing period, and any *khat* pieces that might escape the cheeks and get trapped in the throat would be washed down.

"As a Somali man," said Khalid, "you must always order for your friend what you order for yourself. If your friend is broke, simply pay the bill without hesitation. And do not ask the money of him in future or remind him of it. Your money is yours, but it's also for your relatives and then for your Somali brother. If you

19

want to extend your love beyond the confines of the community, it's your choice. But never let a non-Somali pay your bill at a restaurant. You do the honors, always. We are free people, and therefore we are generous."

"Maybe you should begin to teach him the language," suggested HassanZuu, who had been drinking coconut juice in a corner of the room.

"Thanks for reminding me, Brother Zuu," said Khalid. "We might as well begin the language lessons right away. We don't have the whole year."

James was pleased at the prospect of learning Somali. He had heard Somali being spoken many times, but hadn't been able to make out a word. As a matter of fact, to him the sound of Somali words was similar to the sound of broken glass mixed with water and poured down a zinc roof. He had never been able to conceive how a fellow human being could articulate such sounds.

"We shall begin with the hardest words and gradually move toward the easiest," said Khalid.

"Ok, let's try," said James.

"Say, *Dhicis*. It means 'premature baby.'"

James attempted to say the word: *"Dees."*

"Dhicis!" repeated Khalid.

James tried again: *"Dees."*

"Okay, that's enough," said Khalid. "You realize I am dedicated to your service, don't you?"

"Of course," said James.

"Well then, you have to cooperate with me by all means. I will have you drink a glass of bitter lemon for your throat and try the word again."

HassanZuu handed him the preserved bitter lemon in a steel glass and went out.

"Take it down in one gulp," said Khalid. "Good boy. Let's try again: *Dhicis.*"

Khalid listened as James said the word, asking him to repeat it twice and a third time before standing up to call in HassanZuu from outside. The latter came in with two ropes folded in his right hand. He was accompanied by another young man, a short, muscular fellow, whom he introduced to James as Othis. He handed Khalid one of the ropes, about four feet in length, and quietly took his position next to Othis. Khalid ordered that all *khat* twigs be cleared away from the scene.

"Brother James," he said, twisting and stretching the rope. "We are about to conduct a simple procedure that has the potential to work miracles. The bitter lemon hasn't been successful in getting your throat flexible enough for your Somali articulation. I am certain this little rope here will work."

James looked at Khalid, then at the other two men. He stood up abruptly, ready to defend himself.

"Don't get all worked up," said HassanZuu. "It's just a simple procedure. There's the hard way and the easy way."

"Fellows, get to work!" Khalid ordered.

They seized James by the arms. James, who was stronger than both of them, could have fought himself loose, but he was dizzy from the poor diet and the strange twigs he'd chewed. He fell flat on his chest, and both of his hands were tied behind his back. Khalid made a little knot in the rope he was holding and, when he had the perfect noose, slid it deftly around James's neck. He tightened it, gradually and slowly, until he could hear a certain agitation in James's voice.

"Please don't take this the wrong way," he apologized to James. "This is all for your sake. Your throat must get flexible enough, or you won't learn a single word of this language, not to mention marry my cousin. I am positive this will work. You will be the first Kikuyu ever to pronounce Somali words without an accent."

"This is abuse," moaned James.

"Say that again," said Khalid. James moaned again. Khalid thought he heard a raspy sound in James's voice. He looked at Othis and HassanZuu, nodded, and said to James, "So far that's the closest thing to a Somali word that you've uttered. I told you it can work miracles."

"You might want to loosen the rope, Brother Khalid," warned Othis. "You don't want to make any mistakes."

"Well, so far now," considered Khalid, "I have choked him about eighty percent. If I loosen the rope it may not be as effective unless I extend the timing. We would have to prolong the exercise by two days to produce the same results of this tightness level."

James changed his moans into a series of gasping sounds until Othis, possibly noticing an impending tragedy, hastened to loosen the noose.

"That's it, no looser. Or it won't work." Khalid stopped him lest his heart get in the way of his work.

HassanZuu checked the ropes for the last time, tugging at every knot with caution.

*

For thirteen days James was locked in, neck-tied except during meals and *khat* chewing sessions. He was allowed one meal a day. Every other night Khalid would visit him with a kilo of *khat*, from which he had to chew for at least three hours and listen to the language and cultural lessons. When the chewing was done, Khalid would tighten the strap around his neck and leave. James resisted the daily and nightly procedures at first; however, as time wore on, he became weak and emaciated. On many occasions he tied the rope around his own neck when it was time, making it clear that he preferred "the easy way".

To his surprise, the procedure worked. He pronounced many difficult words that required unusual manipulations of his throat muscles. However, when he repeated complete sentences after Khalid, he perceived an extraordinary change in his own mood. Each time he said a Somali sentence with correctness he felt his temper rise, and lost patience for repetitive lessons. Subsequently he demanded, with a marked urgency, to be taught new words and sentences by the minute, and maintained a choleric, intolerant disposition.

Once HassanZuu sent him his breakfast through Othis and he rejected it. "I don't eat from the hands of one who smells of lake fishes. I am not even sure you are circumcised." He took a long time putting the words together but spoke them with the right pitch and emotion. He raised himself on his knees, wagging his index finger violently at Othis. But unaccustomed to the strain of Somali words, his heart beat too fast, and he placed his right hand on his chest and fell back, out of breath.

*

On the last day of the program, Khalid gave him a summary of all the cultural lessons.

"Your throat will no longer be an obstacle to your learning," he told him. "We will give you skin applications for your neck bruises. Ultimately you will be a man without regrets. The benefits you've gained from this program surpass by far any difficulties you've gone through. One thing you should never forget is that a fellow Somali's interest is always your interest. Never hesitate to help a Somali man who is at war with others."

23

Khalid continued his farewell lesson late into the night. He gave clear directions as to how James should live his Somali life. Thanks to the diet, James' body, according to Khalid, had come to resemble that of the average Somali male. He had lost at least thirty percent of his weight and his cheeks had gotten hollow. True strength, he was told, is in one's soul. Only slaves seek strength in their muscles. If one's fury is intense enough, he can defeat anyone. Khalid also taught him how to live an outgoing, flexible, yet conservative life.

"Do not ever imprison your mind with rules," he was told. "All land belongs to Allah. No government should ever limit or dictate where you can or can't go. Budgets and financial records are a nuisance, created to make lives hard. You will find in being a Somali that money stops being a serious issue. You will learn to spend it even before making it. Money is like women. It comes and goes. You must never for a second think about how much you have left when you want to help a brother; such attitude can only invite poverty into your life. Never hesitate to share what you have with your fellow Somali. Lastly and most importantly, you live for yourself and the community. If you get hungry in a foreign land, join any Somalis who are dining. They should be welcoming unless they have something else in their blood."

"So emotions are good, huh?"

"Well, positive emotions are," answered Khalid. "The kind that you need when saving a brother who is in danger. If you try to be reasonable in such a case you will waste precious time in which you could have served the community. One who defends his own is never at fault. A Somali man must always know his rights. That's why our ancestors, in all their wisdom, said, 'Give a Somali man his right or your head.' You see! You've got to walk away with something: your rights, your Somali brother's rights, or the oppressor's head. Haven't you noticed that oppressive

24

people are happier when their victims are cool and reasonable? Beware! Pacifism is a sanctuary for cowards, the un-revolutionary."

*

Early the next morning James was freed from the bed and the rope around his neck was permanently removed. Ayaan was brought in to see his new, Somalified form.

"Oh Allah!" she gasped. "What have they done to you? Why did you let them do this to you, my love? I hardly recognized you when I walked in. You look like a refugee who's fled on foot for months without food. Allah! Allah!"

"But isn't that the whole idea?" said Khalid. "How else would he lose his Kikuyu muscles, gained by centuries of vegetable farming? You should be glad we didn't take him to the desert to look after camels." But Ayaan's rage was far from being quelled by verbal persuasion. She leaped up and slapped him numerous times, scratching him with her nails and clawing at his shirt.

"You sick brute with a worm-filled head!" she cried. "I thought you were going to teach him the language and the culture. How much of that does he know now? Huh? You sick torturer!"

Khalid gently pulled her hands off him and tried to explain himself. "Teachings, by themselves, are not successful assimilation tools; the individual must change," he said, "physically and psychologically."

Ayaan, now suddenly composed, bent over James and shook his thinned biceps. She touched him about the chest, laid him on his back, and shook his kneecaps. Soon, her lips tensed and she stopped the inspection. Her eyes constricted in renewed rage and she opened her mouth like someone in pain, gritted her teeth, and, clasping her neck-beads, let out such a squeal that HassanZuu and Othis cowered on the floor, terrified. Khalid tried to console her but she shook him off and paced fast across the room, back and forth, before falling almost limply, on top of James. She gathered him by the limbs into her arms and rocked, sobbing.

"My darling," she stammered in Swahili, "what do I do? I can't... I don't..."

Behind her the door creaked, and it didn't take long before everyone saw the intruder. It was the dreaded Sharmake, Ayaan's elder brother. He had followed Ayaan when she suspiciously absconded from the breakfast cooking duties earlier that morning, and from the Somali traditional dagger he carried, his intentions couldn't be clearer. He leaped across the room and seized Ayaan by the hair, throwing her to one side, away from the frail, gaunt figure on the floor. Then he kicked James hard in the mouth and stabbed him twice in the back with the dagger. HassanZuu and Othis, at first frozen with fright and wonder, ran to James' aid and, just in time, wrestled away the assailant.

"Bloody Kikuyu fool!" said Sharmake, amid rapid gasps. "You never get it, do you?"

He tried to kick James again but Khalid blocked him. Ayaan launched at her brother, tearing at him with her henna-colored nails and biting his hands. She called him names and then said a few rude things about his mother, who was her mother too, and then his sister, who was herself.

"I wish James was in a position to listen," thought Khalid. "These would have been useful notes to take." Sharmake pulled his sister by the arm, out of the room. Khalid and HassanZuu bent over the writhing James to assess the injuries.

*

Two days later James woke up in a hospital bed. Khalid and Ayaan were at his side.

"Thank God you're back," said Ayaan.

"You're lucky to be alive," added Khalid. "He hit your spine, you know?"

"My dear," said Ayaan, leaning closer to James, "I must end our relationship. I don't want to risk your life anymore. I am sorry."

She kissed James on the forehead and went out.

"What did she just say?" murmured James.

"Don't worry. You don't need her," said Khalid. "Women, like money, come and go. Now, my brother in Somaliness, I am here for a most important thing."

Khalid bent over James and turned him gently sideways. He inspected the bandaged stab wounds and pouted his lips in grave contentment. Having confirmed the adequate extent of the Somalification, Khalid lifted his right hand in the air like one taking an oath and declared in a solemn, formal voice:

"Brother James, on behalf of the Somali community, I congratulate you on a successful Somalification."

Then he lowered his eyes, waved, and left the room in haste.

AYOBAMI ADEBAYO

EMMANUEL IDUMA: You said reading *A God of Small Things* changed your writing. Why? Are there other books that have had the same affect?

AYOBAMI ADEBAYO: That book changed the way I think about the possibilities of language and imagination in fiction. It removed some limits as to what one could do or not do in fiction. Before I read Arundhati Roy's novel, Wole Soyinka's play *Death and the King's Horseman* also affected the way I thought about language. I am particularly fascinated by the final section; the language of the exchanges between the Iyaloja and Elesin is exquisite. What both works have in common for me is that whenever I read them, I get the feeling that although I'm reading English, it isn't quite English. Even though Roy isn't African, both books are for me practical examples that what Achebe writes about in "The African Writer and the English Language" can be done. He concludes that the English of the African writer "will have to be a new English, still in full communion with its ancestral home but altered to suit its new African surroundings."

Death and the King's Horseman was so much more impactful for me because I could read the Yoruba in the English. When I read books that have such beautiful language, sometimes I feel the writer doesn't have to tell me a story, she or he should just keep turning phrases like that. *A God of Small Things* also tells a powerful story; it is just brilliant. Some of the other books that I keep going back to include Ann Patchett's *Bel Canto*, Toni Morrison's *Beloved*, and Edwidge Danticat's *Krik Krak*.

EI: Do you find that as you mature as a writer, there's a tendency for you to commit more time to a work?

AA: Yes, there is that tendency. I'm not sure why it happens, but if I have to give a reason, I would say I am more aware now that the work could be better if I just work a little harder at it.

EI: What did you think about Occupy Nigeria, especially within the threshold of your artistic viewpoint? Perhaps as a recompense for loss? You know, we come from a context of protest, having attended in Obafemi Awolowo University. And there I believe you stayed aloof to student unionism, which could suffice as activism on a micro-level.

AA: The last part of your question makes me laugh. Why do you assume I was aloof? I suppose you are right, my level of involvement in student unionism didn't go past attending a few congresses and voting in the elections. I do think there is, shall I say, an attitude of protest you almost cannot escape if you attend school in Ife; it is in the water you drink and the air you breathe.

Occupy Nigeria was, among other things, an opportunity for us to articulate the latent anger we feel as Nigerians about the unnecessary breakdown in virtually every sector in this country. It was Nigerians standing up and saying we were tired of paying for the failure in leadership at many levels. From any viewpoint, I stand in awe of the protests. I don't think I have ever been more proud of being a Nigerian or more hopeful about the possibilities for change in this country.

EI: Once you gave the impression that anything was possible within the human mind, the kind of minds that are replicated in your stories. Take your story "Angels of Peace Villa," for instance, and the moment when those daughters leave their father in a room to burn to death. How did this play in your head?

AA: In that particular story, it was about those girls realizing that they could in fact walk away and let this terrible thing happen to their father. Not just that; they could stand there and imagine that the man was not burning, that he did not even exist. They could believe that their father along with all the pain they had experienced—because they were his daughters—did not exist. They stood on the threshold of that possibility in their minds as they watched the house burn. It played out in my mind as these girls discovered that they could, in their minds, get their lives back.

EI: I find that the realm of the political always plays into your writing. Sometimes it's an election (more than once it was an election) or ethnic-related violence. In sum, it's the manner in which the public takes residence in our private spaces. Why do socio-political tendencies fascinate you? Or do they?

AA: Yes, such tendencies do fascinate me. The public (by this I mean government: federal, state, and local) often has little input into our lives in terms of social infrastructure. Most Nigerian families run like miniature local governments. You generate your own power with your "I pass my neighbor" or a Mikano generator. You provide your water with your well or borehole. Yet the public still manages to have a strong impact on our lives, perhaps more so because the public systems have collapsed. It is as though they collapse and having nowhere to crash into, descend upon what you have called "private spaces."

31

EI: Are we obliged to tell how the public collapses into private spaces?

AA: No, I don't think any writer has an obligation to engage such incursions. It just interests me as a person.

EI: Considering your work as fiction editor of *Saraba Magazine*, and the colloquiums and workshops you have facilitated, how do you perceive the business of creating structures for emerging writers?

AA: For me it is this simple: I love to read good stories and good books. Anytime I come across someone whose work I would love to continue reading, I want to make sure that they have access to information and opportunities that would help them fully realize their talents. From there on, the rest is their responsibility. Perhaps, it is really a selfish endeavor that boils down to me thinking, "This person has the ability to write a novel that I would really enjoy reading one day."

EI: Does writing with the pseudonym Ayobami Adebayo make you feel halved, the one who writes and the one who lives?

AA: No. I always think of myself as Ayobami Adebayo. There is only Ayobami Adebayo, the one who writes and the one who lives.

EI: Would you consider the fiction you write as imagined reality? We often take so much from the real, the tangible, enmeshing such details into our characters. Simply, where does fiction and reality intersect for you, considering that even to make that classification is to be beguiled by illusion?

AA: It really is reality for me. These people do exist; I talk to them, sometimes out loud, thankfully only when I'm alone. I think my job is to make them as real to whoever is reading my work as they are to me.

EI: You and I have often discussed your aloofness to new technology. I am eager to put this into a broader frame. Once we talked about how print books have an aesthetic value, how an e-book cannot line a shelf. Anna Quindlen says, "I would be most content if my children grew to be the kind of people who think decorating consists mostly of building enough bookshelves." The critic Dwight Garner responded by taking her side, but suggesting that it's the mental furniture that matters. What is your response?

AA: We are told that eventually books will disappear and everyone will go about with iPads and such. I guess it makes sense to say it is the mental furniture that matters. My stubbornness is perhaps just sentimental. I cannot imagine a world without hard covers; I do not want to. I hope it doesn't happen in my lifetime. I just love the smell of new books and think the whole world should too. I imagine one must get used to these things. Books themselves have not existed since the beginning of time. At some point, they were "new technology."

EI: And extending "mental furniture" to a different terrain—supposing the chief intent of writing is to build lasting furniture in the memory of readers—what ways can we consider what's called non-literary fiction? Could genre fiction—romance, thriller, sci-fi, etc.—climb into the critical space reserved for literary fiction?

AA: Who makes these reservations for literary fiction? How many rooms are available in this hotel called "critical space" anyway? Such delineations cannot be so rigid or shouldn't be. I have read sci-fi that has built not just lasting furniture but duplexes in my mind. I have also read "literary fiction" that didn't leave even a stool in my mind. If you know the good people who own this hotel called "critical space," do tell them to build an extension so they can accommodate more books.

EI: Once, in a conversation on publishing and reading culture, you emphasized that, for want of a better expression, Nigerians "read." And you drew strength from seeing Sidney Sheldon titles in homes while growing up. Our friend, Adebiyi Olusolape, counter-argued that you were speaking literarily, from a privileged position, as your group of Nigerian readers was situated within a particular social class, an academic environment. I cannot remember what your answer was. Could you remind me?

AA: I do believe that Nigerians who can read, do read. It is a question of what we read. Some of the most popular spots in communities are newspaper stands, and I've observed this almost anywhere I've gone, not just in the academic environment where I grew up. Nigerians read newspapers like *The Punch*, *Alaroye*, *City People*, *Hints*. People read a lot of religious literature too, and self-help books.

EI: You might also recall in that same conversation, we equally spoke about publicizing books. Your position was that writers are equally responsible for ensuring their books are sold. How do we balance this responsibility with the disease of completion (that sigh of "oh, I'm through") that follows the publishing of a book?

To tell you the truth, I would love to conserve that energy for the next project!

AA: I really do not know how to balance these things because I have not gotten to that stage. The ultimate responsibility for a writer's career lies with the writer. Fortunately, social media now provides relatively cheap ways for writers to put their names out there. Let me add that the best contribution you can make toward ensuring your books are sold is to put your best into writing the book. After all the marketing is done, it is the quality of your work that will determine whether I would buy your next book or recommend the current one to other people.

EI: Have you ever written poetry? Very few writers achieve success in both genres.

AA: I write poetry when I'm depressed, really horrible poetry. It is so bad that I delete it from my system by the next day so it won't crash the poor laptop.

EI: Are you comfortable in any other genre?

AA: I have only been interested in writing fiction. I have written a play and what you might call nonfiction, but I'm just not interested in them enough to work at them. Perhaps in the future.

EI: So plays in the future?

AA: I'm actually thinking more of nonfiction, but maybe plays too.

EI: I think a lot about digital nativity. Lately, I'm wondering what affect Instant Messaging culture—especially that awful BlackBerry—will have on literature. Should we propose a dictionary of abbreviations? Like it or not, we have been visited by alien smileys! What do you say?

AA: We should have the dictionary for people like me who read comments on their Facebook wall and wonder for the next week, "What does that mean?" But we thank God for smileys, they enable one to mask ignorance or indifference.

EI: Perhaps because of you, Ile-Ife's literary flag might be hoisted on a global stage. I say this to ask if you assume any responsibility to the community that has mentored you.

AA: The question sounds so grand. Perhaps we should wait for that to happen?

EI: You have taught me patience, to keep a watchful gaze for right timing. Is this a necessary strategy for the prolific emerging writer?

AA: I don't think of myself as prolific, but I guess I will always see myself as emerging. Sometimes I think I'm just slow, not patient. But I do think that there are times when the best thing you can do is watch, wait, and keep writing.

EI: But, really, what are we waiting for?

AA: The right opportunity or a series of opportunities. Don't get me wrong, by "wait" I don't mean wait for some fairy godmother to visit your laptop and discover all the wonderful things you have written. Keep writing, apply for everything you are eligible for, submit to every journal or competition. Hopefully pushing yourself this way will help you get much better at your craft. So you are waiting for your efforts to meet with the right opportunity for you.

EI: To what would you attribute the increase of literary platforms on social media? Could it be ease of formation, a cultural awakening, or a sense that things could be lost if not engaged with?

AA: You know me—I never keep up with these things on Facebook. I'm hoping I can get more involved at some point down the road, be a more sociable person.

EI: How often do you write longhand?

AA: Every time I'm stuck in a lecture and I really need to be completing a story. I hope my lecturers never read this.

EI: Could you describe the period before the first sentence of a new story?

AA: It is never the same each time. Sometimes it is beautiful because there is this stupid line in my head that I think is wonderful at the time, but which I will delete with my eyes closed the next morning because I'm too embarrassed to even read it. Other times I keep rewriting that first sentence over and over again. Those are the ones that usually stay. Most times, I write something that I know is rubbish, but I write it, highlight it in red, and move on to the good stuff. It is always exciting to start something new.

EI: And how do you begin the end of a story? Does the end occur to you as an "end"?

AA: I don't think of it as the end, just as the point where that particular story stops. Those people keep on living their lives when I'm not looking.

April 16, 2012

SPENT LIVES

Ayobami Adebayo

She recognized the new tenant from her dreams, but she did not
know this. She assumed that she simply remembered his face
from so long ago, remembered the way his shirt hung on his thin
shoulders like it might on a plastic hanger. The truth was that he
had been muscular when she knew him and his hair had been
black like a moonless, starless night sky. It was now grey all over
like hers and half of it was gone. What was left lay on the sides
above his ears and looked like it would fall off if the fan blew too
hard.

Seated next to the fat estate agent who had come to introduce
him to her, the new tenant looked malnourished. His clothes
hung loose as though he had recently lost a lot of weight, and she
thought that his wife must be too old to cook good meals for him.
It never occurred to her that he never married, that in the end
Ayandele went about playing his drums from city to city,
following a band around, kissing women who stared too long at
him when he played, and hoping to hear her laughter from their
mouths. She had no reason to imagine he would not marry
because her smile was lodged somewhere in his brain. When a
woman left you, you found another woman; it was what one did.
You do not fall from a horse and refuse to climb another one all
your life, how would you go about? On foot from city to city? She
had gotten married within two years from the last time she saw
him.

She was married to her husband for nearly five decades
before he inconvenienced her by dying before she did. She was
sitting in his favorite chair, an old armchair he had refused to let
go of whenever they changed their furniture. Ayandele sat

39

opposite her on a large leather couch. She had never loved him enough to hate him, or to spend too much time in murderous rage over what he did. Her rage had not even been murderous; it had been fleeting, forgotten in a few weeks. He had faded from her mind gradually until she forgot that the beads she wore on her wrist until that day when she saw him again had been something of his that she had tried on and liked.

Still, she often dreamt of him, not just the young man she had known, but the man he became and the old man whom she now saw and recognized immediately. She had seen his first grey hair and the hairline that receded till it disappeared, she had even seen the glasses he now wore, all in her dreams. Only that in the dreams the glasses had green frames. The ones he actually wore had brown frames that matched his skin. She did not know all of this because her mind banished the memories of the dreams before dawn, so that on days she dreamt of Ayandele, she always thought she woke up from dreamless sleep. It was from those dreams that she recognized him.

When he said to her, "Good evening, our mother," she laughed because it was strange to hear him talk to her so reverently. He had never been polite enough for her. He had a terrible habit, saying exactly what he thought about a matter or a person. He never mastered that necessary art of smiling at people while cursing them in his mind.

"Ayandele, son of Ayankunle, you don't remember me?" She did not look at him as she spoke, she stared at a picture that hung on the wall directly opposite her. Her husband had hung that picture so that it was always in his line of sight whenever he was in the sitting room.

He scratched his eyebrow. "Alake? The one who sings *rara?*"

"It is Alake, but I don't sing *rara* anymore. That was child's play." She leaned back in her chair and smiled.

"Child's play? Alake, it was your spirit; *rara* was your life."

She bit her lip. "It was child's play. Don't talk to me about it again. It was child's play."

Ayandele nodded. "So this is your face."

"Abi, can't you see? An old face too, not as wrinkled as yours though."

"You know that this rag was once a fashionable dress. Surely, you remember when my face was smooth."

"Do I remember?" She tapped her forehead with a finger. "I don't think so. Your face was always a rag."

He laughed. There was no awkwardness, perhaps because too much time had passed, perhaps because he knew that the man she had married was dead. The agent had told him the landlady was a widow. He wondered if things would have felt different if he was to be the husband's tenant and was grateful that the man lay six feet under a concrete cross in the front of the house.

"Our mother, so you know the new tenant?" the estate agent asked.

Alake nodded. "When we were young, we attended the same secondary school."

"People really are water." The agent said.

"The stream that flows out of a river will meet the river again further down the road," Ayandele said.

"So should he bring his things? Our mother, you wanted to speak with the new tenant, but since he is a known person, the words..."

"... have spoken themselves." Alake nodded "Abi, Ayandele? Have the words not spoken themselves? The house is yours, bring in your things when you are ready."

*

It was not a house though; it was a room and a parlor downstairs. Alake's sons had lived there as teenagers before they left for the university. The girls lived upstairs, so their parents could pay surprise visits in the middle of the night to make sure they were not out dancing in a disco. The apartment hadn't been occupied since the last boy went off to study engineering in Ukraine.

Ayandele tried to avoid touching anything in the parlor. The room was very dusty and even the green walls looked as though they had been topped off with a light brown coating. The men who were helping him move his things kept coughing.

"Will you help me clean some of the dust?" he said to them as they brought in a settee.

"Baba, you did not pay for that one. You will drop some change." One of the two men replied.

He sighed. He had no money to spend unnecessarily. It was a strange world now, and everything was about the money. He had hoped that the men, both of them barely thirty, would have some respect for his grey hair and spend some minutes cleaning the dust.

"Don't worry, leave the dust," he said.

The movers shrugged.

*

That night, Alake went downstairs to see her tenant. She was eager to meet his wife. She waited impatiently until it was around 8:00 p.m. for the new tenants to come upstairs to greet her, but they did not show up. She hissed under her breath as she knocked on the door, but it was something to do, somewhere to go, some people to speak to other than the house help her children had employed to take care of her.

"Our mother, you have come to greet me," Ayandele said when he saw her on the other side of the door.

Alake laughed. "Is it old age that has done this to you? Who is your mother?" She looked left and right. "Are you seeing ghosts?"

"Come in," he said.

She started to cough immediately after she entered the room; it was still dusty. She concluded that his wife must be a slob; whatever woman could stand in the filth for more than an hour had to be.

"I hope you are enjoying the place." She sat on the only settee in the room.

He nodded.

"How is your wife? Is she enjoying the place too?"

"My wife?" He removed a lantern from its place on a stool.

She put a hand to her throat, thinking the wife must have died. But when? It couldn't be in the period since the agent had first told her about him. Could it? "Ehn, your wife."

"I don't have a wife." He placed the lantern on the floor.

"But, the agent said you have a wife. Has she taken the earth as her blanket?"

He sat on the stool. "Maybe he thought you wouldn't rent the house to me if I had no wife. They say you are a Deaconess, *Iya Ijo*."

He was right, she would never have agreed to even meet with him if she had thought he was widowed.

"Iya Ijo, should I begin to pack my things?"

The lantern wasn't bright and she couldn't see his face clearly. Still she was almost sure he was mocking her. He had never accepted Christianity. Her parents would never have allowed her to marry a pagan.

"You are a known person, there is no need."

"Thank you, Iya Ijo." He did not sound grateful, he sounded tired.

"What happened to her?"

"Who?"

"Your wife. How did she pass away?"

"She did not die."

"She left you?"

"I never married."

She was speechless; it was strange even for him. It was unimaginable, like saying a man existed but he was not born by a woman. It was what people did; they were born, if they lived long enough they got married and then they died, it was a fact of life. She could not think of any man she knew who had never married. Women? Yes, if they were too ugly, too stubborn, too lazy, or even too beautiful. She had been taught since she was a child that a mortal danger awaited any woman, the possibility of being too-something for any man to want her, the possibility of living life unmarried. As far as she knew, men were not in that danger, they would marry even if they were too-everything.

"But, but how have you lived? Without a wife all your life?"

"I have been eating, drinking water, sleeping, waking up, breathing..."

"I am not playing a child's game. How have you lived without a wife?"

"I have always lived with a woman—women—until now."

"A woman?" She spoke as though she had never heard the word.

She hadn't changed at all. There was still only one world for her. A world where people, all people went to church and did what the vicar had instructed all week. When they had been together, they had never even kissed. Perhaps, he thought now, for the first time, that was why he never forgot her.

"Different women," Alake said. In her mouth, the words carried too much weight, the weight of regrets he hadn't known he had until he heard her. "How did you meet them? Who were they?" she asked.

The lights came on suddenly, the way they often did when people had already forgotten there was something called electricity. They both flinched as the light of a lone fluorescent lamp flooded the room. For a while they did not speak. She looked around the room—it looked so terrible. She fought the urge to grab a broom and start cleaning; it was easier to fight the urge now that her knees could no longer be bent without considerable pain. He saw the beads on her wrist. The ones he had given her when they were barely adults, when he had thought for a few days that he might marry her, the way he thought about every woman he had met until he got to know them and marriage didn't seem so necessary anymore.

"You are wearing my beads."

She looked away from the cobwebs that covered the ceiling and squeezed her face.

"On your wrist."

She looked at her wrist and tried to remember where she had gotten the string of beads, from whom she had gotten it. "I can't remember who gave them to me. It was you?"

He nodded.

"They are beautiful."

"They are royal beads." His brother who played drums for the royal family had gotten a dozen of the bracelets as gifts from the king. He had given Ayandele one, the one Alake now wore.

"How did you meet them, the women?"

He could see her face clearly now.

"At parties where I went to play."

"How did you do it? Did the women have no parents? How did you just live with them?"

"Have you not heard of it before?"

"Yes, children of today. But in our time?"

"Some just came to live with me, some had their own houses and I moved in." He felt weary. He wished she would leave.

"Without *idana?* You never asked for their hand?"

"Correct."

"They were not just concubines you went to or who came to you? That one is normal. They actually lived in your house without *idana?*"

"Yes."

"What happened to your house?"

"I never built one." He looked into her eyes when he said this, without shame, without regrets.

"Why not?" It was a reflexive question, she knew why already. It was because he never married a wife. A wife would have given him the common sense he needed to build his own house.

"Why should I build one?"

"Are you... serious?" She had wanted to say crazy but it would not have been proper.

"*Iya Ijo,* did you bury this house with your husband when he died?"

She flinched but he did not apologize. She got up then. It was time to leave.

"I will send my house help to clean this place tomorrow," she said as she hobbled out of the sitting room.

He went to sit in the depression her buttocks had made on the settee; he could still feel her warmth there.

*

Alake did not see him for a few weeks, although she did hear him drumming at different times during the day. She went downstairs in the mornings, to the bathroom in the backyard to take her bath, 5:30 a.m. as always. Except for Wednesday evenings and Sunday mornings when she went to church, she spent her days watching television and talking to her children on the phone.

She also thought about the man downstairs. She thought about the life he had lived. It appeared to her as though he had reached for something intangible and managed to get a hold of it while she had never known that such a thing even existed. She imagined his women to be free and happy, she wanted to know them, to meet them and ask them if they would face death knowing they had lived.

It was by chance that she saw him again. She was on her way to take her bath as usual, was passing by the kitchen when she noticed that a candle was on. She hadn't entered the kitchen for over a year. Her help did all the cooking now. She stood by the window and watched Ayandele bent over a green kerosene stove. He was holding a wooden stick and stirring something in an iron pot.

She had never known a man who could cook. It was something that had simply never occurred to her as a way that men could live. She had never taught her sons to cook or even to wash their plates because she assumed that they did not have the ability. It was a fact of life; it was not their fault. It was simply something they couldn't do, just as they couldn't menstruate. Those sons now cooked in their homes, but their wives were careful to hide the fact when their mother-in-law visited, even the Ukrainian woman that the last boy had married, never allowed him to even make toast whenever Alake was in their home.

47

Watching Ayandele, she was sad that she had never taught the boys how to cook *asaro*, that when the girls had gone off to university she had done all the cooking alone. How could she not have known that it was possible for a man like Ayandele to hold the hot lid of an iron pot without dropping it and injuring himself? Her whole life in that moment felt suspended on that lack of judgment, that one mistake she had not known she had made. Who knew how many other mistakes there were? The questions she had suppressed all her life dominated her mind; could she have had a different life? Had another life always been available to her that she had never known?

She groaned. Ayandele turned and saw her; she noted that he had not been startled. She would have been alarmed and would have overturned the pot. He radiated a kind of peace, a steadiness she never had. She thought that he knew something and because of it he was not afraid to be without a wife, a house, or even children. She wondered if this was what happened to people when they had truly lived, if they developed this quietness that refused to be shaken.

"Iya Ijo, good morning." He said.

"Good morning. Did you wake up well?"

"I am grateful that my eyes opened when I willed them to."

"Thanks be to God. What have you woken up so early to prepare?"

"It is *ewe*, it has been on the stove all night. I said I should come and see if it is cooked."

"Have you added palm oil?"

He shook his head. "It is not ready for palm oil; it still needs to drink a little more water."

"My house help can do these things for you; you just need to give her the foodstuff. She will cook everything." She drew her wrapper tighter around her chest.

When he said nothing she added, "The girl hardly does anything anyway. It as though we have set the money we are paying her on fire. She needs more work so our money won't waste." She spoke in a rush and was breathless when she stopped.

"That will be good. Thank you. Can she come for the cooking materials today?"

She nodded and walked away, a little disappointed in him. She had thought he would refuse her help, that he would remain a shining example of self sufficiency, an embodiment of the life she imagine she could have lived.

*

When Ayandele played his drums, he went from one drum to the next. He played and played and stopped only when his arms ached. Even then he did not let the drums go. He traced their taut skins, allowed his hands to caress the wood or twist the twines of antelope skin at the sides of whichever drum happened to be the last played for the day. On some days, the days he felt like crying, he cradled a small one against his chest, lay on his back, closed his eyes, and willed the spirits to come.

Like bored lovers, the spirits of the drums had left him without a backward glance. He still saw the drums but he knew that there was nothing in them anymore. The sounds that came out when his hands slammed their skins floated into the air, circled above his head and left the room. They did not touch and envelope him like before. The beats did not drown him, did not own him. Still he beat the drums each day, waiting, hoping. Even when the sound that came out irritated him and sounded like a dozen mosquitoes circling his ears, he waited. He waited for the moments he lived for since he was a child—moments when his hand touched the skin of a drum and the sounds that came forth wrapped themselves around him until the world disappeared and nothing else existed besides the beat and him.

Day after day, the world refused to shift away. He could still hear the world. He could hear a goat bleating in the back yard, Alake telling one of her children what she had for lunch. The wall clock ticking away, counting down the time he had left on the earth.

*

Every Wednesday, Alake invited Ayandele to attend the evening's Bible study with her. She never invited him on Sundays; it would have been too aggressive, as though she was trying to convert him. She was not quite sure of what she would be converting him from, since he didn't seem to pay any attention to worshipping the gods of his father. Alake went to him every Wednesday, but not because she had any hope that he would change his mind. The invitations gave her an excuse to enter his sitting room, see the holes in his single settee, and reassure herself that her life had been good. She also got a glimpse of the drums that her hands itched to touch but told herself that they must be dusty and degenerating like everything in the room, like Ayandele himself with his face of crumpled paper.

He always declined with a smile and a request that she pray for him. She never prayed for him, the only prayers she did not read out of a book were for her children. She seldom prayed for herself anymore, and when she did, all she asked was that she would die a good death. She had taken up this prayer after an old friend was mangled in a car accident. There was no lying in state. It seemed so unnecessary that someone so old would die like that when she could have gone in her sleep or after a brief illness.

Alake prayed to die in her sleep, in the afternoon after a good meal of *amala* and *ewedu*. She wanted to leave with a full stomach because she suspected that in heaven, there would be nothing to eat except dry sandwiches cut in perfect triangles. The missionary sisters who had taught her in secondary school loved those miserable sandwiches so much.

The church she attended was an old church, most of the members were old. Many were dead or about to die and every other week there was a fresh obituary fixed to the notice board at the church's entrance.

Transition to Glory

With heavy hearts but also with immense gratitude to God for a life well spent, we regret to announce the passing on to glory of our Mother, Grandmother, and Great Grandmother...

Since Ayandele moved into her house, Alake thought more about her life. How it was like money, currency. What had she spent it on? Had it been well spent? It had been enough before that she was mother, grandmother, great grandmother, but now she felt she could have been more and she hadn't. She was dismayed that though she had some currency left, she had nothing to spend it on. Even her children did not need her help. They always had reasons why they could not visit for the holidays—work, vacation, their children were sick. She hadn't seen any of them in over two years. Even when she spoke to them on the phone, they didn't sound like they were listening. There was always noise in the background, traffic, their children screaming, or just the television. While she prayed for them, she now prayed more for herself. Alake began to pray to spend the rest of her life well, although she was not sure what that would mean in the little time she had left. She continued to plead that the flaming hot deaths that came in accidents and disasters

51

would pass her by, that when death finally came for her it would be of the cool variety.

When one Wednesday Ayandele said he would go to church with her on Sunday, Alake was happy. She heard nothing in the church that evening and for the first time in decades had no contribution to make during the Bible study. She kept thinking of Sunday, thinking how on God's own day she would generously spend some of the little currency she had.

*

Ayandele was ready to be saved, from his badly lit room and parlor, from his drums empty of life and spirits. He was ripe for some kind of ritual, a form of communion that no longer existed in the beat he had lived for. Since the spirits had left his drums, perhaps the peace they brought would be found within the walls of a church. Even if—as he had always suspected—the church was filled not with the warmth of the spirits he sought but the frigidity of too many human spirits, he was ready to have a place to go during the week. He was ready to have the priest pay occasional visits to say prayers, to say anything. He was the last child in his family and his only living sibling was bedridden. No one came to visit him. The few friends he had now lived with their children in Lagos or some other big city. He was still agile. He could walk for miles before getting tired, but he had nowhere to go.

When Sunday came, he was waiting outside his door for Alake and the house help by 9:25 a.m. It was the help alone who came downstairs. "Mama no well, O', she want rest. She say make I follow you go church."

"What is the matter with her? Won't she need you to look after her?"

The girl shrugged. "She say make I follow you go."

"Let me go and check her." He started toward the stairs.

"Mama don' sleep. Maybe she no fit sleep for night."

He stood for a moment longer beside the stairs, and then followed the help out of the house.

Alake stood by her bedroom window and watched him disappear into the distance with her house help. She left the window open, breathless with the possibility that they would turn and see her standing there wide awake. There was sweat between her fingers, like there had been on her first day of school, her first day as a primary school teacher, her last day as a virgin. It had been long since she sweated there. She picked up her keys and went downstairs.

The keys fell from her hands twice before she opened the lock on his room. When she entered, she did not look at the holes in the settee; she went to the corner where he kept his drums. Alake went on her knees and caressed each one, ran her hands over the smooth skins that covered their faces, twisted the twines of antelope hide at the sides of a few of them. She took the smallest one, the size that had been slung around Ayandele's neck from the day he took his first step. She cradled it under her shoulder and left the room.

In her room upstairs, she sat on her bed and began to beat the drum. She didn't sing at first because she knew her voice was too wearied with age to rise to the impossible pitch of a *rara* singer. Like a fish, she opened and shut her mouth several times; only air made it past her dentures, but her hands kept hitting the drum. When a song eventually made its way out of her mouth, it was a hymn.

Ayandele was sweating by the time he got to the church. The sun had risen early that morning and was already at work in the sky. He entered the church as the congregation rose to take the processional hymn. He heard the distinct beats of *gangan* merge with the deep tones of the pipe organ. His eyes went to the boy in choir robes who was beating the talking drum with a curved stick. He held his breath and let the beat hold him. He felt a presence rest on him, like a wet cloth placed over his sweaty face, and he imagined it was peace.

DAMI AJAYI

EMMANUEL IDUMA: Let's begin at a point of intersection—between wisdom and delight. It was no other than W.S. Merwin who quoted the 16th century poet Philip Sidney: "Poetry begins in delight and ends with wisdom." Merwin was of the opinion that, "... people are happy enough to talk about how it ends in wisdom, whatever that may mean, but they don't dwell enough, I think, on the delight." Do you think this is an important distinction? How do you respond, first as a poet, and then as a budding writer of fiction?

DAMI AJAYI: Indeed Philip Sidney's profound quote is a good place to start. It lends itself to many turns and gives tons of meaning and complexities. Delight is an emotion most poets encounter. I have, in my rather short stint with poetry.

There is that giddy way one feels when a phrase begins to pirouette in one's mind, the opening verse of a new poem or a prelude that would lead to one. Wisdom is another emotion I often identify with denouements; it is the grief that occasions the end of a poem, the resolution that follows the justification of a poem, or an attempt at one.

Of course, there is that erroneous and popular belief that poetry and/or literature must give itself to a definite message, that it must speak for a moral, that it must be didactic in its thematic leanings. I suppose one can christen this attribute African, in that our literature shares a firm kinship with folklore, but this is debatable. It is an exorbitant demand that our communal characterization of literature makes in the declaration of its reach.

55

What really strikes me about delight and wisdom in poetry is that it can foretell the course of a poetic career.

Again, to approach the matter differently, the Nigerian poet Remi Raji once said that the poet is the eternal child in everyone. But maturity is a virtue time bestows on poetry; poets grow in the mining of their muse. For instance, take a look at the early stance of poets such as Wisława Szymborska and Miroslav Holub—they embraced communism at first and later gave that up. One can see the wisdom time afforded them, the gift of discernment. So indeed, the life of a poet or poem can begin with delight and culminate in wisdom. I suppose you might have something to say to this, especially with your wealth of interaction with fiction.

EI: For me both qualities are mutually exclusive, even inclusive. By which I mean wisdom is a necessary feature of delight, and vice versa. It's akin to reading the prose of Michael Ondaatje or someone like Susan Vreeland. Perhaps it's in the use of language, the infinite possibilities of word-use, and then again it could be the fact that fiction is a necessity, and given that delight cannot suffice as its singular quality. G. K. Chesterton says literature is luxury and fiction is necessity.

So, why did you write your first work of fiction? I ask this because you write such touching poetry—so delightful, true, so cogent. Are you equally drawn to fiction and poetry?

DA: My first work of fiction is a published short story called "The Love Below," which was an attempt at examining illegal abortion, deploying the point of view of the victim's ghost, recounting her plight, and following the misery of her accomplice and lover. I could have written a poem instead, something like

Lola Shoneyin's poem "For Kittan," which chronicles a lady's abortion experience. The poem was successful in the depiction, the vividness, and the clarity of the gush of emotions.

Anyway, I felt more comfortable with the milieu and mileage of fiction. The complexities of the emotions and circumstances, I felt, deserved the clarity and poise of copious sentences. The hawser of poetry was too taut for what I conceived as an angling foray that required a slack line, hence my choice. I am drawn to the possibilities of fiction, and I consider myself a student of fiction because when it is successful, it gleams. But the practice of fiction is excruciating and often exhausting, and it requires a discipline that is much more than I can afford because of my day job. Perhaps this is why I often ease into poetry.

EI: Do you remember any event as a child that you have always wanted to capture in words? Is this the way with your writing—an attempt to capture, whether or not you succeed, a feeling, a moment, an image?

DA: Oh yes, there are many moments. Many of the stories are unpublished. I have published a few in an essay called "The Economy of Loss," a tale of how I watched my parents lose their loved ones. I was at that time engrossed by grief and how people dealt with it.

I believe that writers are constantly obsessed with X-raying—or Xeroxing, if you wish—images, situations, encounters. Often we do this subliminally, by burdening ourselves with the plight of our characters. Like the Christian assessment of forthright actions, WWJD (What Would Jesus Do?), writers often ask themselves, "What would I do if I were my character?" A thorough and unflinching attempt to answer this is perhaps essential to writing meaningful fiction that will pass the litmus test of reality.

EI: A mutual friend of ours remarked on how in a work the language must exist not just as a vehicle, but as a living being. Does this conform with your view on language and word use?

DA: I often attempt a delightful and thorough depiction of an account, be it fictitious or otherwise. I insist on glorifying an idea or engendering a moment that is as rapturous as words will allow. I am also obsessed with the voice, which must resonate beyond the boundaries and reaches truth and originality.

Language is what we writers subsist on. Language is integral to the concoction of make-believe. Language must become a character in a writer's work. It must pierce the reader's experience—poke at and jar the reader's consciousness. In essence, it must draw the reader into the substance of the piece. I believe in what Borges once said, "He who reads my work, creates them." The writer-reader relationship is not give, give, and give; the reader should not slouch and take and take and take. It must be a collaborative association, an amalgam if you wish. But for one to gain a reader's trust, one's work must thrust at the reader.

Apt word use goes without saying. The writer must carefully choose his words to be clear, crisp, concise, meaningful, and unambiguous. Anything less is fraudulent.

EI: How important to you are the poems you wrote as a medical student?

DA: These poems were very important to me as a fledgling poet. You see, my foray into poetry as a mode of expression coincided with my clinical experience in the Teaching Hospital. My clinical experience as a student was a mixture of thrills and sadness; it was rather a glut of emotions. We can simply say we won some and lost many others—to cancer, to infectious diseases, to trauma. That's the result of failed governance and the tendency of humans to explore danger, which can either be youthful or irresponsible or both. While all these were ongoing, I was also growing in my poetics. And I was just commending my experiences to verse, which is not particularly new to doctors and practitioners of medicine; I have a kinship with the likes of Miroslav Holub and William Carlos Williams. What I did was just to perpetuate a tradition, the obsession of science with humanity.

EI: I haven't seen a collection of poetry from a mainstream publisher in the last decade, except perhaps collections from older Nigerian poets like J. P. Clark or Soyinka. Is this an indication of a greater malaise?

DA: If one wants to be political and go into recent history, poetry has suffered a great deal since the days of the older poets you mentioned. I do not know if you recall the 2009 Nigerian Prize for Literature, where nine poets were shortlisted and a winner did not emerge. The judges argued that their poems were substandard and their books were badly done, and as such, undeserving of such prestige. The money was supposedly given to a phony academy that did not achieve anything tangible with it—at least I am yet to be convinced they did. That is poetry being trampled on the local scene.

And what should one expect from the international scene? The poets of yore were published traditionally in the African Writer Series and their books enjoyed better global coverage than what newer poets enjoy today. Who publishes literature locally these days? A handful of daring publishing houses. How many titles do they churn out? How many of these titles are poetry collections or anthologies?

Poets who are restless about being heard often, if not always, resort to dipping into their own pockets to self-publish, and this is not without its compromises or shortcomings. In fact, I know that the cost—both monetary and kinetic—of self-publishing is probably the same amount of energy needed to produce another manuscript. These are the plagues that befall poets today.

There is the part the Internet and social media play, which is biphasic and not always exhaustive or beneficial. I suppose as a writer who honed his craft on the Internet, you might have one or two things to say to that.

EI: I am very wary of feedback on the Internet, as I've never imagined myself as a social media celebrity. So I really don't take seriously acclaim on social media. Yet, I figure there's a distinction when we refer to the Internet broadly, when we refer to blogs, web journals, etc. Most of my writing has been published on such platforms, and I know the intricacy that goes into writing, editing, publishing.

But I'd like to take you up on that word, *kinetic*. In my mind it represents a sort of diffusing of energy; I have always held the view that self-publishing leaves you fatigued. But I could argue for the poets and how they feel their work demands cogent attention. How do we argue against *kinesis* and yet support *cogency*?

DA: I totally agree that self-publishing is an occupation that can exhaust a writer or make him into a poor one. But again, there is urgency in the need to be heard, which if unattended can starve one's creativity. And there is the miscellaneous risk of not being a genuine voice in the first place or perhaps a voice that has not grown into its own. Then there is kinesis, the writerly stimulus for a reader's attention, and cogency, its merit. I say there must be a balance, as both phenomena are mutually inclusive. A cogent writer must be heard, should be heard, and will.

EI: Would you say the Brunel University African Poetry Prize, which aims to become Africa's biggest poetry prize, will resurrect interest in publishing poetry?

DA: Well, one can't disregard the role poetry prizes or any prize at all play in literature. They often serve as a communal validation of writers; they often go a long way to instill confidence in their beneficiaries. The best quote I can refer to is that of Bernardine Evaristo, who chaired the 2012 Caine Prize. She said the Caine Prize chooses to pour fairy dust on an African writer annually. That is exactly what a big African poetry prize will do. It will make one big name and cheer a myriad of other poets into the possibilities of their craft, if practiced conscientiously and with a touch of genius.

I doubt if it will resurrect interest in poetry.

EI: What will, then?

DA: I know poetry will resurrect itself. I am sure that poetry and its recital will find a way to work itself back into being fashionable and popular. Social media might play a role in that; we can boast of Facebook poets and poetic tweets. Spoken word poetry, a hybrid, is also playing a role. I think I will just stick to the possibilities of poetry as its own messiah.

EI: As co-founders and publishers of *Saraba Magazine*, how do you think we can cross the border into immortality? I know this sounds very metaphysical, but lately I have given thought to cogency as the need to be judged by posterity. How do you think *Saraba* can speak to, about, for, this generation? And is it in an attempt to do this that sustainable literature lies?

DA: I am strongly of the opinion that *Saraba* is doing all these that you ask for and more. *Saraba*, a modest and selfish idea, which we nursed for less than four years, has morphed into an international literary phenomenon publishing as much emerged as emerging voices, as many provincial artists as international artists, collaborating in translation projects and still seeking new ways of being relevant in the literary sphere.

The journalist Akin Ajayi already described the Internet as the home of contemporary African writing. It's unarguable that the internet bypasses the bureaucratic chain of traditional publishing, or quickens it at the very least. *Saraba* is one of the homes of contemporary African writing and I remember that our mission statement is to create unending voices. Ours is to do just that. Immortality often takes care of itself. Besides, who will be here to judge?

EI: One of the arguments we have made together is that a new form of literariness is rising. How is this happening with our generation of Nigerian writers?

DA: I haven't categorized our generation, if it can be so-called, as exceptionally different from the previous. What is a generation anyway? Three decades. When do we start counting our generation? Thirty years forward or thirty years backward? I am more intrigued to hear your thoughts.

EI: I am not really interested in how we might "number" our generation. I am just keen on our shared nuances — such as social media, social technology, collaborative energy. Defined in this manner, we are free from the complexities of age or educational qualification and all the blah blah blah that easily stereotypes.

Specifically, I'd remind you of the International Chain Story Challenge that we both took part in, which we won and earned "international bragging rights." Was that competition an indication of the open-ended possibilities of storytelling, of collaborative energy?

DA: Yes. Yes. It was indeed a successful experiment, which I am very proud of. I risked a day at work in the hospital for it, and I was most delighted that our team — comprised of the youngest and most unevenly matched writers — won. Biyi Olusolape described our victory as a tyranny of heavily skewed social media demographics, but I saw it, rather, as a validation of collaboration as an important venture for the near future. I am in awe of the possibilities that could result from being handed the baton of someone's fiction and wary of how much trust and literary cooperation is needed to build characters. It was a giddy experience and I am also sure you have something to say, especially as you set the ball rolling by imbuing our characters with such emotional landscapes.

EI: I like the idea of the collaboration, even over the story. I wasn't really bothered about winning, so maybe the story didn't particularly interest me. The fact that six writers could tell one short story, tell it well, in about six hours, though they were in separate corners of the world, was simply the triumph for me.

Ah, there are so many points we could consider. Let's consider how much you have been influenced by Eliot (recall that we jointly wrote love poems, copiously referencing him). Now, Eliot acknowledges that Pound "was a marvelous critic because he didn't try to turn you into an imitation of himself. He tried to see what you were trying to do." Has there been anyone with this form of influence in your writing life?

DA: That was another collaborative effort which I enjoyed being part of—writing a corpus of poems that seemed to lure personas and concerns of the 20th century to our time. These poems, autobiographical in their lilt and exuberant in their mode and form, still pierce my consciousness. I must ask how you felt writing that final poem. I recall your lines "Your Eliot-ness/Too much affection/Is cure for caries." I am taken aback by the clarity of this pseudo-maxim and the complexities of its meanings.

To mention people that played the Pound in my career will be to recur the recent past. Between the years 2008-2011, the likes of Biyi Olusolape, you, and Ayo Famurewa were at Ile-Ife and we exchanged ideas and works-in-progress. When I remember, I am filled with nostalgia; I wish I could buy a time machine and visit this period repeatedly.

EI: Also in that regard, there's an obvious attempt in your poetry to name-drop. Take for instance, the sections in the poem "The Suicide Notes." What do you suppose you can achieve with name-dropping?

DA: I refer to this period of my poetry as my fleeting obsession for the mentally morbid. I was rotating through psychiatry, a field of medicine that both confounds and interests me. I was very much interested in suicide, especially among writers. The likes of Hemingway, Sylvia Plath, David Foster Wallace, and Anne Sexton preoccupied my reading list. "The Suicide Notes" was an attempt to condense my summations into poetry and I deplored the metaphysics of a séance, a fictitious letter, and a modern elegy to examine the complexities of mental disequilibrium, the nerve- and life-wracking tendencies of literature and sweet escapism of suicide. A few names dropped inevitably in my attempt, perhaps intentionally as postcards and clues for readers. I would rather deploy a name than launch into an arcane regurgitated biography. I often strongly adhere to the triad of successful poetry: beauty and brevity and precision.

EI: I recall how I celebrated your story "You and I Will Leave at Once," which tried to chronicle a family's ordeal in the Ife-Modakeke crisis. You wrote about an event that could easily be dismissed as inconsequential in the huge montage that is the history of Nigeria. What moved you to work on what many would consider a minor historical event?

DA: Well I suppose a personal fascination with a "small-scale" genocide that has been recurrent, ancestral, and varying in its magnitude might be a good place to start. I have been visiting Ife since childhood, and I also saw a bit of the havoc the war wreaked on society's harmony and the loss of property, without trivializing the death toll. It is unfortunate indeed that this war passed into insignificance in the literary landscape, just like the psychology of middle-class Nigerians during the military dictatorship would have if you hadn't written your novel *Farad*.

EI: Do you suppose we are tasked to speak to collective memory? Mine it? Re-present it?

DA: Yes, yes. We certainly are compelled by the duty of literature and mimesis.

EI: I believe you speak to a universal dilemma in your short story "Henry's Hypothesis," which is captured in the question your character poses, "How could I drown again in rivers of formulas, lakes of measurement, and depths of objectivity?" Do you agree?

DA: Yes I do. Characters can and should often undertake grand conflicts, such as the dichotomy between subjectivity and objectivity and the tenacious stubbornness toward achieving objectivity.

EI: What was your first reaction when you were shortlisted for the Melita Hume Poetry Prize?

DA: I was elated. Often, in secret, I doubt my abilities as a poet and the significance of *Clinical Blues*, as I often refer to it as juvenilia. This was some form of validation for me as a poet and as a writer. To be the only African writer shortlisted for an international poetry prize is a significant feat. Shortly after, *Clinical Blues* was shortlisted for the Erbacce Poetry Prize. This further seals the importance of the collection as a corpus and my major literary preoccupation is to give the collection a life of its own in print.

EI: How have you coped with trying to fulfill the demands of your medical practice? You have been a medical doctor for about a year now, and I know how difficult it has been even for you to maintain personal relationships. Have you considered the need to sacrifice one career for the other? Is there any form of pressure to sacrifice? Or not?

DA: Medicine and Literature are two demanding preoccupations that demand to be practiced conscientiously and whole-heartedly. This past year has been hectic. One often has to give for the other, and I think I am in the best position to understand Anton Chekhov's analogy of medicine being a wife and literature a kept woman.

Often, I have considered sacrificing one for the other. As much as I love to write, I also enjoy saving lives. And medicine is what pays the rent and puts food on the table for now. So I must say that literature will continue to come between my matrimony with medicine, or better yet, be thrown into the polygamous mix.

EI: Was *Clinical Blues* an attempt to reflect the science of being human?

DA: I once wrote about how in his collection *Satellites*, the Gambian poet Lenrie Peters showed me how poetry could measure humanity in the realms of medicine. So, yes I agree, *Clinical Blues* is an attempt to reflect the humanity in science.

EI: Which globally-acclaimed writers have influenced your life the most? Let me add that when I speak of life, I am interested in books and writers that have an affect not merely on your writing, but on your nuances, perceptions, outlook, gaze.

DA: I will always go with books rather than authors, although there are a handful of authors whose careers have been resplendent with enviable literary accomplishments—the likes of John Irving, Wole Soyinka, Toni Morrison, and John Updike.

I really can't lay a finger on what I owe to the authors who are my influences. I suppose it is a gift from God, or that I might need a truckload of critics to unpack them. I am drawn to the poetry of D.H. Lawrence, *Pansies* is an all-time favorite; the short stories of Borges, E.L. Doctorow, Steven Millhauser; the magic in the prose of Rawi Hage's *De Niro's Game*; the breathtaking oratory tendencies of Maya Angelou's poems; the distinctive identity of the poetry of Lenrie Peters, Kwesi Brew, Gabriel Okara, etc. My influences are numerous. Can I add to that the exuberant innovations of Lil Wayne, Terry G, and Beau Sia as my influences?

EI: If you were to pay some form of homage to Nigerian writers of our generation, not simply for their prolificacy, but for their outlook, which writers would you name? And why? Do you agree this is important for the simple reason that recognition carries with it and imposes a baggage of temerity?

DA: Rotimi Babatunde's devotion to craft is just delightful. Niran Okewole's poetics make me giddy. Ifesinachi Okoli-Okpagu's seamless fiction measures up to reality appreciably. Sylva Ifedigbo Nze's essays remind me of conscientiousness often expected of valuable writers. Your meta-psychological tendencies in fiction pummel my soft spots.

I am proud to be associated with our collective corpus as a worthy tract of our movement and, most of all, our individual works, which speak at length about our devotion to craft and our conscientiousness to our time.

August 7, 2012

TALK TO ME

Dami Ajayi

We are in this room. And we are not.

Our spaces seem divided, partitioned by an impenetrable firewall.

The damn sound comes again. It's the ding of your BlackBerry and I realize that you are still in this room with me after all.

My eyes rove around my small room and sometimes around you, but you stay in that pose with your phone nestled in the embrace of your interlocking fingers. Your free thumbs stroke and stroke and stroke your new-found love.

I see the smile you do not try to hide. Every so often, the sound punctuates our silence. I see the chuckle too, and that laugh that is not directed at me. I see you don't regard my presence. I pull out the bedside drawer, lift out the crumpled pack of cigarettes you do not know I still have. The nicotine patch you bought had long worn out, the chewing gum also exhausted.

And you don't show concern anymore.

You do not see my sunken eyes, my lost appetite, the change in my attitude, the itch, the red eyes, the runny nose—you don't see all my signs of need. I'm withdrawing fast into myself, imploding under the cold turkey cessation of an addiction, and you just keep pinging, laughing, chuckling, smiling, waiting for that stupid jingle.

71

My cigarette glows for a bit before you acknowledge it. You look at me for a while, momentarily abandoning your text conversation. What do you see? My skinny hairless legs, my pork chop thighs, the waistband of my boxer shorts that doesn't quite hold my spilling pot belly, my hairy chest, the tufts of hair around my breasts, the stubble I'm nursing, dry pink lips from which the glowing cigarette dangles?

You let out a loud hiss, a hiss that almost coincides with another tinkle, then you look at your phone again and I watch the taut facial muscles congeal into a smile that almost, almost becomes a chuckle. Then you stand and shuffle your feet toward the creaking door, eyes and fingers still hoisting your phone.

*

Some three hours later, nineteen sticks puffed, half a bottle of gin quaffed, the door jerks open and you cough your disapproval, your arrival. The clouds of smoke wreathe the ceiling and the night is airless and the windows are shut and the throbbing air conditioner needs servicing. You walk to the open wardrobe, wriggle out of your clothes, jeans first, blouse, the left strap of your bra... You pick your lingerie, the blue satin one with lace trimmings, my gift last Valentine's Day, and you pull it over your head, letting it slide downward, gracefully. You bend to pick up your clothes and I see the outline of your panties through the sheer satin. Your bundle of clothes drops in the middle tier of the wardrobe and you head out of the room again, not a glance at me, not a word, grunt, hiss, hesitation, and just before the door closes with a thud, I again hear the ding of your newly found love and my heart sinks.

I sigh. I drag the bottle of gin to myself and uncap, let the liquid swill at the tip of my tongue, at the back of my mouth, down my throat, down into my stomach with a peppery heat trail. I stub the stiff filter in my ashtray; it used to be your favorite soup bowl until it broke.

I run a forefinger over my forehead and sweep the beads of sweat. I throw on some clothes, a dirty pair of jeans and shirt, both retrieved from the laundry pile. I head out of the room, into the adjoining living room where I find you awake, still cradling your phone. A light keeps flashing at its top-right corner, varying colors—red, blue, orange—like miniature strobe lights. Then I remember how we met, just before I leave the room.

*

We met while I was still a student, in my last days, when the zeal and bravado of being a student had begun to fail me. I was exhausted from the long hours I kept in medical school. I noticed you at Mole's Bar, where I drank in the company of friends.

I noticed you dressed to suit your mood. How on your exotic days, you donned wool jackets. On days you felt exquisite, you wore short gowns stopping short of your knees, and on moody days, you wore jeans and a leather jacket and drank only table water.

I am not sure you noticed me back then. My friends and I, we sat at the back of Mole's Bar and our table was always cluttered with a variety of alcohol brands, and the air around us was foggy from tobacco smoke. You should have noticed how we never came to the bar with girls; how our conversation never strayed from the hospital; how we discussed patients and their ailments, killing time, and feasting our eyes on the barely-clad bodies of ladies who frequented Mole's, especially on Friday nights, when Mr. Mole switched on his strobe lights and hired a deejay from Gold FM.

We met on one of those Friday nights. I was meeting an older colleague who was in town. Although I was tired after a very long ward round and not financially sound for a raucous Friday night, I chose to show up. I had just finished a phone call outside Mole's Bar when you and your three friends walked toward the bar, giggling, dressed in short floral-patterned gowns, long artificial weaves, beads cluttering your necks, and wooden bracelets obliterating the entire length of your forearms. You and your sorority sisters could have passed for postmodern suffragettes.

Your head was slightly bowed when you walked in just as I put a propane lighter to the cigarette hanging from my mouth. I was surprised when you came outside two songs later to beg for a cigarette.

I was tempted to say no, or ask why I should spare you a cigarette, but it seemed inappropriate, and the way your eyes glistened in the dark and looked up at me in a coquettish manner touched my heart. So I slipped my fingers into my pocket and slid open the pack for you to pick one of the rumpled cigarettes.

Your fingers dipped in and lingered. You looked at me twice and then eased the cigarette out slowly, as though you were detaching it methodically, like a surgeon removing a benign growth. While you did, you kept giving a reassuring smile; your smile was asking questions, dancing in my face, and the air around us became still and our emotions began to swirl and my mouth became dry. I wanted to put my lips on yours in a throaty, fleeting, Friday nightclub kiss, which invariably usually led to sex and a sleepover and an awkward morning after.

As though you sensed the sensual workings of my mind, you quickly withdrew the cigarette and walked on by. I lost the moment in a flash. I put another cigarette to my lips and I stared down at my watch again, wondering what kept my colleague from showing up.

Eight songs later, I walked into Mole's bar and I caught you in mid-dance, drenched in sweat. You and your sorority sisters were the gift of the night, dancing spiritedly, and the alcohol had emboldened you so that when you heard your favorite dancehall song, you climbed on a table and danced provocatively. In the dimly lit bar, the strobe lights casted several colors on walls and faces; I saw your eyes searching mine and when you found them, you kept looking into them. Your eyes danced around me in slow deliberate circles and I was tempted to prance toward you, let you dance to me, with me, for me, within a more intimate reach. But my zeal and bravado had left me. I put a champagne-filled flute in the air, raised it further to acknowledge you. My senior colleague had begun to dance and I headed out urgently in need of a piss.

When I returned, I found you leaning against the wall outside.

"Why didn't you want to dance with me?" you asked in an audacious voice.

I was tempted to tell you why, but in a lighter mood, I said, "You did not ask me nicely."

"What exactly do you mean?"

"Exactly, what I said. There is a nice way of asking people to a dance, just as it is proper to say thank you if someone obliged your request like sparing you a cigarette."

"Duhhh." You made a face I could barely see, then continued. "So you took that personal, that I didn't say a proper thank you?"

In a second, you advanced toward me and hungrily put your lips on mine and my response was overwhelming, a cataclysm of desire, and, moments later, we were in bed doing what most people do after kissing on a Friday night.

*

I choose the worst time of the night to clear my head with a walk. I discover this only after walking for a while, heading in the direction of the main campus. It is annoying that cars put their headlamps at full intensity so that it shines into my face. Sometimes I raise a hand to block out the beams.

After walking for about thirty minutes, I approach campus. The air and the trees that mark the boulevard on campus are still. I walk past a few stray students with their books and bags and flasks holding tea or coffee. Some are in twos, heading to dark crannies, like we used to.

Do you remember the night that we walked into the desolate ruins of the former Faculty of Agriculture? That night you chose not to wear underpants, and just as we got to the topmost floor, after climbing the rather shaky stairs, you lifted your dress above your waist and lunged at me, with your body, the glistening of your lips. And when our bodies touched, you sighed and moaned.

We made love, your hands fastened to the wall, your body hunched so that I took you from behind. I observed the aerial view of our university, like a pilot observing the ground on which to descend, its outlay sprawled for our benefit. We ravished ourselves through several orgasms and left the place spent.

But those days have long passed. I'm now a House Officer at the Teaching Hospital who keeps several nights on call, fixing ailing bodies with drips and drugs by taking instructions and being supervised, while you are in your final year writing a long essay on "The Autobiographical Influences on the Earlier Works of T.S. Eliot." We are both buried in our work. You are at the top of your class and you have barely a semester left to win the Best Graduating Student Prize.

That was why I bought the BlackBerry for you, when you thrilled me with a whopping 4.53 GPA. I hadn't thought you to be a bright kid back then when you and your cohorts kept occasional nights at Mole's Bar, getting high and dancing wild. I sent you the phone as a birthday gift through the campus courier, not because I was on call that night and needed to exorcise myself of the guilt that I was going to miss your birthday party. I wanted to give you something to be proud of. I wanted to give your friends something to gossip about.

I eventually stole out of my call, having explained my predicament to my Registrar, a hopeless romantic who had just returned from her honeymoon. I returned home to find you nestled on the couch, sleeping in the living room, wearing one of my T-shirts, your favorite.

Your breaths were noisy because your head wasn't well rested on the pillow. An intact phone package and a bottle of champagne lay on the rugged floor beside you, as if you were waiting for me to return, so we could open both together.

You were still fast asleep when I peeled off my tie, my shirt, shoes, trousers, and I fastened myself to your body. It didn't matter that the couch was quite small and that there was not much room on it. I wanted to lie next to you, hear you breathe. You felt warm against my thighs and I became aroused, just before I fell asleep.

I woke to a nicely made breakfast; we opened the champagne that you had put in the fridge. Then we activated your BlackBerry service.

And that was the end of us as I knew it. Your courtship with a new friend began, so that when we are together on the few nights that I'm not on call, I can hardly sleep from the loud dings and your chuckles. When I'm driving, you fix your face on your phone. When we talk, you are absent from the conversation. When we are in bed, making love, every beep distracts you. Even when we go to drink at Mole's Bar, you hardly ever dance anymore.

I feel alienated from you. My friends are all gone, doing their internships elsewhere. I chose to stay around, chose to be with you, and now you are with something else, something inanimate, bought from the sweat of my labor.

I step into Mole's Bar, it's a Friday night, and so I have to greet everyone I know around the bar. Alcohol acquaintances request a few bottles on my account, but I genially decline; I am in no mood to buy drinks.

A bottle of beer later, I step out and bump into a junior colleague from the hospital. He is now in his final year. I ask him to drop me off at home.

*

I sometimes wonder about the paradox of it all, the irony. The fact that a mobile phone which should enhance communication broke ours down. How my decision not to also own a smartphone thwarted our relationship.

I wonder how that stupid sound, at best a casual call from a faraway friend, means much more than the warmth of my body on the other side of the bed, how my breath passes into insignificance, usurped by the beep of your phone's weakening battery.

But this happened to us.

I walk into the house, and you are still awake, reading, I suspect, my copy of *Prufrock and Other Observations* that I lent you for your long essay. Your phone is not far from you, so that its slightest whimper will not go unattended.

You regard me in my entirety. The scorn in your eyes sets me ablaze, and I feel sorry for putting you in this place, even though I only meant well.

I'm here in this room, as urgent as the next rush of air that becomes your breath, but I don't matter much, do I? I'm just a vague object of attraction, not your favorite virtual friend on BlackBerry Messenger, not the guy that you once told that you wanted to be a part of his world. Not the lad whose brown eyes you wished upon our kids. Not the dude whom you once helped to fight a nicotine habit. Just another guy with a growing potbelly and responsibilities.

I feel sorry for you, for giving me up as a sacrifice to fashionable trends and vacuous popular behavior. I feel sorry for your long essay that suffers from your growing distraction, your GPA that might become irredeemably damaged from the midnight candles that burn from this little phone.

I walk briskly toward you, snatch the phone and head for my room.

You rush after me with outstretched hands, inaudible words of protest, then I turn to face you and you retreat.

Your silence speaks more than words.

It is then that I realize you have been irredeemably bought, lost to my own gift. I can see that your focus has been transferred to the pings and dings; they arouse you better than I do. I see in your eyes that our relationship has been pummeled by the sledgehammer of my generosity, the popularity of enhanced communication, that provisional immediacy short of physical presence that removes the encumbrance of physicality and replaces it with a memento, a presence that is absent.

With all the energy I can muster, I slam your phone into the wall and watch the smithereens come at you.

RICHARD ALI

EMMANUEL IDUMA: When did you become conscious of the contribution you could make to life?

RICHARD ALI: I remember the period, not a specific time, and it happened in the resort city of Jos, Nigeria where I grew up—I must have been about seven or eight at that time. It came about as a result of a television series, *The Wonder Years*, about the junior high school years of a boy named Arnold—the way the episodes were shot and directed, there was a narrator speaking out the thoughts of Arnold, such that the viewer could hear this character think. For me, a somewhat introverted child, this was revolutionary—it opened a whole new world of thought to me. I could actually observe myself thinking, talking in my head just as Arnold in the show. With thought, of course, came all sorts of experiments. But I remember I was about eight years old then. I lived in a middle-class part of town and had a life just like Arnold's with a bike and friends, and my days and holidays were spiced with playing *baram*, a hockey-like local game, against his baseball, and of course, my catapults and bird catching and mango tree disturbing were other pastimes. I realized that thoughts were a thing, very malleable like plastic, something I could play with while doing other things—a private place.

While the seeds of the sense of my Self came from then, it took a while to make the connection that thought could create impressions for other people, that one's thoughts could be made into a context for other people to enter and live. That came in secondary school at Emmanuel College in Jos, in the friendship of my late friend Faruk Ibrahim Hamza. Prior to this, I was an avid reader of books and magazines wherever I found them. I started reading *Time* and *Newsweek* in the early '90s, regularly; I'd also read story books of the children's variety and then my father's books, which were an eclectic mix—I remember reading James Hadley Chase's *No Orchids for Miss Blandish*, dozens of African Writer Series books—of which Peter Abrahams' *Mine Boy* and Ferdinand Oyono's *The Old Man and the Medal* are the first in my mind. Tayeb Salih's *Season of Migration to the North* as well. All these were, shall I say, cosmetic readings in the sense that the sole job of these books was to feed my thoughts, to populate my mental spaces.

Things changed when Faruk, my tragic friend, discovered books on philosophy in the course of a holiday and shared his discoveries with our little clique. It was as if, you know that trick where a tablecloth is quickly pulled off a table so the tea set on it stays exactly where it was? Everything changed. That was Faruk. I remember him asking if we could be sure that the blackboard was in fact black. Relativism, the primacy of definition, rationality, heady stuff from Faruk's reading that set my thoughts in frenzy. I saw that, like those philosophers who had created worlds of ideas for other people to think in, I could do the same thing. I was about thirteen; Faruk was a year younger. Faruk Hamza died the next year in a freak car accident in Kaduna. By the time I arrived in Zaria as an undergraduate and met the work of Leftist historians who had had their heyday in the '70s and '80s and begun my own student union activities, contributing to Life with a capital L was something I had already started doing and felt I would do even more definitively in time.

EI: Do you remember the first thing you wrote, and the feeling afterward? Is this akin to the feeling of being a first time author? Or has maturity replaced naiveté?

RA: I do hope some sort of maturity is evident in my present work—we are all dying and I don't think the fate of Benjamin Button is a particularly pleasant one. The novel *City of Memories* is my first major writing out in the public, but it comes latest merely in a line of less, to use your word, *mature* writing. My very first writings were memoirs and I was about thirteen—about the same time my conscious thinking started, my fourth year in secondary school. I had no idea that thirteen year-olds had no business writing memoirs, so I bought a notebook and skipping the first page, I wrote "Memoirs" in as stylish a script as my scrawl would allow. I remember it took many weeks before I returned to that page and wrote my full name at the bottom of the page—it was a heady feeling, to be a writer without his words yet. Perhaps later that night, I wrote my first entry.

My "Memoirs" was populated by thoughts about the world and about other people and why they were the way they were. I remember an essay on a friend who was heartbroken; I remember another about a girl who had bent an infant's fingers backwards to spite its mother. This was my first writing—trying to understand the world in words, for I was introverted and never was a physically significant child. I consider these juvenilia and much of my early poetry as well, until about 2007; all these are mostly juvenilia and the sole purpose of such writing is to find the core ideas for the rest of one's life—lacking elegance, the first task for a writer is to make his ideas elegant. Poetry came with taking Literature-in-English in secondary school and learning the dynamics of the genre. I was fascinated with English poetry and tried, as Robert Louis Stevenson exhorts us to try and fail, to copy their style. I never had the ear for the falling and rising notes of the iambic pentameter, but I contented myself with counting the syllables on each line and playing around with rhymes and rhyming schemes.

The first major break came in 2007 when, having stopped my imitations of the traditional English, I wrote a poem "Buddha Child," which Chuma Nwokolo published in his *African Writing* journal. After this, my poetry became better as I had found the core of my poetics. So, yes, to my mind there has been a lot of maturing over the last decade.

EI: Are there schizophrenic tendencies in choosing whether to read or to write? I often feel tempted to write when I am reading, and a parallel feeling when I am writing. Perhaps it's the same with you?

RA: Schizophrenic is a good word. It also means withdrawn, doesn't it, to be withdrawn into oneself? I would use that word to describe the difficult feeling you ask about, but with a nuance. For me the choice is not between choosing to read or choosing to write, these two are so related as to be Siamese. On the other side is thinking. Thought. Especially with fiction. I'll tell you about the cliché effect; it is the tendency to write what you have read—a lot of minor plagiarism is birthed in this tendency. Even major cases of plagiarism, paragraphs or pages long for example, these are sometimes innocent doings of people who can remember extremely long passages, but not where they got them from— quite understandable, even if rightly prosecuted. What a writer needs to develop, and the earlier he does this the better, is the core of writing—the dynamics—and for me these always border around very existential questions. The nature of truth and reality, for example, as seen in the theme of identity. Causality, as seen in exploring the context of actions, to better understand events and happenings.

Then there's the question of freedom and how to be free—is it by knowing more or by knowing less, how does what other people know affect us? All these are for me a writer's core negotiations and the answers to these inform literature truly, whether poetry or prose. If a writer has this at the back of his mind, if he wrestles mentally with these, if he has an active imagination, and even if he has just average skills in craft, such a writer will write true literature. That is why we feel Okonkwo from *Things Fall Apart*, even by German or Inuit readers, because Chinua Achebe's existential, philosophical concerns, coupled with his imagination, saw him write a book that mined the human experience at its most basic. We must imagine Okonkwo, as we must imagine Arthur Miller's character Willy Loman, or J. D. Salinger's Holden Caulfield, as Adamic or Babelian. Adamic in the broadest, most inclusive, most human sense of the word. Babelian not as dissonance, but as a One.

This does not come from reading books or writing books but by thinking, and this sort of thinking requires a style of schizophrenia. The reading-writing dichotomy, to use a very distrusted word, really depends on what you are reading, whether popular fiction or literary fiction within these two extremes. For example, if you are reading an Anne Rice book and you want to write, there is a choice between pleasure and effort. But if you were reading Umberto Eco and wanted to write, it is a less clear choice, because both are extremely similar things. I'll give you an example from poetry; it is not possible, I think, to read T. S. Eliot or Yeats and not stop in places, bookmark, take a pen, and write—even if it is marginal notes. Difficulty in choice only comes when there is difference. Reading and writing what I consider to be true literature is a Siamese relationship.

Let me return to my earlier idea: it is dangerous to read too much true literature, because of the clichés of perception that this sublimates in a reader. The writer must create new perceptions, not the mimesis of others' perceptions, however well-perceived these may be.

EI: It seems to me that you draw sensibilities from nationalistic concerns? Is it a sense of duty to a troubled nation like ours, or an attempt to extricate yourself from the laziness of being an onlooker?

RA: I wouldn't say my sensibilities are "nationalist;" I would prefer humanist. But I am more interested in my local context than in larger, perhaps international or even interplanetary contexts. This local interest, often coinciding with very recognizable national settings in my writing, especially prose, comes from a belief that the universal is in the particular. I will illustrate this with the universality of myth. We have these grand Scandinavian myths of Loki and the Babylonian-Persian myths recorded in the Upanishads and we have the Ifa myths that predate the present Yoruba people, and all these are attempts to understand the elemental world. Yet, all these myths have similar, near archetypal characters—we have the Hindu deity Agni and Agni is similar to the Yoruba god Sango. Take a look at the Christian trinity and its Egyptian precursor, or its various Middle Eastern triune gods. I think these theologies are not only related, but are in fact the same thing. Imagine a plumb line into the core of what it is to be a human being or imagine various shafts leading to a common mother lode. I am interested in my path, my local environment, because I know it leads to the same place as his and hers and theirs, because it is as much human as his or hers or theirs. The nation is a microcosm of the world, my street is a microcosm of the nation—microcosms have all you want and you see the details of everything, the Larger Story, clearer than ever there.

EI: Why do you write?

RA: I assume you mean my fiction? Out of responsibility—to the authors and the books I have read, primarily. Perhaps I've read five hundred books in the last decade. Most of these have been literary fiction: Milan Kundera, the truly great Ondaatje, J. M. Coetzee down to Achebe and Soyinka, and all these writers have contributed the nuance of their understanding to the larger human story. I think a sense of indebtedness arises from having read all these—it is the sort of crucial indebtedness which, as a matter of honor, you seek to discharge and memorialize as soon as you receive that unexpected patrimony. This drives all writers, I think—the conviction that they too have something to say, something to add to the human story. Everyone has a range that their talent and experience allows them to observe. I never tire of restating the Igbo proverb about the inability to view a masquerade from one spot—you can only truly experience the spectacle of culture, literary culture in this case, and the humanity or humanism that underlies it, by a synthesis of vantages. These vantages are provided by various writers.

To write is to affirm—I also saw the masquerade, and this is what I saw! All the while you are aware that the larger spectacle is truly a collective one. An example comes to mind, a quilt! Each fiction, literary fiction, is a patch in a quilt.

The second reason why I write is because I enjoy working on my writing, both the stringing of words together and the finessing afterward. I think some of the most beautiful sentences in Nigerian writing belong to Wole Soyinka, many from his *Prison Notes*. When I write, I see the sheer beauty in Soyinka's language. I know that beauty is accessible to me and I try to mine that aesthetic field and make my words latent with beauty and power as well.

EI: What is it about Jos that is endearingly beautiful? In your new novel your celebration of Jos might, to the careless reader, seem contrived. Did you seek to unravel the state of being in that city? What do you seek to do when making a work out of Jos?

RA: The city of Jos, for me, symbolizes the center of everything and I put my native city at the heart of my novel to further ground that symbolism—writers are allowed to play such private tricks. My sense of the world largely revolves and resolves itself into the religious Sufi idea of Oneness of God. Put simply, it means that while there may be Two and Three and Ten and possibly a universe full of numeric deviations, all these have a common *fons et origo*, and this is the One, and this One is the same numeric value as Zero and Infinity. All religious ideas, especially the great monotheisms, are mirroring of one thing. I am interested in what casts the reflection, less in the glass that reflects, and this primacy of interest is what Sufism is about. In the same sense, countries, modern African countries with their major issues and problems, always have a way-they-were-before. Jos is a resort town right in the center of the country; the first fact means it is a cosmopolis and the second dramatizes the idea of centrality.

Let me say something about centrality—the most artistically sophisticated culture in Ancient Nigeria was the Nok Culture, which thrived in the Jos-Southern Kaduna area at about the same time Xerxes was building Persepolis and the Greeks started writing. It means we were there as well; we, Nigerians, contributed to the world story—significantly. This is the meaning of Jos, the sense of historical authenticity that comes from always having been in the pulse of historical events, knowing that your story is wide enough and resilient enough to absorb all the sub-stories, seemingly discordant, forcedly antagonistic, that modern Africa teems with. There is nothing contrived about it, it is rather something challenging—if you can dare to imagine the Largest Possible Picture, you will find yourself in Jos, in Babel, in Eden, cosmopolises such as these. The modern city of Jos has seen a lot of politico-economic (masked as ethno-religious) eruptions in the last quarter century and many think adversely about Jos-ness. Yet, what is 25 years when your history is as long as 1500 years? When I write about Jos, this is where I write from.

EI: You write in "How Wild Horses Die," an unpublished poem, "everything reels in a swirl of images." To me the image is the trajectory of feeling. And evoking feeling is an important duty of the novelist. How do you manage, if you wish to plumb my analogy, to create reels in a swirl of imagery? Or do you feel obliged, even?

RA: I use a "swirl of images" there in the sense of a mental swirl; an image is something that exists but has yet to be experienced. Perhaps I could use your analogy and say mental images are feelings that have the promise to be experienced. You are right to say the novelist's job is to evoke feeling. I think this is not so difficult to do, for the novelist is among the most observant people on the planet. Orhan Pamuk sits writing a book in Aladdin's coffee shop in Istanbul and decides to pepper his story with descriptions of the real coffee house in fiction. What he has done is to take something very public, perhaps a hundred thousand people go through that same coffee house each year, and make it significant by writing about it. The same things happen to us all, what sets the writer apart and above the rest is that he writes about it—re-invokes it, such that the others to whom these things did happen, might have happened, or sought to have happen, identify themselves in his re-invocation. And, if a writer succeeds, how he saw what happened, becomes how it happened for other people for whom the events of course happened differently. In this sense, the novelist is a politician. He politicizes what to emphasize in his world through his fiction.

EI: How do you navigate the demands of the image as a poet or a novelist?

RA: Both are one and there really is no great dispute between a Poetry Faction and a Prose Faction in my head. Let's say there are certain things that I would naturally tackle in poetry and others that have to be written in prose. I think poetry, at least my poetry, is the genre in which I try to find and express the truth of things. Poetry is difficult for me, yet I derive the most pleasure from my poems, because it's difficult to write, I have very few poems and am only just thinking seriously of a collection. Some poets seem to have poetic lips or spirits or whatever, such that anything they see they can, forgive me, poeticize. I don't begrudge these poets, though they do have a tendency to somehow write good verse on trivial topics and shift the burden of depth, and possibly truth, to the reader. I think this is a mischief.

The novel is far more luxurious, far more leisurely. As I said earlier, the most important thing about the novel for a writer is the form of the novel, which is very, very fluid. A writer should feel free and confident to experiment. Be aware of tradition, then set out to create a new tradition, each and every time. I try this in my novel, leaving some questions unanswered, involving the reader in a play of language while doing subtle tricks with plot— whether I have pulled it off or not remains to be seen. A novel is a thing that can be planned; as I sit here, I can see sketches of my next novel on the back of a calendar on the table and when the actual writing starts in a year's time, this schema will be subordinate to the words and ways of plot that cannot be argued with. The demand of each is different, prose and poetry.

EI: In the last two, three years you have indulgently, even fascinatingly, edited *Sentinel Nigeria*. When did you consider you could facilitate that platform? What demands has it made?

RA: *Sentinel Nigeria* is one of the success stories of the Internet; it couldn't have happened without the World Wide Web. Back in the early 2000s, in the pre-Facebook days, I was a member of a Yahoo! Group—the Sentinel Poetry Group—in which most of the "third generation" of Nigerian writers shared their writing and opinions, engaged in controversies, and we even had a monthly competition. I took to the Internet as soon as it arrived in Nigeria, having read about it in *Time* and *Newsweek* in the late '90s. I was fascinated and when it became reasonably cheaper, I think 500 naira (~$3) for 30 minutes, I joined the online community. People like Adebola Rayo and I were the green ones, in silence learning

93

from our elders, most of whom had left Nigeria for various reasons in the '80s and '90s.

Five years later I got an e-mail from Nnorom Azuonye, who had set up the Sentinel Poetry Group, offering me an opportunity to set up the *Sentinel Nigeria* magazine. I accepted. At the time of setting up the editorial team, comprising Nze Sylva Ifedigbo and Unoma Azuah initially, I hadn't met either of them. I finally met Nze in Abuja after our third issue, and met Unoma after our seventh. As of our tenth issue, I have never met my boss and publisher, Nnorom Azuonye. Ivor Hartmann, I've never met him. Its demands have been considerable, but I have a solid team behind me and I enjoy what we do at *Sentinel.* We are all working pro-bono, so it's a labor of love. I actually love editing together with the sub-editors, and I love it when an editorial comes out well. But editorials, like poems, are difficult to write; thankfully, I go through the trials of it only once every three months. Its demands are considerable, but they also bring pleasure.

EI: Let's expand the conversation. There is the argument for home-grown literature, that we ought to globalize the local. I wonder if the present circumstances of being Nigerian supports this view. Compared to a decade ago, is the work being done inside Nigeria of interest to those outside the country?

RA: I don't agree with "globalizing the local." In that process, essence is lost and to be candid, any writing that is capable of or in need of being "globalized" is of doubtful quality. Did Chinua Achebe globalize *Things Fall Apart*? Cyprian Ekwensi's novellas, did he globalize them, measure them up to some O' Henry or XYZ somewhere "there"? Tayeb Salih? None of these guys internationalized anything they wrote. I've spoken on this earlier, but I'll tell you again why they did not—because they wrote the core of the human experience and what is human in Umuofia is recognizable instantly in Beirut, and what is human in Vladivostok is easily identified with by just about anyone. Look at Anna Akhmatova's poems! Or look at *The Gulag Archipelago*, yes, Solzhenitsyn versus Wole Soyinka's *Prison Notes*. If Wole Soyinka's *The Man Died* was translated to Russian, and a political detainee of the Soviets back in the days had read it, would he have needed any globalist modifications to identify completely with the persona? I doubt it. Both books go to the core of what it means to be human.

You only need to use artificial lighting when there is no natural lighting. No, I'm not a believer in globalizing literature—take the form of the novel, take the tradition of poetry, take what has come before, study it and re-imagine something new. If you have done your intellectual job well, the product of your re-imagination is instantly recognized without recourse to "globalization" or the wearing of similar funny hats.

EI: It might be simpler to ask—why should we be concerned with globalizing the local? Is the local not enough? And I think you misunderstand me—I argue from the point of your conclusion, that the local is eventually universalized, and so we shouldn't struggle with the need of being globalized.

RA: My point exactly. We have no concern with globalizing the local in the same manner a man with full limbs has no need for a crutch. I'll take your second question in two senses. In the sense of content, the fidelity of content, the local is self-sufficient because the core of the global is embedded in it. The only time when it is not is if the necessary mental effort hasn't been expended and if the local is improperly imagined whether by mistake or mischief. In these cases, this is only a local so-called, an imposter local.

The second sense is that of market; if the local market for fiction is not enough, then why would a writer want to sell copies of his book in Ukraine and Alaska? The reason for this is vanity, and it is a very excusable vanity—to want to be read widely. Writers need to be able to say they got fan mail from some remote part of Australia; it sounds good and is sure to earn you points with women or men. I want to be read everywhere, like any other writer. But even more than being read in a nonexistent Everywhereland, I want to be read at home by my own country, my own continent—Nigeria, Africa first—because the story I am telling is one that's theirs, happening down the street or in the country just two or three border crossings away. They should identify themselves and their environment in my writing.

To your last question: the revealing query is, at whose instance does the local become globalized? This is so immensely important that to assume it is not important is the single greatest mischief that can exist. I say the global must accept the local and come to seek it in its habitat, humbly and respectfully, not demanding and proud and rude like the Spanish Armada. The local must never give a quarter in the name of globalizing, for the simple truth is that the so-called global is someone's local backed with a dubious power. This global, actually a scam-local, can, at best, be only parallel to my own local.

EI: You once mentioned Orhan Pamuk's internationalization as a useful model for Nigerian literature. Could you elaborate on this?

RA: I read Pamuk after he won the 2006 Nobel. I read the Nobel Lectures of all literature laureates because, regardless of claims of "politics," all laureates are at the very height of true literature — literary fiction especially. I then read his *My Name is Red* and his essays in *Other Colors*. Pamuk's *My Name is Red*, as all his books, was written originally in Turkish and this came from a tradition of writing books since the early '80s that routinely sold tens of thousands of copies. *My Name is Red* itself sold over a hundred thousand copies in Turkey in its first week. The point is, Pamuk wrote for his countrymen first — the streets of Istanbul he describes are their own streets and he doesn't fill in details of explanations as one would find in a tour book; he simply describes his settings elegantly. And the local Turkish market rewarded him for this by buying unheard of amounts of his books. In Turkish. When the West saw these sales figures, they came to him, bearing publishing deals and fellowships in America — I believe it was Columbia first among others. His books make no apologies, they wear no funny hats to impress. He was, to use your word, internationalized, via translation, on his own terms. When you read his essays, you understand why — and you understand that his concentration on Turkey did not mean he had a congenial career in the country, he had all the controversies and fights that make for intellectual ferment and creativity.

So, why are Nigerian and African writers not doing the same thing? Why should a Malawian be more interested in a bad review in the *New Yorker* than in a positive review in the Kenyan *Daily Chronicle*? I know dozens of writers who have spent money vanity-publishing themselves in America, some small press in Kalamazoo, and their books, sometimes their very first books, are not available in the book store at the corner of the street in the town where they live—a town in which their writing is set. If a writer writes as best as he can, his first market will be the one he breathes the same air with. Others come later. I intend to be around for a while and write a hopeful four more novels—yet, I am still thinking whether or not to get an agent and if I would accept a publishing deal from one of the majors were it offered for any of my subsequent writing.

EI: Should writers read the kind of books they want to write next?

RA: I don't think you should read the sort of book you would like to write next. I'm a believer in originality and, above that, authenticity. The easiest way to lend yourself to deliberate or mistaken plagiarisms is to read about the next book you wish to write—believe me, the temptation to not attribute sources, where such unoriginal unauthentic ideas exists, is a strong one, one that may even require, to use Wilde's quip, great strength to not fall into.

But then, maybe I'm doctrinaire? I know a young man, one of the more talented younger Nigerian writers, who declared he was not original and that being authentic was not a goal he wished to aspire to. I smiled, because I knew then that pretty as his writing ever would be, it would be of little value to me—for he as a person simply had no core to him. So, I do not agree with this theory of yours, for it is incompatible with my cherished ideas of originality and, possibly, authenticity. Now, look at it this way, between me and the young writer I just mentioned: if he is right and I am wrong, what would that prove if not that we are all damned already? Redemption, not damnation, should be the idea associated with creative artists.

EI: I like you for many reasons, one of which is the divergence of your preoccupations—from Coldplay to Occupy Nigeria to Sufism, and more. Do you see beauty in this collagist identity?

RA: Sufism guides my life and these seemingly disparate personalities are all in harmony—and yes, I think I am beautiful. I started pluralizing myself quite early, maybe even as early as the phase I realized the action of thought during the time of *The Wonder Years*. I have spoken of the Sufi idea in answer to an earlier question, so let me seek another illustration, a chemical one, to capture what I feel to be this collagist identity. The core of this is informed by being from central Nigeria and living in Jos, at least in part.

Manifestations of Self, in its protean variety, feeds into the master work of my life. It is a work I cannot say anything about, quite in the same way a patchwork in a quilt cannot describe the quilt of which it is a part.

This reality brings up a number of possible reactions, the most obvious of which is existentialism in the French sense of it, as alienation and the sense of living life as being absurd. My point of departure from Camus' existentialism, however, is that there is no dichotomy between man and the world—we do not have the one seeking order and the other being definitively chaotic. If this dichotomy does not exist, it follows that there can be no "absurdity" and suicide does not come up in my world. For me, both man and the world are all, to use not the best term, matter, beneath their seeming natures. If one probes deep enough, you will find a basic harmony. This puts me to mind of the dialectics of Hegel, Marx, and their descendants. Unlike them, I am interested only in working backward and finding the One rather than working forward and predicting the future. This is how I see my protean personalities, as feeding a deeper logic of my Life — all these, all Me, are beautiful like the skirt of a Sufi dancer spinning round and round in one spot in love for the One.

EI: Have you ever responded to an online debate as though you faced your opponent in real life?

RA: I always respond to online debates as if I were facing my opponents across the table. The image in my mind is of those great disputations, the First Council of Nicaea, right down to the Renaissance disputes. I admire the Renaissance thinker Pico della Mirandola who, in sheer audacity, offered to debate any of his 900 theses with any man alive — the gesture presupposes that Mirandola had thought out each of these theses and had a firm position in his own mind about each of them. For me, Mirandola is the archetype of The Thinker.

Setting out one's ideas is a serious business; it is to ask normal people to trust the product of your Thought; it is also to ask fellow thinkers to test the fidelity of your Thought. In these situations, I remember when Einstein said God did not play dice. I similarly see no reason to give quarter. In the folly of intellectuals lies the ruin of civilizations, and the ruin of civilizations is not a joke. This informs my contributions to disputes.

Yet, Time has taught me to stop engaging in online debates or disputes. This is because without a raconteur, without a court registrar, there is a perverse species of disputant who enjoys dispute for its own sake, who have no true stake, and so do not mind imagining they argue cyclically, even when chunks of the circumference of their arguments have been carved out by their opposition.

EI: I suppose you're a lover-man. Otherwise I find no other explanation for the blissful imprudence in the final stanza of "She-Shell" (unpublished):

> *Between eternities, my mind explores the subterns – whiffs*
> *Of perfume, cadenced laughter, chance glances glimpsed*
> *At market squares, and such ephemera. Dreams are groves in psyche*
> *Beckoning to our trust. I close my eyes and melt into her dream.*

RA: I guess you can say that—I love women very much and they inspire a lot of my poetry. Yet, in these love poems, I also try to code the idea of love for God that informs the poetry of my predecessors, such as the sublime Rumi. Some poems are merely carnal love, others bear love for what is greater than mere carnal love. That poem was written for a girl, Elizabeth, who I came to love at her core. Sometimes you are lucky and a woman bares herself in a way that is done hardly, and sometimes what you see is beautiful. So, you love. In that affair, we can say both sorts of love poetry found balance. It is one of my favorite poems.

EI: I always get the feeling that you believe in this generation of Nigerian writers more than the earlier ones. Is this correct? Do we have a "unique selling point"? Has this informed your efforts with *Sentinel* and your publishing firm Parrésia?

RA: Absolutely. I think this new generation of Nigerian writers is more home-grown than the last, the so-called Third Generation, who are still mostly diaspora-based. This generation, unlike the Third, do not have to bother about the geo-psychological politics of expatriate, exile, or émigré life—all those tedious, false, immensely crucial arguments with self about proximity from "home," hyphenation, and so on. All those real and imaginary things that plagued the creative phase of the Third generation, we do not have those concerns. Nnorom Azuonye, Esiaba Irobi, Olu Oguibe, and Victor Ehikhamenor—these guys were plucked in their twenties and put under the immense pressures of forced acculturation. I cannot imagine that really; I can only deeply empathize. We, on the other hand, are in our own country, albeit one that is rapidly dysfunctional. We are the parallels of the First Generation of Nigerian writers, Wole Soyinka, J. P. Clark, Achebe, et al. We are in times of great social ferment and perhaps this informs the vibrancy of our writing. It must, in the very least, be closely related. Read up on Ukamaka Evelyn Olisakwe and Ifesinachi Okoli, read up on Abubakar Adam Ibrahim and you too, Emmanuel, and one can't help feeling the pulse of new creativity. This is a generation that is defining itself by itself, like the pre-independence guys. There are no foreign influences, so there is less a need to place funny hats on this generation's creativity.

The increasing availability of the Internet, of objectionable quality but nonetheless available in urban areas at least, has seen great intra-generation communication and collaboration. I told you about the way *Sentinel Nigeria* is run. Parrésia is run the same way, with a heavy reliance on e-mail and Skype and Internet services. Our key files are backed up on cloud computing services that are remotely accessible, such that if there is a hardware loss we can be up and running in next to no time. BlackBerry Messenger is another platform, allowing for intimate groups of just 30 people who share their most private ideas and develop authentic senses of themselves each day. Our unique selling point is that we are the Unapologetic Generation. I foresee the rise of ideologies of Nigerian and African writing from this generation; we will have ideas and factions and schisms—the whole works. And we will leave a mark. We are already making an impact, because for us the purpose of tradition is to aid us to be at the start of a new tradition. There are no foreign influences to overwhelm, for we have seen the harm of unoriginality and, I am hopeful, we largely value our creative authenticity.

EI: In my review of your new novel, I accused you of attempting to soak "us in the beauty of language, of philosophic declarations, that we forget the loose ends that are tied up in other, less ambitious stories." Could you speak for yourself?

RA: I liked that sentence in your review. It marked you as a perceptive reader. I'll tell you that I believe a novel should have something inexplicable, the explanation of which the reader will bring out by various techniques—textual criticism, imagination, whatever. An example of such a question is: why does Eunice Pam, one of the characters in my novel, take the fatal step to aiding genocide? I do not answer it and deliver you a novel that is neat as a box of chocolates. I leave the action inexplicable because, in playing with the form of the novel, I wished to mirror life. Why did Hitler take the fatal step of solving the Jewish Question in the manner he did, such that by 1944 trains headed to Treblinka and Auschwitz had more priority over those taking material to the war front of his speedily shrinking Third Reich? That is the Inexplicable. Why did Pol Pot start killing intellectuals, making anyone with even a pair of glasses a counterrevolutionary liable to be shot, even as his Marxism came from an intellectual tradition? That is the Inexplicable in life. In my experimentation with the novel, I include the reality of the Inexplicable.

As for language, I am pleased that you ascribe beauty to mine. Writing is, in a sense, a labor of immense love and nowhere is the nature of this love shown than in what a writer does with sentences. Read Hemingway's sentences, read Michael Ondaatje's—each sentence exists as the heir of perhaps fifteen that were erased, deleted, re-formed. Read Ondaatje's *In the Skin of a Lion* and *Divisadero*, also *The English Patient*. Do you remember in *The English Patient* where Almásy instructs Hana on how to read the first paragraph of Kip? It is because what a writer does to sentences, how they rise and fall, where the pauses are, the commas, therein lies all the labor of love that some have called style. I try to make my language beautiful because I love words. I love my story and I love my readers and I can only give them the best of me and the best of me is, I do not doubt it, beautiful in my variedness. The trick, of course, is to do this and not impede the plot. Did I succeed in doing that? I am waiting to read further criticism in the hope that some other critical reader might pick up on what you've sniffed out.

EI: I am curious—your book is dedicated to two daughters and "their" mothers. Do you have a flawless argument for polygamy, or two marriages?

RA: Oh no, far from it. I do not believe in marriage. This unbelief comes from two perspectives. The first is that my chosen, maybe coined, philosophy in gender relations is described only possibly as post-feminist. It means that I assume that the objectives of feminism have been achieved and that the assumption of absolute gender equality informs my relationship with women.

With all women, but especially with women who have had the benefits of a liberal education of which feminist ideology and gender studies are a part. This gender equality is borne on the back of physiology, which has shown conclusively that there is no difference between the brains of either gender, and that the sexual differences are more adaptive than definitive. Following all this, why should one party, one gender, "marry" the other? That would undo the entire gains of the feminism that informs my post-feminism, wouldn't it? Marriage is an anachronism from the patriarchal, pre-neo-feminist social structure and it has little place in a feminist world and no place at all in a post-feminist one. What we can have is negotiations by competent, equal parties. My daughters Zourain and Semira were born as a result of such negotiations—the particulars of these negotiations are my private life and I cannot share these here.

The second perspective informing my unbelief is an artistic one, that which seeks to avoid all clichés of perception. One of these clichés of perception I would rather do without is that marriage is beneficial in any way to men, women, or their children. Sadly, this cliché of perception is ingrained in boys and girls each and every day by our mis-educational system. I choose not to be mis-educated, while respecting everyone else's right to participate wholly in their own mis-education. The key to harmonious gender and parental relations is love, mutual respect, seeking to aid self-realization, and emotional availability. I am less interested in the filigree around a keyhole, more interested in having the right key in my hand.

EI: Do you face the difficulty of alternating between careers—that of a writer, a publisher, an editor, a lawyer, an administrator, a man? Maybe there's a formulaic manner you deal with this difficulty?

RA: The difficulty is of course that the time in each day is finite and the demands tend to make outrageous, jealous demands. But then, I try my best and I hope to learn to delegate responsibilities even more. I did recently discover a system, you will be surprised I came so late to it. I leave reminders and alarms on my smartphone, synchronizing everything.

Smartphones always remember, see, that must be why they are smart, no? So, I re-remember to do things in their own time, whipped on my slave master of a silicon chip made by RIM. All said, I have a philosophy that what is meant to be will be and what is not fated to be would not happen regardless of how much one tries. You might have heard that? My nuance is that I assume everything is meant to be until it is apparent that it was not. The glorious Koran states famously, "Maktub; It is written." But you will remember Ali in David Lean's *Lawrence of Arabia*— he replied, "For some men, nothing is written unless they write it."

May 24, 2012

HELD IN PLACE

Richard Ali

I was naked in the unfamiliar bathroom, aware of my penis standing out from my body like something foreign and menacing. The bathroom was barely six meters square and it had a neatness absent in the room I had passed through, where my clothes now lay on the bed of this girl I only just met. Generic white tiles on the wall, a sloping floor, a tap on the wall running water into a red plastic bucket. I smiled to see the placement of the soap holder containing a jellied blue-green Palmolive soap—it was in the exact same location in my own bathroom.

"What's funny?" Arikan asked.

"Me."

She shrugged at that, turned off the tap. "Let's bathe. *I dey fear cold water sha.*"

"Really? We should have boiled the water then."

"You don't like cold water?"

"Not particularly."

"Not particularly," she repeated, snorting.

It was about 10 p.m. and I was locked in with Arikan in a hot and sweaty, lagoon-cradled corner of Lagos. The city was a lifelong love story for me, dreamed of as a child in my city of Jos three thousand kilometers away and the same number of feet above sea level. Jos was another country, a place where we lived life with the ease of mats in the breeze and ate fried Irish potatoes and drank coffee for breakfast. Lagos was a rush of serious faces everywhere, expensive cars, yellow buses, and the haranguing of bus conductors who looked like mafia hoodlums—all this mix was modern, exciting, and dangerous. I had been in the midst of it for a fortnight, attending a creative writing workshop.

The journey to this bathroom smelling of lavender air freshener started with me leaving with my cronies for Freedom Park after my reading at a Yaba bookshop. Arikan had been in the audience of about sixty, wearing a pastel lime green skirt with black palm fronds seeming as if sketched onto the fabric, and a white semi-transparent blouse. There was something potent, yet muted, beneath her appraising eye when I caught it eventually.

A car horn sounded from far outside her apartment.

"You come from Jos," she said, chuckling, placing her arm against the wall of the bathroom so I could see the concave of her shaved armpit. "Jos is really cold, isn't it? *You suppose don dey used to the cold na.*"

"*You no well,*" I replied, "*person fit dey used to cold?* Maybe that's all the more reason to be wary of cold water, isn't it?" But, compared to hers, I felt the inferiority of my pidgin English—she came from Warri in the heart of pidgin country. What could I speak but to approximate? None of that phrasing was mine. I looked her in the eye. We had to bathe. And I had to ignore my penis.

"Okay, let me help you," I said. I cupped a palm full of water from the bucket, she watched me amused as I let it drip to her chest and run over her breasts. She tensed when the water touched her.

"First cut is the deepest," I said, aware of the recklessness of this night. Then I had a vision of Medusa and I thought of the snap of a vagina slicing my penis off. So I fetched a bowlful of cold water and poured it over my head, feeling the sudden shock of it, then the pleasurable rush of heat as my skin sought to make amends.

"Your turn."

I poured some water on her body, her low moans when the water touched her excited me. Then I rubbed the Palmolive over my body, was she appraising me? I touched her then, this girl my eyes had met by chance hours before. I lathered the soap on to her skin, her chest, arms, between her breasts which were palm sized, yet full. She was silent. I exhaled.

We were having our bath.

Reaching her part of town from Obalende had taken three bus changes and the best of an hour and a half. At the back of my mind all the while was a faint buzz of danger, excitement, or desire—I could not say which exactly. We had been sitting with drinks with a few friends from the book reading at Freedom Park, built on an old Colonial Prison, when she said she liked intelligent men. I looked in her eyes and found the veil of a suggestion there. I took the bait without thinking, like a fool when he wants a woman. An hour after she said this, our little group of six dispersed, leaving her and me with the burden of deciding what to do with ourselves—it was 8 p.m. We walked from the Park through the CMS bookstore to get to the bus stop. Somewhere before the bookshop, I put her palm in mine. She did not resist when I slipped it out and placed my palm, confident and protective, on the side of her hips as we walked in step like lovers through the dwindling urban crowd.

As I bathed, I watched her clean herself. I watched her run the water over her body, brown and voluptuous and watched her palms, in silence, run over her skin, washing it clean of sweat and concerns. I thought how there was always a price to pay and suspected that her price would be nothing and that that would bankrupt me.

I watched her squat a little and wash her vagina and it gave me a perverted pleasure — perhaps no luxury is equal to watching a woman bathe? I had not imbibed this since Tutu left me. And, even with Tutu, we had stopped being intimate a full year before the farce of our dazzling affair came undone, clear as it had been to everyone else. And now, here I was feasting on Arikan, this girl who liked intelligent men. And I wondered if she kept intelligent men, like in a button collection. I wondered if I was intelligent, or just, as a writer, intelligent enough. Was I a con man, aspiring to something higher than I could ever be?

I felt possessed by a madness to touch her. Instead I ran more water over my torso and took down the towel and dried myself.

"I'm done," I said, opening the bathroom door.

I remembered a juvenile short story I had written of Spain — there had been wild flamenco dancing and sangria drinking, a country where everyone is dark haired and care is abandoned. There was no sea in that fiction. Now, I thought I should find and rewrite it, so I could put a sea in. If I rewrote the story, I would set it in Cadiz in Andalucía, a city by the sea, just like Lagos. Cadiz slant rhymes with sea — a sea of people had come to see the bullfight Federico Lorca made memorable, hadn't they?

Alone in Arikan's room I thought of another memory. It was of a hall with a knife thrower and a girl behind a shroud — his daggers flew and pinned her outline to the board behind her. There was stillness in the audience as they held their breath and watched — then applause, long and orgasmic. I think of those daggers flying to find their mark and I wonder what two daggers say to each other when they meet in the air on their way to stopping. Daggers such as Arikan and me?

And fate, how powerful was Fate?

My mind skipped to the long trail we had walked from the main road to her house.

"We should stop at a pharmacy," I said.

"Why?"

"To get condoms."

"You've already decided I'll sleep with you?"

"I haven't, cannot. But I hope you do."

"You're presumptuous."

"I like that word."

Silence wrapped around us like a prophecy intent on coming true. What was I doing so late at night heading to the lair of a girl I just met? Everything was dark and forbidden, like my thoughts of Spain and of the Gorgon Medusa, and of *vagina dentata*. But my palms had been on Arikan's hips all the way and our steps were light and steady.

"My house is a fifteen-minute walk away. You may think I'm taking you to a ritualist's den some parts of the way, but *no fear heh*?"

"Why?"

"Who knows why?"

She came out of the bathroom naked. I watched her put on a flower print nightgown. We watched each other without a word. She came to the bed and sat at its edge.

"So, what's your story?" I asked finally.

She did not answer. She now lay across the bed, face down looking at me. I erased the distance of a few feet between us and when I reached her, I hiked up the flower-print shimmy, taking in the back of her thighs. I kissed her left buttock and drew her up to face me. Words would come later, and something happened to my fears as well. We fucked with only the sounds of moans of various surrenders. Sometimes I saw her dreadlocks waving about, tips like the heads of snakes taunting me, and I would try to reach out for salvation. But my arms never made it except to hold her waist onto me. She dripped with sweat and I thought of a story of a woman who had risen out of the sea—a story scattered in my recollection. We fucked and we ran through the four condoms in the pack.

She said she liked intelligent men. I thought of the Prophet Ibrahim and that ram he was to sacrifice in place of his son, Isaac. I saw the lamb and the patriarch suspended above the sea. And it seemed normal to be here in her arms, this strange girl, Arikan, a gypsy like me. And I felt the knife plunge into my vein, above the sea, and felt all the blood in my body become one drop and I imagined it falling off me, like reason, and heard it hit the surface of the water. And the entire world turned crimson.

Gypsies have no use for words.

*

The sex was so-so.

I watched him watching me in the bathroom as if I was a meal—he did not touch me. I wanted to be savored and he savored me. I watched him watching me. I liked that when he bathed me, he didn't linger on my breasts, did not squeeze. And that was when I decided to sleep with him. Not before, not even when we met and his smile did something decadent and wrong to my insides. I liked him, yes, and now I just slept with him. And we just met today. Arikan!

We met at his book reading, his book, and he had arrived late—an hour late. The emcee improvised until in came this man in a milk-colored northern kaftan, with an outlandish black backpack hanging behind him off one arm only. I had just bought his book—it was dedicated to his daughters and their mothers.

112

There was something irresponsible about that. He had kept us waiting and, without meeting him, I thought he kept us waiting deliberately. He came in with a woman, his publisher. Quickly he was ushered to the little dais. He wore a bracelet on his left wrist—what sort of man wears a bracelet on his wrist? Was he a homosexual? I had heard stories about men fucking men in northern Nigeria.

My next memory is of the fluorescent light suffused Freedom Park near Obalende.

But, before that, other details exist that I recall hazily. He had spent the first few minutes on the dais joking and cracking up the hall; he did it well and I forgave him for coming late. The emcee read his bio—he had sinned a lot of sins in his short life it seemed. He wasn't yet thirty. He did not believe in marriage. I want to get married. I believe in marriage. What sort of man says he doesn't believe in marriage? Aren't men supposed to lead women on and then break our hearts with, what is it: *I don't think I'm ready to settle down yet?* He was such a conceited, cute bastard. His eyes raked over the hall but they did not find me. I was just any girl. Then he settled in to read. I hated him, the confidence of his bowed, balding head as he read from his novel; I hated his voice, how sure it sounded, and I hated the mole on his cheek. He was reading about a girl who was ripping a sheet of paper to shreds. I caught his eyes mid-sentence when he looked up—he winked and smiled. I remember him signing my book and saying with his eyes to wait.

Next thing, we were at Freedom Park with his cronies drinking beer and pepper soup. It was getting close to 8 p.m. when they left. He paid.

"So, Arikan, what do we do with us?"

"I'm going home."

"And you're asking if I'll come with you?"

We scraped our white plastic seats on the dirty terrazzo floor of the bar and stood to leave. It was a calm Lagos evening, the air from the sea making my lungs buoyant and my heart expansive as we walked silently through the inner marina. We made to cross an intersection and he put his palm on my hips to steady me—I let him leave it there. I leaned into him and I wondered whether he was circumcised or not. I'd heard stories of northerners being uncircumcised. He stopped in front of CMS Bookstore, gasping—"My God! It's so historic," he said.

I crossed the street and stood in front of the bookstore so he could take a photo. Then he crossed over to join me, kissed me, and we walked on to the bus stop. The night market was just starting. I wondered if he noticed that the lanterns cast golden light on the faces—I wondered what he saw, and if he was looking at us as I was.

"I stay far away."

"At sea?"

"No."

"Then let's go."

It took us two hours and three bus changes to reach my house. I felt him become afraid during the fifteen-minute walk from the road to my little apartment at the heart of Ajah. I joked. He relaxed, but said he would spend an hour and leave for his friend's house at Lekki. I found that funny.

Now he was lying on the bed, glorious and naked, naked as me. He had asked what my story was again. Sonofabitch, what sort of man asks that—what sort of a man asks that on a one-night-stand?

I told him about my parents and my schooling in the Niger Delta—about studying English language at the University of Port Harcourt and the essay prize I had won five years ago—an essay on pidgin English. I told him about the Montessori school where I taught (and hated), and about the two years I had spent in Lagos when I left home with a man who was to marry me but didn't. I told him about how I had chased another man with a knife and he chuckled. I told him about the year I had been alone and homeless in this Lagos and I knew he guessed more than what I had said, but I did not contradict him—why should I?

"You must see me as a Lagos girl," I said eventually.

"What's that?"

"Girl in her late twenties, unmarried, with a job and an apartment, who sleeps with strangers on Saturday nights. Someone once told me all I needed to complete being a Lagos girl was a car. *When you buy a car, Arikan, you'll be a true Lagos girl.* I hated him."

He drew me close to his body. He was spent, maybe too much excitement, the sex had been so-so and two of the condoms had been more or less wasted—but then, he had used his tongue and brought me to climax. Yet, he drew me close to him so my body lay across his on my scattered bed in my cramped little apartment. We were draped on each other.

"I'm not that sort of man," he said and kissed my brow. "I'm proud of you, even if I'm just knowing you. I was afraid of you for a while, but now I'm proud." He liked kissing. He kissed everywhere. I liked that, his touch and his tiny kisses like little fish lips nibbling my flesh. *Arikan, keep your heart away*, I said to myself.

"Afraid? Proud?"

"You're a frontierswoman, Arikan, I can see that, like a gypsy way out there. I was afraid because of myths I had been thinking about, errant memories that had escaped from my writings into my mind."

"*I no understand wetin you dey talk so.*"

115

"Love, I'm speaking of love, Arikan. Who knows why we want to fall in love? Somehow, from all you've told me, you don't sound cynical about men or life or pity yourself or, you know. . . those damned things. But I want to fall in love with you because you seem like a girl manning a fort, and you do it so matter of factly, so easily."

I didn't know what to say, so I said nothing.

"Arikan," he said after a while, his finger tracing squiggles across my stomach, "what is this little apartment but a frontier position? I think there's a battle going on."

"A battle?" *Which kind thing this man dey talk?*

"Yeah, for your place in the world. Between Arikan and the stereotype of you that people like your friend come up with—a Lagos girl. And I've taken sides already. Arikan will win, just wait and see. And when you do, I'll say—*I told you so.*"

I pulled away so I could look at him; he stared back with his brows unruffled. Most men can't look honest when they are naked. A woman always just knows. I have often had to pretend to not know when they are bullshitting me. Then I would disappear and never see them again, content to be a fleeting conquest in their minds, knowing that I, instead, had been reprieved from pretending not to know if I met them again. But he seemed honest. What sort of man seems honest while naked, for God's sake?

"Arikan, I'm sleepy. Leaving Lagos tomorrow. But, we've gone far today, tonight. A marker for tomorrow—you'll see. My gypsy. . ." he said, drawing me to him again until he fell asleep. I watched the heaving of his chest for a long time and noticed how little he breathed, naked except for the bronze bracelet on his wrist. I fingered his bracelet. He didn't snore.

The Chinese clock I'd bought months ago started chiming midnight and I picked out the shadows falling on my curtains from the outside, from a vague place, like uncharted territory. I felt held in place as I watched him sleep, and I prayed for dawn not to come.

ABUBAKAR ADAM IBRAHIM

EMMANUEL IDUMA: Do you ever think there are too many writers out there? Do you have the fear of becoming obscure, glossed over by the astounding work of older, more accomplished writers?

ABUBAKAR ADAM IBRAHIM: I think every writer must believe in his story if that story is going to be successful. When you think of the older writers and all they have achieved, you are awed, but when you think of the younger writers breaking through, you are inspired. Every writer must find his story and his voice and his belief in these, and that determines how far he will go. Sometimes, the stories might even echo an older work and still be successful. When two raconteurs tell the same story, each will bring his flair and unique experience into it such that the stories come out completely different. Take for instance Ola Rotimi's "The Gods are not to Blame," which is a pastiche of "Oedipus Rex" by Sophocles. Somehow, the two stories appealed to a lot of people across generations and continents.

The way I see it, there are seven billion people in the world and perhaps three times as many stories. A young writer just has to find his voice and believe in it.

EI: Which characters in books have influenced you the most?

AI: Well, I don't know if they have influenced me. I would say I liked some of them, like Cash Daddy in Adaobi Tricia

Nwaubani's *I Do Not Come to You by Chance*. He was quite similar to Calamatus Jumai in Chuma Nwokolo's *Diaries of a Dead African*. I almost fell in love with Nina while I was writing my first book *The Quest for Nina*. I think I found Yambo in Umberto Eco's *The Mysterious Flame of Queen Loana* a bit intriguing.

EI: If you didn't write in English, which language would you have tried? Why?

AI: Well, I have experimented with writing in Hausa. I had a manuscript in fact, which I have lost. But I am not thinking of writing in Hausa anymore, at least not in the near future.

There is something appealing about Arabic. It is a beautiful, poetic language and I have actually fancied myself writing in Arabic at some point. But that is just a fantasy for now. I will be sticking with English for the foreseeable future.

EI: That's interesting. The love for Arabic is shared. Have you considered taking lessons, or visiting Arab-speaking countries? That might help.

AI: Yes, I studied Arabic for some years in Jos. I'm not as eloquent as I would like to be, but I get by.

EI: Given our underrepresentation, and the quest for validation from institutions that define contemporary literature, emerging African writers might give in to the need to have big breaks (winning a prize, for instance) before publishing their first books. Is this a dangerous need? What, in your opinion, is the most essential need of an emerging African writer?

AI: Oh, certainly, it is not healthy for our literature. It is even more so when you consider that the few good publishing houses we have here are waiting for works to be published elsewhere before they take them on here. So we end up compromising our standards, telling our stories by borrowing stories, looking at our lives through rented lenses, which is not ideal.

But as a proverb goes, if you consider the thief, you should also consider the person running after the thief. Writers here are too impatient to get published, which of course is understandable when you consider the urge of the muse. However, we have to accept that some of the works we rush to publish are simply not good enough. I think we will be better off if we are able to critique our own works and have the courage to dismiss them when they don't meet up. We should be able to challenge ourselves as writers to constantly improve our art.

What every emerging writer wants is to be published; what an emerging writer needs is patience and perseverance—the patience to allow your voice to develop, to perfect your craft, and the perseverance to deal with rejection. If J. K. Rowling had given up after *Harry Potter* was turned down twelve times, she wouldn't have been one of the richest writers alive today. If William Golding had given up on *Lord of the Flies* after publishers turned it down twenty times, we wouldn't be talking about it today half a century since it was published.

EI: By saying we must challenge ourselves, do you suppose that young writers must chart their literary destinies, define their own standards?

AI: We live in a dynamic world and we must learn to keep up if we are not setting pace. I think emerging writers must have the courage to set a high standard for themselves and constantly raise the bar. Writing is a very challenging art and you must constantly push yourself to get the best out of yourself.

EI: Speaking of validation, the Internet does offer an interesting perspective to publishing. And if we are speculating correctly, the emerging African writer seems overwhelmed by a new medium—overwhelmed because danger and promise are equally offered in this new medium. What do you say? You have several "links" to your name!

AI: I think there is opportunity on the Internet. I think it is revolutionizing literature and publishing. It gives a platform for emerging writers to showcase their works, get feedback, and improve their creativity. Yes, in most cases, you don't get paid to be published online, but for an emerging writer, being read and having a fan base is—I think—a more immediate need.

But now we have e-books as well, and while some people may see that as a threat to conventional publishing, others see it differently. Amanda Hockings, for instance, self-published an e-book after she had been turned down by conventional publishers and has made millions from it. Now she is going through the conventional publishing and editing process, which shows you that the two media, the old and the new, can co-exist. Publishers wouldn't have taken notice if she hadn't taken it into her own hands. So the Internet creates greater opportunities for emerging writers to get noticed.

EI: And you conceive that noticing as a precursor to what? What possibilities exist afterward?

AI: A million and one possibilities—the possibility of becoming a bestselling author, the possibility of being discovered by the right people, the possibility of achieving your dream, the possibility of having your work critiqued by some intelligent people who will help improve your craft. Endless possibilities.

EI: The matter of literary demographics will necessarily come into this conversation, seeing you are from northern Nigeria. You will agree that there have been few writers from northern Nigeria who attained monumental acclaim. Early on, there was Ahmed Yerima, Abubakar Gimba, Zaynab Alkali, and Abubakar Imam (even though he wrote in Hausa). Last decade there was Helon Habila. Incidentally, in Nigerian literature there are occurrences of romanticizing the north—recall Cyprian Ekwensi's *Jagua Nana* and *The Passport of Mallam Ilia*. The point of this rambling is to ask if you see yourself in the forefront of putting northern Nigerian literature in a place it scarcely occupied.

AI: You really had to bring that up, didn't you, Emmanuel? Well, I see myself as a Nigerian writer from the north. I don't want to endorse this idea of a dichotomy of northern and southern Nigerian literature. Regardless, I am from the north and my stories reflect, to some extent, the peculiarities of the north of Nigeria, which is culturally and socially distinct from the south. I feel the north has wonderful stories that have not been adequately captured in the collective body of Nigerian literature; I feel it is important that a region as vast as the north be adequately represented in literature and the idiosyncrasies of its peoples and their cultures be projected to the world. I think that is very important. But in contrast to the idea of romanticizing the north as has been done by the likes of Ekwensi, who I admire a lot, I think we stand to gain more by focusing on the human experience of the peoples of this region. I think that way Nigerians will understand each other more and the world will take note. That is the direction my work is taking now.

I don't know if I am at the forefront of putting writing from the north on a larger platform. I am doing my bit. But I know there are other young, vibrant, and exciting voices from the north who will hit the international limelight in the nearest future. There is so much promise from this side of the Niger and I am excited about the prospect.

EI: Can you name some of these young voices?

AI: There are a lot. Richard Ali. Gimba Kakanda shows so much promise. There is Awaal Gata, there is Hajo Isa the poet, there is Sage Hasson doing great things with spoken word poetry. Ahmed Maiwada isn't as young as all these writers, but he's making waves. There are a lot of people.

EI: Does writing make you feel responsible?

AI: It most certainly does. I think knowing that you have a voice and that people are willing to read what you have written comes with an enormous sense of responsibility. Perhaps because of my background in the media, which suggests that one should be socially responsible, I find that writers are obliged to consider the social implications of what they write. This is what American writer Frank Norris argues in his essay, "The Responsibilities of the Novelist," which I think is an excellent piece. He says the fact that your writing can influence a number of people places upon you the responsibility of not misguiding such people who have placed their trust in you by reading what you have written. And that is why stereotyping puts me off. Yes, people may have a general trait, but that doesn't mean they are all the same and it doesn't help if you demoralize or vilify them simply because you have the talent to write. I think it is an abuse of one's responsibility as a writer.

EI: Let's return to the question of demographics. There's a curious term, ELDS, which is Educationally Less Developed States. The argument is that prospective undergraduates from states in Nigeria with this tag have less-stringent requirements for entry into universities. And there are several northern states tagged ELDS. Does this bother you, to be a writer from/in a region with many uneducated people?

AI: It is a constant worry, not necessarily for me as a writer. It is a social problem, because you have an army of people who do not even understand basic social concepts and so are easily bamboozled into irrational acts by politicians with dubious intents. This affects the way people elsewhere perceive you and relate with you. It puts you on the defensive for whatever prejudice some of "your people" have been taught to believe. There was a person I met who thought I must have attended an elite school to have turned out the way I did because "my people" are not usually like that. That is why I think it is important to succeed as a writer, so that people can say, oh yes, he is a writer, I want to be like him, and they will read and broaden their horizons.

But in truth, the ELDS are a product of social and cultural misadventure and a failure of the system. Children now don't repeat classes in private schools because the proprietors don't want parents thinking their wards are not being well taught. In public schools, students fail because the teachers want to be bribed.

EI: Suppose African writers are powerlessly deadlocked. Suppose that we cannot stay aloof to the subtleties of national life, the ineptitude around us. What do you think this will do to an expectation to tell stories that are "just stories"?

AI: I think that will make us romantics and how will that benefit anyone? I think literature should serve a higher purpose than just entertainment. When you consider our folklore, besides entertaining they serve to affect thinking and behavior. To expect a writer to tell stories that are "just stories" is to strip the writer of his purpose and reduce him to escapism. Eventually, the reader will have to put the book down and confront reality.

EI: What is the writer's purpose?

AI: Is there a universal accord for the purpose of the writer? I think it is relative. It depends on the time, on the situation, on individuals. Essentially, I think the purpose of the writer is to cast light on the dark side of things—of feelings and thoughts and actions that define the way we live and the way we perceive things. I think the writer is the chronicler of the human experience against the backdrop of change, which in itself is constant.

EI: What was growing up like? Do you recall anything from your childhood that helped you decide to become a writer, a user of language?

AI: Not particularly. I just found myself in love with stories and the business of creating them. I grew up reading the books available to me and I grew up trying to create my own stories. I remember reading Soyinka's *The Man Died* when I was twelve. And I suppose reading Anthony Hope's *The Prisoner of Zenda* all those years ago sparked the interest in writing. The defining moment, however, came when I was an adolescent, when my brother and I heard this call for entries for a radio play and he said "Come on, you've got to enter." I suppose that was the moment I decided that, yes, I want to take writing more seriously.

EI: What was the first story you wrote?

AI: Wow! My first story? I can't really remember. My earliest writings were in the form of graphic novellas. I drew the pictures and wrote the dialogue. I wrote fragments of stories that came to my head, bits and pieces like that. I had quite a stack of these juvenilia until I lost them recently.

EI: How did you feel when you lost them?

AI: Your writing becomes a part of you, essentially, and when, for some reason, you lose any of it—especially a whole lot of it, as I did—it is demoralizing. It is a loss that cannot be replenished. And you grieve in isolation because not many people understand the gravity of your loss. It took me a while to recover and I am not sure I can completely get over it.

127

EI: As a writer, is it dangerous to feel capable?

AI: Well, it is important to have confidence and belief in yourself, but it is also wise to realize there are always avenues where you can improve. I have seen writers who think they are the ultimate. They have mastered the art, but when you read what they put out, you realize there is a lot missing, and because they are not open to criticism and suggestions, their work suffers. That is why as a writer you can't live in a cocoon. Your writer friends and colleagues should feel free to comment honestly on your works and you should be open to suggestions about your work before you even think of going public with it.

EI: Which authors do you love most?

AI: There are lots of writers whose works fascinate me, and every day I discover more. I admire Flaubert for daring to expand the boundaries of literature with *Madame Bovary*. I admire Racine for the elegance of his works. Gabriel Garcia Marquez remains a favorite. There is Helon Habila too, Isabelle Allende, Toni Morrison. Lots of them.

EI: Your story "Closure" conveys how difficult it is to let go, how memory haunts even the most inconspicuous of persons. Is this what you had in mind? Is there an overarching political slant we can bring to this? Perhaps that as Nigerians we will never forget our past glory, that just like the character Sadiya we are unwilling to part with our hopes even when those hopes are being bashed irreverently.

AI: If there is a political slant in that, it is that there is a breaking point for everyone, there is a limit to tolerance, as we have seen with the recent protests in the country. There is a point in life you reach and you know you can sacrifice your little comforts for something more profound. Nigerians showed that they could sacrifice their differences for the collective good; they were willing to sleep on the streets, to defy the marauding police, to say enough of these exploitations, enough of this corruption. Now we know the taste of people power; we know what we can achieve when we speak with the same voice. We have precedence.

EI: Does tragedy fascinate you? Does ill-fate confer believability on a story? There's, for instance, Santi's failure to exonerate himself in your story "Night Calls," even the capitulation of the Mayaki family in *The Quest for Nina*. And to speak the truth, tragedy can be fascinating, perhaps even instructive and compellingly introspective. What do you think?

AI: There is this line from a movie where one character says, "Tragedy, every good movie must have one." I love that line. But basically, I have long been fascinated by tragedy; it is such a moving phenomenon. It is shocking and sometimes shock is necessary to bring someone to face reality, and that is what I want to achieve. Tragedies are unforgettable. We are still talking about the Greek tragedies after all these years because of the lasting impression they have made. I want my stories to linger in the mind of the reader. But I don't see myself as a tragedian. Sometimes humor can be as shocking. They say humor is a rubber sword by which you make a point without drawing blood.

EI: Let's examine the question of genre fiction. *The Quest for Nina* traverses a thin line between a thriller novel and literary fiction.

Few people have found that distinction between genre and literary fiction curious, even dubious. What's your take? Is there a way, as your book seemed to seek, to hybridize those forms? And what's the future of genre fiction in Nigeria or Africa, if you might wish to predict?

AI: Well, while *The Quest for Nina* was largely experimental—I did write it quite early on—I don't think there was a conscious effort to hybridize genres. I just felt at the time that that was the best way the story could be told. I probably wouldn't have taken that approach if I were writing it now because my writing is moving in a different direction. It may not be so obvious, but the book is a sort of social critique, inspired by the revelations of the Oputa Panel; it seeks to explore the impact of unraveling all those long buried secrets, if it's good or bad for us.

Having said that, I don't think writers should be straight-jacketed into compliance. I prefer to allow my stories to take on a life of their own instead of boxing them into convention. I am not too big a fan of genre fiction; I think they merely offer temporary escape from reality and I have noted with delight the growing appeal of literary fiction. More and more young writers are tilting in this direction, and I think that is very good.

EI: You've lived in Jos. What has changed, if anything? Has this affected your writing in any way? Maybe it's better to ask: what has changed since the Boko Haram insurgency?

AI: I have lived most of my life in Jos. It was a wonderful place until the politicians came and spread bad blood. The violence began in 2001 and has gone on for over a decade now, things haven't been the same. You can't move around freely. There are all these wonderful folks you talk literature with and exchange books with; now you can't visit their homes without fear simply because they are on the "other side" of town. It is quite unfortunate. But Jos will always remain special to me, even though I lost most of my early writings there. It has a special place in my heart and I hope that someday we can put all this behind us and move on.

And like Chinua Achebe said, literature should reflect situations on the ground and yes, once in a while you think about how you can use your writing to capture some of these things that are happening.

And now with the Boko Haram situation, it is quite unfortunate that it has put people like me on the defensive because of the name we bear and the faith we profess. I am thinking of starting a project on this, on stories that reflect the human condition in these troubling times. I hope we can use literature to affect perceptions and inspire change in the way our society is governed, in the way we think and behave.

EI: You lost some writing in Jos?

AI: Yes, I did. I was away in Abuja when yet another crisis broke out and my house was razed to the ground. I lost everything in that unfortunate incident. My entire stack of juvenilia was lost— manuscripts dating as far back as I can recall, not to mention all my documents, all the books I read growing up, mementos of my ever being young once.

EI: That's quite sad, very sad.

Is there anything being a journalist adds to you as a writer of fiction? That's considering the fact that journalism is an art inscribed in the public space, more or less a rendition of sensational, sometimes tawdry, facts. And that fiction requires, as you say, countless hours of solitude.

AI: Being a journalist was a conscious effort. I actually studied sciences in secondary school, but fortunately I realized early enough that my future was in writing and instead of veering to study English or literature in the university, I decided to study journalism because I wanted the exposure and access this would give me. Now I have met all sorts of people—junkies, seers, ordinary folks in extraordinary situations, politicians, intellectuals, the aloof trader by the roadside, and security operatives. I have had cause to interact with them and ask them questions, and these experiences are benefiting my writing in terms of creating more believable characters, more believable stories. The problem is working as a journalist has made it quite difficult to find time to write as much one would have wanted.

I know some journalists have lost their flourish as writers because of the demand of the trade and when they struggle to bring out something, it is too stripped of emotion and reads like journalese. I have met such writers. I also know of the likes of Marquez, who was a journalist but continued to write fiction with flourish. My being a journalist was to further my goal of being a better writer and I think it is playing out well so far.

EI: Would you consider becoming a full-time writer? That's if journalism doesn't happen to provide continued exposure and access.

AI: Journalism will always give access and exposure. But yes, someday I would like to wake up and have nothing to do but to write the stories I like writing. Perhaps someday.

EI: Faulkner says a writer's only responsibility is to his art—if he has to rob his mother he will. What's the worth of your art? Family? Perhaps money? This might not be a great question, but supposing it comes close, what are you willing to sacrifice?

AI: This is a difficult question, Emmanuel. Writing has given me a lot; it has taken me places physically and emotionally. Writing is a part of me. Without my family I have no idea what life would have been like. We appreciate each other and fortunately they know how important writing is for me. I hope it never comes to that, choosing between my family and my writing.

February 1, 2012

DAUGHTERS OF BAPPA AVENUE

Abubakar Adam Ibrahim

The house woke up around her and the aroma of her meat pies hanging indolently in the air. Asabe was three days into building her pastry empire, which she hoped would expand beyond the confines of Magajiya's grubby house. She had saved carefully, stuffing money she earned from braiding hair into a piggy bank.

After spending many nights making plans and drawing up recipes while chewing on her pen, she decided it was time. She held the piggy bank high above her head and dropped it. The sound of the ceramic smashing would linger. Later she would remember it as the sound of dreams breaking.

"Will that be enough?" her mother asked from the mattress, looking at the scattered notes. "If it's not, tell me."

"It will be," Asabe said shortly, gathering the bills around her.

"You can't . . ."

"Mom, I can handle it," she said, looking at her mother. "I will handle it."

She started on Saturday morning, dishing out complimentary tasters to the women in Magajiya's house, who insisted on being called ladies. By Monday she was ready to take it beyond the house. She went out into the compound, where she and her mother cooked just by the door, and startled the groggy morning with the aroma of her dreams.

Just when a fresh batch of meat pies was protesting in the hot oil, Magajiya's portly head popped out from behind her wooden door at the far end of the long compound.

"Asabe, for God's sake, what are you up to?!"

"Good morning, Magajiya," Asabe sang.

"What on earth are you up to, child? There are people here still sleeping."

"Almost done, Magajiya," Asabe said, not looking up from kneading her dough. She didn't want Magajiya's swarthy face with the usual run-down make-up from the previous night to bring her bad luck.

"Where is your mother, girl?"

"Out since last night, Magajiya."

"You and that mother of yours are nothing but trouble, I tell you. And better be careful so you don't burn down my house, you hear." Magajiya hissed just before her door creaked shut.

"Hag," Asabe muttered.

Ngozi, the slim, childlike woman, who lived two doors away, came out in her pink chemise, one strap having slipped off her shoulder.

"Asabe, how far?"

Asabe looked up at Ngozi's tired face and couldn't help noticing how flat her chest was without the padded bra. (By evening, her boobs would miraculously be transformed into luscious lumps). Ngozi, like Asabe's mother, was one of the dozen resident ladies at Magajiya's house. There were also the twenty or so off campus ladies who only rented rooms by the hour for their business, but lived elsewhere and actually had some kind of other life during the day.

"Ngo, I thought you were out for the night."

Ngozi hissed. "Don't mind those useless men. They just wasted my time for nothing. Why are you working so early, is the business booming already?"

"I hope so. I want to take some to school and see how it goes."

"Good girl. You have a good business head, you know. I hope you turn out better than your mother."

"Will you help me sell some here while I'm away at school?"

"Sure, why not. You make good pies and people like them already."

"Thanks."

Ngozi yawned, and patted her dishevelled hair. "Will you braid my hair when you return from school?"

"No problem," Asabe said and focused on the stuffing.

Ngozi carried her yellow and blue plastic pail and shuffled to the well in the middle of the compound.

Tired looking women with ruffled hair and smeared make-up emerged from rooms with creaky doors. Men also came out, some of them staggering slightly from the previous night's booze and exertions. For those whose memories of the night's escapades still lingered, they made to grab the skimpily dressed ladies as they walked past to the well or the bathrooms. The women laughed lewdly and slapped away the men's hands.

While Asabe stood outside the door, looking at her face in a handheld mirror, one of the men on his way out stopped and looked her over.

"Fresh one," he said. "When will you give me some, eh?"

"Go home, your wife is waiting," she said, patting down her school uniform.

"Ah, come, I will make it worth your while," he said, feigning a lunge for her.

"Dogo! You are drunk already this early morning!" Ngozi shouted from her door. "Don't you know a child when you see one? Or is she older than your daughter?"

Dogo considered Asabe with a smirk. "Old enough, I think."

"You know her mother very well. If she catches you eyeing that girl you are in serious soup, shameless man!"

Dogo scoffed and staggered out. Asabe blinked away tears and hurried back into the room.

*

After her classmate Mariya Jangali, also fifteen, who lived way up Bappa Avenue, had raised Asabe's dream high above her head and let it drop, the sound of the piggy bank breaking came back to her. That was when she knew for certain that the sound of dreams breaking was not unlike that of a piggy bank being smashed. It also smelled like singed meat pie garnished with cayenne and green onions.

Asabe cried all the way back from school. It was a long walk, made longer by the interminable length of Bappa Avenue, like a nebulous dream. It wasn't really an avenue, just a long street sticking out of a sprawling flea market with most of the trees eaten by houses and power poles.

Magajiya's house, infamous for its resident and off campus *ladies*, sat on a rock at one end of the street, close to the mechanic's garage and not too far from the cattle market. When she finally got home, her mother, Laure, lay spread-eagled on the bed, her mouth open and her snores filling the tiny room. Asabe sat, wishing her mother would stop snoring and stop breathing, and just stop being there. As Asabe lay on the carpet among the clutter of phone chargers, extension cords, and displaced books, she wished her mother would just stop existing.

*

Laure heard it first from Ngozi, who had noticed how a reticent Asabe braided her hair with tears in her eyes. Ngozi had inquired from some of the students who lived up the avenue. She heard how Asabe's meat pies had sold out at school in minutes before Mariya lifted one and made a declaration.

"I've just discovered why Asabe's pies are so tasty! It's because her mother, Laure—the greatest whore on Bappa Avenue—washed her privates in the dough. It's black magic, can't you see?" Mariya had said, dropping the pie on the floor. Laure stormed back into the room where Asabe was still lying on the floor among the clutter, sinking deeper into her head, away from the jeers and curses and catcalls that had chased her out of school.

"How can you keep this away from me, eh, Asabe?" Laure demanded, her petite frame shaking so much Asabe feared she would spring up to the rain-stained ceilings. "How could that little tramp say such things to you? I will deal with her father because she's too small to bear the weight of my rage!"

She marched out of Magajiya's house, leaving some of the ladies sniggering as she went, and she stormed up Bappa Avenue, through the flea market to Nura Jangali's grain shop. He was busy measuring out guinea corn to a customer when Laure pounced on him. When he managed to get away from her claws, he asked what the problem was.

As Laure spoke and a crowd gathered, Jangali was as fascinated by this little woman as he was when he first saw her. She was fifteen then, with her shoulder bag and a lost look in her eyes that made him stow her in his shop for days. He remembered their moments on the bean bags until he had been forced to give her up by his new wife's increasing suspicions and the nosy neighbors' inquisitiveness. Now, she slapped him across the face and the crowd murmured. There was confusion in his eyes as he looked at her, as if he had just been plucked from another time.

"If your daughter dares insult mine again, Bappa Avenue will be too small to contain me and you!" She hissed, spat at his foot and stormed off amidst a tempest of laughter and jeers.

The next day, Asabe refused to leave Magajiya's house—not even for school or to help the ladies with shopping. She stayed indoors all day and all night, dreaming of bright blue dragonflies dancing over white streams. She would follow the streams to faraway lands where the hills were rubicund and the trees had lilacs for leaves.

It was easy to forget where she was in the afternoons because of the silence; the ladies of Magajiya's house were nocturnal. In the evenings, they would wake from their day-long slumber, make up their faces and sit in the compound playing ludo, talking about men, and waiting for the early comers—the mechanics from the neighboring garage, traders from the flea market, and the truck drivers who usually stayed overnight.

By nightfall (which was when the off campus ladies appeared), they would move out to the front and stand under the lampposts that held long-dead bulbs high up in the dusky sky. Sometimes Laure brought men home to the adjoining room, which Asabe had been asked not to enter. "It's the office, you shouldn't be coming in here, you know."

Once they were in, the R&B music of P-Square or D'banj's dance beats would stream in through the chinks of the adjoining door. Beneath the music, Asabe could sometimes hear them if the men were loud or the bed creaked too much. When that happened, Asabe would put on headphones and attach them to the television.

On other nights, Laure would call her phone and say, "Baby, take care of yourself until morning."

The night after Mariya Jangali smashed her dreams, a ruckus broke out when the self-styled Lady B started screaming. Asabe ran out and saw a hefty man dragging the ample Lady B by her hair across the ground. When he kicked her across the face, Asabe flinched and turned her back. Despite Lady B being one of the off campus ladies, some ladies rushed out and pounced on the man. Others stood by their doors, snickering with their arms folded across their chests.

"She was trying to steal my wallet, see," the man said, holding up the wallet to the ones by the door and shrugging off the women still clinging to him.

"Stop that nonsense now!" Magajiya thundered. "This is a business place, not a place for fighting, you hear me!"

Asabe turned and went back to the room. She sat on the mattress and hugged herself. She could still hear the commotion outside. Each time the image of the man's leg connecting with Lady B's mouth flashed across her mind, she tried to shrink farther into the wall. When she reached for her headphones, she saw that her hands were trembling.

Laure heard about Lady B's bashed teeth the next morning upon her return, when one of the residents stopped her outside and told her.

"Stupid off campus ladies," Laure hissed. "You see now, most of them steal customers' money and think they are better than the rest of us." She hissed again and went into her room.

When she saw Asabe sitting against the wall staring into space, she said, "My baby, how are you?"

"Welcome," Asabe mumbled.

"What's wrong?"

"Nothing."

"You're not going to school today?"

When Asabe said nothing, Laure sighed and sat down beside her. "Look, this is life. You don't live it in a shell because someone said something nasty to you. I work my butt off to make sure you have a better life than I do, so that you go to school and become something. You think I am happy doing this or what?"

"You could do something else. I'm always being insulted because of what you do," Asabe sulked.

When Laure sniffled, Asabe looked up scornfully.

"You think I chose to be this? You think I like it?" Laure asked, wiping her tears. "Goddamnit. I was your age when I left home because they wanted me to marry some toothless buffoon with three wives who were older than my mother. Everything I've done ever since has been for you. I have been through a lot and I won't have you judging me, you hear!"

She got up and Asabe watched her walk out, wiping her tired eyes as she went.

*

Since what was left of Ngozi—without her padded bra—was discovered in a ditch, things weren't the same at Magajiya's house. The mournful wailings were over and it had begun to sink in. The music did not blare from the rooms and even the clients came with bowed heads.

Magajiya herself delivered the news, knocking on doors and screaming, something she only did when some of the ladies defaulted on her commission or weekly rent. Amid thunderous sobs and great heaves of her gargantuan bosom, the ladies learned how Magajiya's police friend called her to identify the corpse.

"They must have killed her for rituals," Lady B summed up through her bashed mouth. The other ladies shuddered in horror.

"That's what the police said," Magajiya said. She kept repeating it through her tears until it turned into a mantra for her grief.

Teary-eyed, Asabe watched the mournful ladies tire of rolling on the ground and tearing out their hair. They eventually

142

retreated to their thresholds and sat staring blankly into the approaching dusk.

When men, whose hankering belied grief, came calling, the ladies disappeared with them into their rooms.

Asabe was still sitting with her mother well after sunset, thinking of the feel of Ngozi's soft hair in her hand as she braided it the day she disappeared, when Nura Jangali came in with two plastic bags bulging with sachets of beverages, milk, sugar, and fancy snacks and candies and made straight for Laure's "office." When Laure tried to squeeze Asabe's shoulder and the girl shrugged her off, she sighed, got up, and slapped the dust off her butt. Asabe saw her mother wipe away teardrops with the corner of her wrapper as she went dolefully after the man.

They showed respect for the dead; they didn't turn on the music. When their excited noises stretched out beyond the room and yanked at Asabe's grieving heart, she rose quietly and went for a walk in the night. She couldn't go far, though, because she kept imagining Ngozi's mutilated body festering in the murky ditch waters.

Nura Jangali was emerging from the "office" when she returned. She felt something like the tickle of a spider on the inside of her ribs. She didn't like the way he looked at her.

"Have you started working already?" he leaned forward and whispered.

"What work?"

"You know," he said with a gesture that took in the whole of Magajiya's house.

She hissed.

"I will pay you twice what I pay your mother, I swear."

The tears stung as she swept past him toward the room. That was when Laure came at him, tearing through the curtain with a club. He recovered from the first blow and didn't wait for the second. She chased him all the way up Bappa Avenue until he disappeared into the flea market. She bit her finger and whipped the air with it before turning back.

She sat down panting next to Asabe, who sat on the mattress, tears streaming down her face. Laure shifted and bit her lip, but that couldn't keep down the sobs. She slumped and cried, her tears seeping into the floral print bedcover.

*

"I need to get you out of here," Laure said at last. "I am tired of this life."

Asabe leaned back into the wall and said nothing.

"Look what happened to Ngo, eh, just like that. Look at that Lady B with broken teeth," she said, shaking her head and making a clicking sound from the back of her throat.

"We will move somewhere else and I will get you into another school. You will have a better life, I swear."

Asabe looked at her and saw the distant look in her eyes. But it was gone when Laure turned to her and held her cheeks.

"Promise me you will go to school, promise me you will."

"I will," Asabe said, a little breathless.

Laure nodded and rose.

Three days after Ngozi's corpse was found floating in a ditch, the music subtly returned to Magajiya's. At first it sounded like someone playing a song under a quilt, but as the days went by the decibels increased. The men, too, like moths to the lights, returned. But the ladies never strayed too far.

Tracy Chapman's songs (Laure's latest passion) blared constantly from the "office" while Asabe sat reading a book or watching TV. Sometimes, when Momoh came, she would sneak out and meet him under the eucalyptus tree down the street. He was nothing like Bako, the boy from school who had first called himself her boyfriend. Bako had unceremoniously plucked at her breasts one night and she had slapped him, also unceremoniously. She was stunned by the sound of her violence and the shock on his face. He had reached into his pocket and held up some notes. She slapped him again and fled, crying all the way home.

Momoh was not like that. He would lean against the eucalyptus tree biting his nails and say, "You know, someday, I'm going to take you away from here. Someday." But he was only eighteen and was an apprentice mechanic at the garage up Bappa Avenue. She went because she liked the way he talked and how he didn't take her clothes off with his eyes.

Each time she heard Tracy Chapman, which now started in the early evening, she would wait until sunset before slipping out of the house to wait for Momoh under the tree. He would stop and talk to her on his way home.

"Asabe isn't your birth name, is it?" he asked one night.

"I don't have a birth name," she said. She was sitting on the exposed root of the tree, prodding her toe with a toothpick.

"Of course you do. Everyone does," Momoh replied.

"When I was born, my mother didn't have the money to buy a ram for my naming. Men didn't want her then because she was pregnant, you know. So she just called me Asabe because I was born on a Saturday," she said.

He rubbed his jaw and said, "Asabe is fine. My grandma was also called Asabe."

Asabe laughed and said, "No, she wasn't."

"No, seriously, you know." He too laughed. She laughed, but there was no joy in her eyes. Her laughter gradually ceased as the tears streamed down. He knelt down in front of her and for a while his hands hovered uncertainly before her.

145

"Asabe is fine. Asabe is good," he kept saying. Finally, he held her hands and allowed her to cry.

*

Laure was often too tired and only woke up to eat before dozing off again. On some days, she would stuff stacks of cash in her handbag and say, "I'm going to the bank. I will be back soon."

"What about Magajiya's rent? She's been asking all week," Asabe said on one such day.

Laure looked around furtively. She came closer and lowered her voice. "Look, baby, we need all the money we can get when we leave this place..."

"When?"

"Very soon, baby, very soon. I don't know when exactly and I don't know where we are going, but we are going to need lots of money for the rent elsewhere and your school fees and whatever business I'm going to do." She clutched her head and sat down on the mattress. "I am not so good at thinking and planning things you know. This is so confusing, I don't know."

"We could go home, you know, to your parents."

Laure looked at her and shook her head slowly. "No, no, that won't work."

"Why?"

"Because I don't want to."

"Well, I want to know your people. I don't know who my father is and I don't know who your parents are, but I know you have parents. I need to have some kind of family you know, Mom."

Laure sighed. When she spoke, her voice was quieter and sounded defeated. "A few weeks after you were born, I went back home to make up with my parents so they would take us back, but they said I had soiled the family's name and brought a bastard home. They wanted to throw you in a well so the village wouldn't know what I came with. So I fled, again." She started crying.

"It's alright mother, we don't have to go back," Asabe said. "We could go somewhere else."

"Yes, yes, we will, I promise. Just give me some time to save up, okay?"

Asabe nodded and her mother patted her on the head. Laure dabbed her eyes and rose.

*

After Magajiya hung a feathered talisman over the entrance to the house, the ladies started going out all night again. She had been to marabouts, those holy men, and handed out bean cakes to the street kids. She brought a pastor in and he went round the house slapping the devil with his fiery tongue and the book in his hand. Finally, she went to the Indian temple and got the talisman that would guarantee protection for her ladies.

Two weeks after, because it was more lucrative, Laure called and said, "Baby, take care of yourself until morning."

Asabe slept and again dreamed of Ngozi without her padded bra floating in a ditch. She sat up and turned on the TV. At about midnight she was startled by knocks on the door. When she opened it, Magajiya's bulk filled the door.

"Where is your mother, girl?" Magajiya bellowed, sending sprays of saliva into Asabe's face.

"Out for the night, Magajiya."

"Well, when she comes back tell her I have tolerated her enough. She isn't paying her rent and she is holding down my business space. All these off campus ladies are looking for a room and your mother has occupied two and is not paying. Tell her I said she should pay up or else . . . "

Asabe shrank back from the spray and was relieved when Magajiya turned and left.

When next there was a knock on the door, she rose groggily and opened it. She was startled by the sunlight.

"Where is your mother?" a male voice asked.

When her eyes adjusted to the light, she saw Nura Jangali looking at her with a smirk on his face. She placed her arms across her chest and said her mother wasn't in.

He looked around furtively and leaned closer to her, holding up a plastic bag of provision in her face. "Well, how about you let me in, eh?"

This time, she put her weight behind the door.

"Come on, girl, be smart. Your mother was about your age when she first came here and she knew how to use what she has to get what she wants. I'll give you this," he pushed the bag into her face, "and money. Lots of it."

"No, no, no. I'll tell my mother," she said.

He straightened. "I simply can't understand why you are so dumb." He turned and left with his plastic bag.

*

When her mother called and asked her to take care of herself until morning, she said, "Mom, Magajiya was here this evening threatening to throw us out if we don't pay up."

"Don't worry, baby, we will be out of there for good soon."

"Really?"

"Yes, baby, what do you think I've been doing all this time?"

"Can't wait, Mom. I really can't." Asabe wanted to get as far away as she could from Magajiya's house.

"I know, baby. Hey, I've got to go now so . . ."

"I know, I'll take care of myself until morning."

"Yes, baby. Until morning."

Asabe rolled on the mattress and cried. That night, she didn't dream of Ngozi in the ditch.

At midmorning the next day, Magajiya knocked on the door and bellowed like a maddened bull, rousing half the compound. When she left, Asabe dialed her mother's number. The phone was switched off. At noon she tried again with no luck. She cooked some noodles and lounged on the mattress, flipping through a magazine until she fell asleep.

Toward evening, the ladies of Magajiya's house washed, painted their faces, sat to play ludo in the compound, and waited for the early comers.

"Asabe, if you aren't too busy, would you braid my hair?" Kande, one of the resident ladies whose room was close to the bathroom, asked as Asabe wandered into the compound. "Where is your mother? I haven't seen her all day."

"She went out last night and hasn't returned," Asabe said and tears streamed from her eyes.

"What do you mean?" Lady B asked, gasping.

The ladies looked at each other meaningfully. Zahra, the off-campus lady with a nose stud pulled out her phone and dialed. The others waited anxiously.

"Switched off," Zahra announced.

"Hey!" Chioma shouted, startling Asabe. "Jesus!" she added, placing both hands on her head.

Asabe started crying.

*

Three days later, Magajiya came with a carpenter who replaced the lock on her mother's office.

"Your mother's things are on one side, you hear," Magajiya said tenderly.

Asabe nodded. Magajiya sighed, placed a fat hand on Asabe's head and walked away.

That evening, as Asabe lay on the mattress with tear tracks on her face, Sean Paul's music tumbled in from under the adjoining door to the office. Later, it was replaced by Rihanna's "Unfaithful," which played repeatedly well into the night. Then Michael Jackson and Janet Jackson kept screaming from the speakers. Before she slept, 2Face was crooning "Only Me." When she dreamed, it was of Ngozi in the ditch—only this time, Ngozi had her mother's face.

A week later, Magajiya gave her some money. "For transport, you hear?"

"Transport? To where?"

"To your folks or wherever. Don't be asking me stupid questions, girl."

Asabe looked at her with hurt eyes and even Magajiya sighed. She twirled one of the gold rings on her finger and said tenderly, "I want to use the room and you aren't paying rent or commission. Too many off campus ladies need a place for business. "

Asabe went into the room and threw a couple of her things in a bag. She looked around and didn't know what else to pick. She had always wanted to leave Magajiya's house, but now she didn't know where to go. So she lay on the mattress and drenched it with her tears.

Each time she walked past, Magajiya would eye her and snort. Two weeks passed. The little food her mother had left before she disappeared finished. What was left of Magajiya's transport money could only buy a box of matches.

She went to Chioma's door to ask if she wanted her hair braided.

"No, not today," Chioma said. "You look like a scarecrow, you should eat better."

Later, when Asabe was heading to the toilet, she saw Chioma sitting in the compound, her head between Kande's thighs.

"You said you won't braid your hair today," she said.

"Yes, I changed my mind," Chioma said and turned her face the other way.

In the morning when she went to the well to fetch water, a hush fell over the ladies who had lined up there. Titi, the fat one, harumphed and carried her empty pail back to her room. One after the other, the women hurriedly left with their empty pails until Asabe was standing alone, wondering what had happened.

When she bumped into Cynthia, one of the off-campus ladies in the corridor, the woman screamed, "Jesus! She has rubbed her bad luck on me. Blood of Jesus cover me!"

*

Three days later, Asabe washed and sat before the mirror, painting her face like she had seen her mother do. She puckered her lips and painted them with blood red lipstick. She added a dot of eye pencil between her eyes and on the tip of her nose.

When she sat on the threshold in the mild evening sun, the ladies playing ludo stopped and looked at her in her mother's tight fits, which hung loosely about her. Kande rose and came to her. She looked at her, knelt, and used her thumb to wipe away the dot on Asabe's nose tip and pinched her cheeks. When she turned, there were tears in her eyes.

151

When the men came, they stood and watched Asabe ruining her makeup with her tears. They shook their heads and allowed the experienced women to pull them away into their offices.

Just after sunset, Nura Jangali came with his bag of goodies. He was a bit startled to see Asabe in her mother's clothes sitting on the threshold.

"Your mother isn't coming back, is she?" he asked.

Asabe shook her head and fresh tears ran down her cheeks. Nura Jangali stooped before her and wiped them away. "Come now, no need to cry. You must take care of yourself now," he said, pushing the bag into her hand.

He held her by the other hand and she allowed him to lead her into the room.

DANGO MKANDAWIRE

EMMANUEL IDUMA: What does it mean to live in Malawi today?

DANGO MKANDAWIRE: I think it means the same as living everywhere else and in every age that has ever been.

EI: Do you consider yourself an inside-outsider to Malawi? That, being a Malawian, there are things you do not understand about your country?

DM: Who has a country? What is a Malawian or a Nigerian or a Swede? There has been a lot of debate between my friends and I about this, about what it means to belong, considering the history of the lands we occupy. There was a time when—if you were born in a certain place—you spoke the language of that land, you ate the food of that season, and bowed your knee to the God of your fathers. Your idea of yourself was (and still is) partly formed by your wonder and ignorance of other people who were so different to you in clothing, manners, and tongue that it aroused feelings of "apartness."

You and I, my friend, were born in the age of the Internet. We embrace any idea we wish. Boundaries are broken. We are the New Man, waves rather than particles, overlapping and fluid, constantly in flux. I am Malawian in the sense that I have a history here and am gladly attached to it, having a special affinity towards our beautiful lake and any confusions I have about

Malawi are the same confusions I have about Chad or Australia or even the home of Superman—Krypton.

EI: Are you advocating that we listen for the sounds of inter-cultural dialogue? Is it dangerous being a wave, where the tempestuous notoriety of multifaceted existence could disorient you? I know we are in this age of the University of Google, the world being at our fingertips. But this vast reachability becomes unnerving when considered in the sense of everything-but-nothing. What do you say?

DM: You are right, Emmanuel. There is the danger of everything becoming nothing, and the truth is that the vast majority of people do not actually realize the knowledge resource that we actually have in the modern world. We take it for granted that there are documents that were sealed away, even for centuries, by an elite priesthood of knowledge from the general public that can be downloaded for free in an instant. There is the danger that we may lose the idea that anything can be sacred. But overall I do not see how—if we net all the effects together—we could be in deficit. These are exciting times my friend. It may be disorienting, but we are now waves.

EI: Are there things that you write about that, until the moment of writing, were unknown to you, unfelt, as it were?

DM: Yes. It's almost like sitting in a trance between worlds not sure what the other side will communicate, and you just sort of find yourself expressing things you hadn't known would come out that way. Some of the stories I started writing rather half-heartedly only to find myself grossly engaged in them while others, having initially the spark of excitement, fizzled out into my recycle bin amongst the other clutter. The surprises are wonderful.

EI: How do you go about the business of characterization? In my head, characterization is akin to life being breathed into the nostrils of a lifeless, yet already shaped, being.

DM: I like your analogy. It's sharp. I take writing as an act of faith. I simply begin with an intuition and follow it through. That's it really. I believe that the characters will live, for they were destined to live, to breathe. In Christendom we are told that God created men and women, but it seems even He didn't have full control over them. Here pops up the issue of free will, which I am unqualified to discuss.

Anyway as the story goes, they rebel; they eat forbidden fruit and go about ruining themselves and are in need of a savior. They went rogue. Those are my characters. At some point they listen to me, obediently following my every pen stroke, but then they gain consciousness, rebel, and follow their own path, and all I do is watch from the recesses of my imagination. Sometimes I save them, redeem them from their calamity, but at other times I leave them wallowing in their ways. Some of them become great, transcending themselves and I am terribly moved by them. Others have repulsed me, while still others have been so overly boring as to make me question the reason of writing about them in the first place, but they act as the mesh and framework for truly interesting personas.

But back to what you said about breathing life into something lifeless that already has a shape: every story I write has background and some kind of theme that I am working with and pondering.

EI: I suppose "some kind of theme" presupposes the fluidity of your concerns, even their lack of theme. You don't necessarily work with attention-grabbing themes, do you? But then the question of what could become viral is something beyond our noses.

DM: I really do not think there is any way you could reliably predict that something will become viral. It's like why we cannot accurately predict the weather. There are just too many things that have to happen in tandem and we can't keep track of them. I have an aversion to sensationalism and will pick the kinds of topics that may not be the most hard-hitting to the senses, like rape or murder or war, but are the topics that you can quietly ponder for the rest of your life. I prefer stories like that.

EI: Are you often conscious of how your words shape worlds? Is it always an intentional part of writing to define terrains of existence, one that accommodates the plot being configured?

DM: To be a master writer I feel is to build worlds of many layers, and the atoms of these worlds are words. The world as we know it has only 118 elements, and from these few blocks the whole creation resonates. I am conscious of every word when I write, whether it fits appropriately, whether it explains sufficiently, for if you misplace them you will create a whole different meaning. In fact that was what I was trying to convey in my story "Voice of the Gods," that an ancient line of leaders are chosen to rule on the basis of their command of language and are independent even of kings, because of the potency of the spoken word.

And yes I do feel that it is an intentional part of writing to define your terrain of existence. You are a builder, an architect of that world, and if you do not pay ample attention, it decays and ultimately collapses. Compare Earth to the moon or Mars. This is a better world. Brighter. In fact I find that it is when I have finished a story that I have the most trouble with it, because I now have the arduous task of reviewing every single word. Balzac said: "When the artist is giving the finishing stroke to his creation, the last touches require more time than the whole background of the picture." The final touches are what highlight the work. Brevity and clarity in description. This is what makes a story timeless.

EI: In working out a story like "Scarlet Robe," do you contemplate the plot first, or the metaphysical questions? For instance, questions of essence and morality are raised in that story, asked so intricately that there are no doubts that you are as perplexed as everyone else about our common destiny.

DM: I start with an intuition and go with it within a theme, so I guess I think of the metaphysical questions first. I have to be interested in the story myself before I get to the point of writing it. It has to swim and vibrate in my head, make me want to drop everything and rush to write it. That's the point I start writing. Initially I intended "Scarlet Robe" to be a much longer story, with more characters but somewhere I found myself leaving it as a short story.

EI: Incidentally, I have a similar writing process. The thinking always takes more than half of the time. The actual writing, if you ask me, is secondary. Do you agree that one becomes a better writer over the years because he has mastered the art of introspection?

DM: This is a truth. The writing is the end product. The bulk of the work is in your head, how you feel about it, what you think of it. Some seeds in nature spend years beneath the soil before sprouting. No one must despise the quiet phases and unseen intricacies of any process. It may appear futile and laborious, but those micro-systems are what make any work stand out. Your mind needs exposure.

There are certain illusions that befall the unexposed mind and the first one is usually that your idea is novel, new to the world. No it isn't. Great writers rarely say anything new. I can see a few cringes from readers who are also writers who understand what I am saying. For the best writers, look at the amount of research and background work they put in and you understand why their work stands out. What they are doing is masterfully putting it all together. It's almost like they are artisans with a heavily stocked tool shed and are able to cut the same pieces of wood we all have access to into shapes we could never replicate because we don't have that particular tool. That tool could be knowledge or experience or some other resource gained with time and effort. This is not to rob any artist of their own creativity, but we must be humble enough to accept that we can hear the echoes of those who came before us. To be a good writer you must be a good reader. I do not think there is any way around this.

EI: Where do you draw the line between the worldview of your characters and your own?

DM: We must take human nature as we find it. I try, to my best ability, to be fair to my characters. There are some I strongly identify with, there are others I feel are fundamentally different from me, but they are what they are. Good or Evil, we are all people, and in my stories everyone must be given their time under the spotlight. A mirror can reflect the beauty of the auroras, but it can also show us things that frighten us, that cause us to turn away in shame. But all this is to be human.

EI: In reading your story "Voice of The Gods," we could come away with the feeling that the past is being retold; that although being retold it is still the past, quite dissimilar in the face of contemporaneity. What do you say to this?

DM: "Voice of the Gods" is dear to me because it's the first story I ever wrote. When I was writing it I was trying to imagine a past that was not told and yet could pass as tangible. A past that was plausible, unfettered by mythology. You see, Emmanuel, it seems the dimmer the past, the more likely we tend to populate it with phantoms, beasts, and men whose faces we cannot recognize. I wanted the characters to be a little more familiar, accessible. I actually got so involved I picked up from the short story and wrote a whole novel of it. Only my brother has read it.

EI: Do you suppose we have lost something major, as Africans, given that most of what you describe has been replaced by newer ways of being, of initiation into society? Or should I be asking if these newer ways of initiation into society suffices as much as older modes did?

DM: Society is like a drunkard stumbling along a street trying to keep balance. You can sort of hear and understand what it's trying to say and where it's trying to go, but its speech is slurred and its steps are wobbly. The frustration we all face stems from our attempt to slot ourselves into society without being swallowed whole and suffocated by it, or to withdraw from it sufficiently enough without freezing from the cold. That's the friction of living in society and it stays with us our whole lives. New modes or old, fundamentally this is the struggle. Losing here is gaining there. And if you wish to loosen this friction, a little contradiction is necessary in everyone. Just a little. It acts as grease.

EI: We hear a lot about style. What does it mean to you?

DM: To be honest, I have never formally or rigidly thought about things like style and technique, though they are without doubt important. I begin from a different angle altogether. I imagine myself split into two. I then imagine this other me sitting opposite my table listening to everything I write. If he doesn't like the last sentence I have written, he frowns and then tells me to delete it. If he thinks I should spend a little more time on a certain section then I prolong that part. Ultimately if he likes it, I write it. That's the rule I follow. If it's not interesting to me, then why would I punish other people in reading it? But maybe that in itself is a technique. I do appreciate a little humor though. I try to be a little lighthearted at times, even when referring to things that are fundamentally heavy. Sometimes laughter is the only valve against misery and if you forget to laugh, or at least giggle, the flood of despair will sweep you away.

EI: I recall reading: "Agreed, there's a lot of talent, but it is never enough." Does this inadequacy stem from the number of people willing to hone their talent, the number of people who strive determinedly towards mastery? What does mastery even mean?

DM: Hmmm. Mastery. There is a story of a professor in psychology who every year in the first semester would tell his class to spend the first week reading Dostoevsky. He then based the subject matter of his course on the characters in Dostoevsky's novels. Writing stories with many layers. This is mastery. You have to see the world from above, alongside the eagles. To do this you must elevate yourself beyond your own feelings and prejudices, beyond your opinions and beliefs. You must ascend. This way, though everyone who reads your story will relate to it differently, it remains relevant to everybody. Not everyone can do this. As a writer you are concentrating knowledge, every thought, feeling, emotion, and idea into points gelled by words, and to keep it all together requires a thorough mind.

Discipline. You have to take the time to cultivate your imagination, to feed it so it becomes fertile. I expose myself to anything that will arouse "thought bolts" in my mind, to keep it active. My interests range from quantum physics to Sufi Islam, to Japanese anime, to SpongeBob SquarePants, and my favorite program on television: *The Penguins from Madagascar.* Many cartoons actually make intelligent programming if you listen closely.

In short, as it has been said, "Conversation enriches understanding, but solitude is the school of genius." Take the time to think. Read.

EI: Before you studied economics and statistics, did you consider being a writer?

DM: I hadn't considered it even fleetingly. I started writing relatively recently. A few years ago, actually. "Voice of the Gods" was my first story, other than the compositions I wrote back in high school as part of the curriculum. There are two people I have to credit for becoming a writer, or at least some sort of eager imitation. The first person is directly responsible for me being a writer and I really cared about that person; they really cared about me. That person brought it out of me. The second person, Joseph Tendai Milburn indirectly brought me here, after unknowingly teaching me probably the most important lesson of my life: "If you are brave enough to be yourself, despite how awkward it may sometimes appear to others, you will find your natural path in life and some happiness. You are who you are." Observing Joe and his sometimes eclectic behavior made me, me. Thanks, Joe.

EI: How do you know when it's time to write?

DM: The sparkle precipitates from nowhere. But it will come. I will just wake up one morning with a glow in my chest.

EI: Reading your stories, there's a feeling of a mishmash of voices, as though your work is polyphonic. I felt this particularly in "The Times." I especially like stories that are occupied by the voices of more than a single character.

DM: My brother, Mgawa—who may be my most ardent supporter—was the first person to point this out. I feel no character is so colossal as to singularly cast his shadow on the full expanse of a story. Relational beings are what we are. So I try to have quiet voices, loud ones, gruff ones, squeaky ones, all kinds. The danger I have always faced by having all these voices is that the result is noise rather than music. This has happened a few times without me being aware, for in my head, the gel still holds. This is where my brother comes in as a maestro to help me put harmony to the notes.

EI: Is there anything about the label "emerging writer" that makes you feel responsible? Does it humble you because you are not in full glare at the moment? I suppose you wonder what it would mean to become a famous writer, what responsibilities it may entail, especially.

DM: Being labeled an "emerging writer" (if that is what I am labeled) would exclude me from a lot of responsibility, and the lack of responsibility in the early phases of anyone's growth is a welcome and necessary part of a healthy evolution. Responsibility can breed bitterness. Ask all those who found themselves in a position where they had to assume it before their time. Even if they end up succeeding against the odds, they lose the glimmer in their eyes.

For now I am just happy to write stories that are entertaining. That's my main aim. Would someone sit down for a good hour and read this stuff? That's what I ask. As for fame, I cannot really imagine what that would mean. I think it's a gift and a curse really. Pedestals are lonely places. Not much room to maneuver. One has to stand with a pose. It's bad posture, harmful for your spine.

March 16, 2012

THE JONATHAN GRAY AFFAIR

Dango Mkandawire

His shirt was a slashed canvas, and taken collectively, the blood trickling down his right nostril, the salty white streak of a dried tear on his left cheek, and the mud on his forehead made him look quite ragged. He stood in a place that was between pitiful and comedic, whimpering as he breathed.

"Pemphero, what happened to you?" she half-screamed, pulling him into the house and holding him, before softly pushing him away in disbelief to have another glance at his fragile body. "Goodness gracious look at you. What village did you stumble into? What would the neighbors think? Where is your asthma pump?" her questions darted without intermission as Pemphero timidly pulled his inhaler out of his pocket and stretched it out with both hands, as though presenting a placating offering to an agitated deity. "Are you wheezing?" She queried. "Why are you always fighting? Almost every day, fights."

She wrapped a bandage on a shallow cut on his arm. "Always fighting! For what?" She asked again, louder, looking over the generational gap into her son's eyes for insight, perplexed as to why a group of spoiled and pampered boys at such an expensive school would lower themselves to the primitive customs of barbarians.

Pemphero was silent as he received his scolding, his mind numbed and illuminated with the flashes of violence. Acute bursts of pain rushed up his torso like a slithering phantom lurking within his joints.

"Who did this to you?" Mother asked.

"No one."

"Oh, so you mean these bruises appeared by themselves. Was this at school?"

"Ma, just leave it alone."

"No. No. Unacceptable! Your father didn't work for nothing. We do not spend a sizable fortune to send you to a school three-quarters white and expatriate to be slapped around rather than to learn to play Vivaldi. I will find out who did this and have them expelled immediately."

Pemphero was beginning to regain his composure, but was now feeling something previously unfamiliar within him. It was a squeaky feeling in his chest; the more mother questioned him, the more accentuated it became. "What do you mean you can't tell me? Who did this?"

Silence.

"Pemphero, who did this?"

"I can't say..." he replied, looking downward and finally walking away, much to her surprise.

"Why not? You are the one getting hurt. Just tell me and let me help you."

"I am fine!" he exclaimed from behind his bedroom door. "It's nothing."

Clocks can be brutal—the revolving hand a constant reminder of things pending, issues unresolved and, ultimately, the scarcity of time left. It's as though we invented it to better define our mortality, to quantify it, and thus, in our quest for progress, we mistakenly added to our misery. It was three rows away from a subtle but nagging clock that Pemphero sat pondering nervously. It was 15:25 and the clock face hypnotized him as he considered the dark shades of his immediate future. At 15:30 the bell would ring, the door would swing open, and people would rush out feeling liberated from the burden of study. He had spent the greater part of the previous night maneuvering between nightmares, and when he had woken, he heard the chirping birds outside his window as a dirge signaling his demise. He was in school again. Mr. Mumford was in full swing once more, a disciple of physics oscillating left and right across the chalkboard in his usual infectious enthusiasm, divulging the laws of motion as though they were eternal truths to starving soul searchers. He was the sort of man who hadn't a job, but a vocation, and he spoke naturally of physics beneath the equations, as a poet would speak of poetry behind the letters.

"You see, Isaac Newton did more than describe everything that moves. He showed us that the whole world, the universe in fact, was mechanical. No spirits magically transporting stars. No unearthly giants with mercurial shoulders upholding the galaxy's orbs. Every path is determinable and predictable. And from that viewpoint it changed our whole perspective of reality. That was the essence of his genius."

Mr. Mumford paused and thought momentarily, searching his mind's inner troves.

"And it was genius because he had to shut his eyes from heaven, just for a moment, so he could look clearly at the Earth. And in that regard he was the first man who had ever seen the Earth clearly. As it was. To go from seeing the world as a fantastic and haphazard place, where gods occasionally take strolls for their leisure to the confounding of men, to seeing it as no different to … to … this clock here."

He pointed to the clock, adding to Pemphero's calamity. It was 15:27.

"...this clock here. Mechanical. This was a revolutionary step. The world was never the same again. This was Newton. And now you learn the ways of motion."

He returned to the board and the lesson, realizing he had digressed somewhat. The students blinked and looked at one another in amused bewilderment. He would often say things beyond their scope, but he did so deliberately, so that he could fish out the most precocious of them, the one whose reach was highest up so that he could reach down and raise him to whatever limit lay within him. He was no fool; he knew full-well that a teacher's hell was no more terrifying than a classroom with no promising apprentices. Had he a keener eye, he would have scouted the trepidation on the face of his star pupil, Pemphero. Today, everything Mr. Mumford said was alien to him and calculus, which Pemphero excelled at, appeared as obscure hieroglyphs pasted across the board. He wore a blank stare caused by the listlessness one experiences on the eve of an unavoidable calamity. The second hand on the clock ticked silently before the bell rang with a thunderous clamor.

"God please save me," Pemphero whispered to himself as the class cleared with the speed of a gale wind. Today he would try something different. Instead of attempting to be the first one out and speeding home before giving anyone the chance to see him, he would remain behind, wait for the room to clear, close the door, and wait until he was camouflaged in darkness if need be, before going home. Arriving after dark would mean trouble at home. But trouble at home was a lesser evil than the trouble he had here.

"Pempro," Mr. Mumford called from behind his desk, having surrendered forever any further attempt to learn the proper pronunciation of his full name "Pempheroyanga." "Pempro. The bell rang a while ago. Surely you noticed. Do you have any questions?"

"No sir. I am just finishing up my homework."

"Well, I have always been an advocate for hard work, but this isn't home, is it?"

"No sir, but I just like to finish it as soon as possible." Mr. Mumford sensing something mischievous yet having no evidence of foul play, packed his bag and left.

"You behave now, you hear," he said from outside the door, before disappearing into the distance and into his mental world of equations, calculus, and his beloved Newton. Pemphero sat alone with vacuous pupils waiting for an event he couldn't define, alert to nonexistent signals. He changed desks three times, wrote nonsense on the chalkboard, and even did some push-ups to pass the time. Half an hour into his self-imposed exile, he heard footsteps, first ethereal and quasi-imaginary, then heavier and certain. Two voices playfully mingled from behind the door but Pemphero couldn't make out what was being said. One was female and giggling, incessantly jovial, the other was hoarse and familiar and at its resonance, Pemphero wished he could sink into his shadow beneath him and disappear. His thoughts became scrambled and he considered rushing to the door and leaning against it, so that it would appear locked when someone tried to open it, but he knew that obviously wouldn't work. The hinges squeaked, the door opened, and his nemesis stumbled in walking backward, his face buried in the bosom of his buxom female companion.

"Oh!" she said jumping up and back, covering her half-bare chest with her sweater, after realizing that they had company. Pemphero stood timidly in the corner of the room, like a hamster in the corner of a cage. He swallowed hard.

"Pempro!" Jonathan shouted, who unlike Mr. Mumford, had not even remotely considered that it was courteous to at least attempt to say the name Pempheroyanga. Jonathan needed a name to identify him for beatings. Pempro was that name; it was no different than a number to him, an identifier.

"Why are you here!? Will you ever stop being such a rotten nuisance!?" Jonathan slammed his fist into the desk beside him, his brain buzzing off a cocktail of hormones and meanness.

"Jonathan, it's ok, let's just go," she said, pulling him by the arm with no effect, wishing to avoid trouble.

"No, Laura. It's not ok." He quickly replied, strutting toward Pemphero and rolling up his sleeve.

"Jonathan just leave it, we can always come back tomorrow."

"Tomorrow," he said aghast. "I want it now! There is no way in hell I would allow this little shithole to get in the way of my boner." He towered above Pemphero, but somewhere between clenching his fist and swinging it into Pemphero's face, the throbbing bulge in his trousers became unbearable. "Pempro you will wait outside for me. I want to have ample time to settle this between you and me. If you dare run I will kill you. You understand?" Pemphero felt as though his insides had hollowed out and filled with lead. His knees were quivering.

"You understand?" he repeated, at which point Pemphero nodded rapidly. The girl rushed to Jonathan's side again and an argument broke out, she Pemphero's representative, arguing his cause, mustering all her tenderness to soothe the flares that were emanating from her boyfriend. It was no use. She looked at Pemphero with a limp face, a half-placated face that showed compassion but not conviction.

"I am sorry," she whispered. "I tried."

"Here's an idea." Jonathan suddenly lit up. "You be our guard. Stand by the door and warn us if you see anyone coming. Be my watchman. After all, we have no keys."

Pemphero stood outside the door awaiting his judgment, the school football field not far away. The openness of the landscape before him and the whistling of the sweeping winds stirred something base within him and he felt the need to run—to run violently in all directions at once with no purpose into the distance. He closed his eyes and dreamed of the day he would be good enough to make the team, when he could wear the school colors and go on sports trips, possibly win Player of the Year or some other laurel he could display before an applauding crowd. But he knew he was asthmatic and could run neither far nor fast. Above the layer of this dream, this simmering ambition, he could hear them: the moans, the groans, the shifting chair against the floor, the entangling flesh. He knew the girl. Who didn't? She was Laura Belcoe. He, along with every boy in the school, had a crush on her, though he was sure that within his heart, his adoration burned with the greatest fervor. Yet here he was, standing guard at the door in the humiliating service of his enemy as he casually had his way with her.

Soon the lovers emerged, their hair frazzled and tilted to the sides with looks of satisfaction across their faces. This time she walked past him without so much as blinking, and as she disappeared into his peripheral vision, he wished he could explain to her that he wasn't always like this, that today was a strange day. Jonathan stepped outside and looked down at him.

"Now... where were we?"

Zione Chisale had found her son Pemphero squatting in the store room holding a mirror and using a makeup sponge to cover the bruises on his face. It was a poor choice of a hideout and he had made a complete mess of things, looking worse off with the brown powder smeared generously on his face, so that he would have been better disguised with a clean abrasion. She asked him repeatedly what had happened and he kept insisting that he fell off a bicycle and landed on the tarmac.

"Pempheroyanga Taonga Chisale," she said, quoting his name in full with arms crossed. "We both know you don't have a bicycle."

"It was Mark's. I fell. On the way home."

Looking down at him, his eyelids trembling in the dim light, she knew he needed to speak to his father, but sadly he died years ago. In his place acting as a surrogate was Badu, Pemphero's uncle who, coincidentally, was arriving that evening. Badu was not her perfect choice as a role model. In the past she had done all that she could to shield Pemphero from him, not completely cutting him off but limiting contact. Badu was a rough man, a man of the world. He had disappeared for seven years without contact and only resurfaced at his brother's funeral, reassuring the distraught widow.

"It is difficult, but we shall persevere," he repeated as the coffin was buried. It was this gap in his life, this mysterious seven-year absence that irked Zione. He had never clarified it, and he had the demeanor of a man who daily carried with him an unpleasant secret. She didn't like surprises. He had never married, always arriving with a young slender lady on his sleeve always introduced as "my pretty friend." This had never sat well with Zione. But alas, Badu was the closest family Pemphero had left and, considering the nature of the recent troubles, she capitulated.

Soon after his arrival, this time surprisingly alone, she pulled Badu aside and explained what had transpired in the house since his last visit. He listened intently, nodding intermittently before shuffling over to Pemphero's room where he found him asleep. He tapped Pemphero on his shoulders, waking him. He wasted no time getting to the point.

"Pemphero, life isn't easy. Your mother tells me you have been having some problems at school." Phempero could only half hear what was being said to him and was blinking rapidly, exorcising the sleep out of himself. "Whether you love peace or crave the fight, the truth is that the battle comes to you and you have no say in the matter. The world has weapons, some sharp, others blunt, all lethal. If the world had no arms, then we would be lying in green fields basking in the sun. We would be living the life described by the religions, where every tear is wiped from our eyes. We would be carefree and happy all the time. We would be in paradise. We would be surrounded by people who love us."

Pemphero looked up at Uncle Badu and with all his resolve blocked the warm tears welling in his eyes. Uncle Badu was a near replica of his late father.

"But the weapons exist, lying about and ready to be wielded either by you, in which case you are defended, or by someone else, in which case you are defenseless. Better the former."

Pemphero didn't understand all that was being said or alluded to, but the parts that filtered through resonated with him. He felt the words more than he comprehended them.

"Things just happen to us without our consent. Your father's death in that car accident. No one wanted it, but it happened anyway. This is the world." He reached out his hands and raised Pemphero's chin, the bruises on his face now faint but visible. "What happened?"

Pemphero felt tense and sat up straight. He couldn't lie to Uncle Badu as he had to his mother, and he began to recount the familiar events that led to his weekly beating: first the taunts, then the slaps, and finally the punches.

"What's his name? No, never mind. You needn't tell me. They are all the same, Pemphero. They don't deserve special mention. That would be an honor they don't deserve." Uncle Badu stood up suddenly, put his hands into his pockets, and looked up at the ceiling as though recollecting a fleeting memory.

"And the teachers? Do they know about this? About what has been happening to you?"

"No."

"Why don't you tell them?"

"I'm afraid."

"Afraid of what?"

"Afraid of Jonathan Gra—"

"No. No. No. I do not need to know his name. They are all the same. Come with me." They walked out of the house and were immediately serenaded by the soothing, cool, summer breeze whistling beneath a seraphic sky. A small bar was at the corner and Badu walked to it, pulled out a bottle of brandy and two glasses.

"Brandy was your father's favorite drink. Have a seat." Pemphero sat on one of the lawn chairs directly facing his uncle. "You say you were afraid? Afraid of what?"

"I was afraid of him."

"Fear. Never give in to it." Badu paused and suspected his next words may have little immediate effect. Yet he hoped that on some later day, when the spin and tilt of the world was better understood by the young man, he would look back and this conversation would act as an anchor to steady him.

"We all start off afraid. It begins with the fear of the dark, and then it spreads to too many things. Many, many things." Badu continued, "But it is your responsibility alone to draw the limit and proclaim, 'No more! I will not fear beyond this mark!' Cowards are people who neglected this duty when they were young and as the years pass, they become worn down. Fear is like a tide. It rolls toward you in spiraling waves and unless you set up a levee, you slowly drown. Fear is deceptive, Pemphero. It induces panic. In some cases people have drowned in shallow waters for failing to simply stand up."

He sipped his brandy and licked his lips. "Do you want a sip?"

"No thank you."

"Started drinking?"

"No."

"No need to lie. Especially not to your dear uncle. "

"Well ... a little. But I have never been drunk."

"I knew it. You see this is why I appreciate our customs of circumcision or other rites of passage. There is a clear separation as to how society must treat you before and after. If we were back in Africa, after your rite of passage I would simply have poured some brandy into the other glass without too much caution. But these days, in these modern times, we go by speculation. I have to guess as to whether you have become a man. Oh well. Here you go."

Uncle Badu poured a little brandy into the other glass which was full of ice and passed it to Pemphero, who received it timidly, feeling a surge of pride strike his chest. This was the first time an adult had presented him a drink, and not any drink—his father's favorite drink. Badu looked at him searchingly.

"Pemphero. We are going to assume you have passed your rite of passage and we shall speak as equals. We shall speak as men. We are going to speak of war." He changed his posture, straightening his back.

"Do not think of war as violence and murder. First and foremost, think of it merely as conflict resolution, an expression of the friction that exists between men and nations. Business executives the world over read manuals that were written by military generals. There is a reason. Think of war as the sparks of fire that intermittently appear when different interests grind against each other. This is war. And unfortunately, it is inevitable, because all of us have different interests. Even between you and me. Our interests differ, but in our case they do not differ so much as to cause us to wage war, for we are family. Hopefully and probably you and I may never have to be involved in an actual physical war, but the fact that we live means we struggle and must learn warrior codes. To learn these codes we must look to those who have excelled at war. There are several generals who never lost a battle."

At this point he took a monster sip, squinted his eyes and became transformed in a reverential countenance. "Julius Caesar—Rome. Ban Qi—China. Alexander Suvorov—Russia. Arthur Wellesley—England. And of course that most illustrious and famous of generals, Alexander, who is called 'The Great.' Now I need you to understand this. These men were like you and me, flesh and blood, but there are reasons why they excelled. It isn't secret knowledge. One needs only to look closely and study the circumstances surrounding their lives."

"Uncle Badu, I appreciate what you are saying to me, but how does all this matter to me?" Pemphero asked confusedly, already soothed by the brown liquid in his glass.

"Patience, Pemphero. Later you will understand. Firstly, you must dry your eye when you look at the battlefield. Tears blur your sight. You need to carefully mark the terrain. You need to be honest with me. Why are you being targeted? Is it because you are black? You see the blacks and the Jews have historically—"

"No uncle, it's not that."

"So you have had no troubles with racism. From what your mother tells me you are the only black person at your school, right? That's always tricky. There are few things more taxing on a soul than doing your very best to fit in somewhere and never really knowing whether you have succeeded in chiseling yourself into the right acceptable shape to fit in the slots set for you by society."

Pemphero thought about it a little before responding.

"Obviously I can't be friends with everyone, but in the beginning when I first arrived, people wouldn't really talk to me. They only did so after I scored really well in our first test. I got the highest mark. I think this shocked them or something and maybe they became curious about me, and after that I got along okay with most people.

"Okay. Just checking. With us, Pemphero, you can never know... are you alone?"

"How do you mean?"

"Does he pick on you alone, or are there others?"

"There are others."

"Ah. Those are your allies, and the best kind. Alliances formed in the face of a common enemy are the strongest, much more lasting than those formed on common views. Next, define your enemy. What is his advantage over you?"

"How do you mean?" Pemphero asked again.

"What advantage does he have over you? Is he bigger?"

"Yes, most certainly. Much bigger."

"Gangs? Is he in one? Do you have them at your school?"

"No. No gangs. And he has no friends. Not even one. He is too horrible for friends. He is several years older than us."

"So the only advantage he has is size."

"Yes."

"Over a majority, with no gang."

"Yes."

"Ha!" He exclaimed." Trifle matter. We have nothing to worry about then. Stand up."

Pemphero stood up and Uncle Badu's eyes swept across him then scanned him, first down and then back up.

"Extend your arm." Pemphero did so feeling as though he were being examined by a doctor. "You have always been small. Now I know they say you shouldn't, but do you like fighting? Be honest."

"No."

"Why?"

"It's wrong."

"What if I told you it wasn't wrong. Not always."

A pregnant pause followed. Uncle Badu smiled.

"Sit down. If you do not start standing up for yourself now, it will spill over to the rest of your life. You will grow accustomed to being shoved out of the way and trampled upon and ultimately, you may grow to hate yourself. And I will tell you right now... this... okay. Tell me his name."

"Jonathan Gray."

"This Jonathan Gray is only the beginning and he is nothing but a conniving little goblin. As you get older, and the walls of your school give way to the mountains of the world, the monsters grow bigger, the stakes are higher, and the courage necessary to face them multiplies. There are some natural fighters in the world. You aren't one of them. Even as a child you were timid, and if a child shows himself to be fiery, that fire is his true nature. You were always shy. And your asthma had always bothered you. But don't worry." He refilled his own glass; he was already on the third one. "From my experience some of those who are physically docile are mentally ferocious in their aggression. I could teach you to box. I was university champion three years in a row. But it's not for you. I will teach you a greater discipline. To wage war."

"Do you know the story of David and Goliath?"

"Yes."

"David and Goliath. There is nothing inspirational about that story. It is merely educational. But inspirational? No. Not in the least bit. David being beaten into a pulp while fighting back with every fiber of his being and never retreating, that would have been inspirational. That would have been the story of someone in a hopeless situation clinging to hope against ghastly odds, never surrendering his soul. In David's case the odds were in his favor. The story of David and Goliath teaches us that the fastest way to rise in the world and to overcome your obstacles is not necessarily to work hard, but to outmaneuver others and circumstances. And this is the art of war."

"Wait. Uncle. What do you mean the odds were in David's favor? As I remember it, Goliath was a giant and David a boy."

"And who said being a giant is always an advantage? David killed only one man and became an instant legend. There were other soldiers, warriors of note who had labored their entire lives, forever forgotten because they hadn't stepped up at the right moment. There was nothing particularly special about David. He was no different than anyone else—at least at that point in his life. They say he had been a shepherd and had gained experience by defending sheep in the fields against wolves and lions. There were plenty of other shepherds. He just had a plan. The odds were in his favor. He simply looked up, realized that Goliath had a fatal opening, and attacked that opening. Goliath had a gap in his helmet, and as the story goes he shot a rock by a sling through that gap. Goliath was too lanky to catch David anyway, so there was really no threat of him being mauled. In short, he was never really going to lose. He knew that. But no one else did. Pemphero... This Jonathan Gray affair is not just about being bullied at a high school. It is about life and how you shall live. And life is a serious matter. That's why I am taking my time with you on this. This is the secret of successful people."

He leaned in and motioned for Pemphero to lend him his ear before whispering, "Successful people have a plan that fits really well to their surrounding circumstances. Thus, they end up looking smarter, braver, and more resourceful than others when in fact they have simply outmaneuvered. HA!" He laughed sitting up again. "That's all there is to it. After Goliath had fallen like a heap of stones onto the floor and David was assaulted by songs of praise heralding his courage, I am sure he was uncomfortable, if he were honest. It was more tactics than courage. War, victory, success, is to outmaneuver. Have you ever heard of something called the Exploitation of the Great by the Small?"

Pemphero shook his head, putting his glass down, his head warm.

Uncle Badu was undeterred: "The Exploitation of the Great by the Small happens when smaller units hold a large unit ransom. The tables suddenly turn and an advantage—whether it be muscle, intelligence, or any other resource becomes a liability. The underdog rises and wipes his sullied paws on the elephant. Who are your friends? Real friends, not acquaintances. Acquaintances are like cockroaches. When problems come to light, they disappear so fast one wonders whether they were really there to begin with. Who are your real friends?"

"Mark Coleman and Thomas Milburn."

"And where were they when you were being pounded?"

"Also being pounded, just in different places and at different times."

"Ok. Those are your primary allies. Organize yourselves. Obviously there are others being bullied, yes?"

"Yes."

"They shall also play a part. This is what you are to do..."

Mr. Mumford was once again gliding across the chalkboard, enchanted by the sleek shape of the integral symbol in Calculus.

"The integral symbol is cooler than the Nike swoosh," he casually comments with a cheeky smile. He stood in front of the students like a maestro orchestrating the flow of the logic, each successive line immutably confirming the previous.

"You just have to be logical. It's hard to see at first. But you just have to be logical. People struggle with mathematics, but it's because they don't see it like a language—like English or Mandarin. The more you speak a language, the better you become. Speak mathematics, students. Speak it."

He stopped suddenly, in mid-equation, and turned to face them. "You see the problem with society is that it's bad enough that we are semi-literate, but we are much more innumerate. Ask someone to calculate a percentage and they fall flat on their faces. Even the *brightest* person fails the simplest arithmetic. And it's because we don't stress it. Nope! Someone being illiterate is a tragedy! A human rights violation! But someone innumerate? That's normal. Division is hard by default they say. Yet we all want to make more money, and money itself is absolutely numerate. The more of it the better, right? Yet most people can't count. And if they can't count, how can they know if they are rich or poor? Math. Practice, practice, practice." He turned around again and continued his lesson and as usual the students smiled in amused bewilderment.

Pemphero was at his desk still feeling the struggle within himself, but Mr. Mumford's musings between exercises always cheered him. The clock was as it always was—reminding him of things pending and issues unresolved. The bell rang and as always the room cleared in a flash. He sat calmly and Mr. Mumford cleared his blackboard. He was the only teacher who didn't assign anyone to clear it, or write on it for that matter. He almost treated it as though it was a sacred shrine and he was the only initiate.

"Pempro, staying behind again?" he asked. "You are doing well enough to play a little. You must remember..." he wagged his finger in the air, "Albert Einstein discovered relativity by daydreaming sitting at a clerk's desk! HA!" He laughed. "Imagine that. Arguably the most intelligent man in the world sitting at a clerk's desk filling registers. Leave room for play. Go outside."

"I will. I was just clearing my desk, sir."

The sun assaulted him as soon as he stepped out, and the noise of the chattering students laughing and giggling seized him. He was absorbing everything around him like a sponge. His friends Mark and Thomas joined him strutting nervously.

"You have everything?"

"Yes," Mark replied nervously looking into his backpack. "But are you sure about this, Pempheroyanga?"

Apart from his mother, Mark and Thomas were the only two people he knew in the whole world who called him by his full name.

"Mark," Pemphero returned. "We have been through this before."

"Ok, ok. Sorry. I'm just nervous that's all."

"Thomas, how are you feeling?"

Thomas was steadier and had been nonchalant about the whole thing since Pemphero suggested it to them.

"The Exploitation of the Great by the Small?" he asked wiping his palms against his trousers. "That's some wild idea man. But fuck it, I'm just tired of being slapped everyday and being relieved of my pocket money."

Jonathan Gray appeared from around the corner with his girlfriend Laura beside him. It was easy to see that she adored him and was walking (almost skipping actually) slightly behind him while he looked utterly bored and unconcerned. The boys gritted their teeth as he approached, the very clothes he was wearing having been taken from each of them. His cap belonged to Pemphero, his trainers were once Mark's, and the belt around his waist with the flashy buckle was at some time the property of Thomas—a belt which he would periodically unbuckle and administer a beating to the backside of its previous owner.

"Guys, I need some money. Me and Laura are hungry. We need to buy lunch," he casually said, placing his hand on Pemphero's shoulder. Mark and Thomas retreated. "And where are your friends going?" he asked. "I guess you can afford it by yourself. Shitty friends you have. Pay up."

"At least I have friends."

"What was that?" he reacted leaning forward.

"Jonathan, please." Laura interjected. "I have enough money. Let's go."

"No. You my girl. No need for you to spend anything while I'm around. I will take care of you."

He kissed her on the cheek.

"I will let that pass, Pempro. Laura doesn't like it when I upset people. And I do that often. Pay up."

"No."

"What do you mean, no?" He returned, now furious.

"No." Pemphero repeated. "No more."

Jonathan's eyes screwed, his blood boiled and swirled within his veins, and he clenched his right fist. The others stood hesitantly in the perimeter, the lonesome figure of Pemphero standing alone beneath the heaving danger that towered above him.

"I guess I just need to teach you a lesson then, little man, and in front of all your puny friends as well." He looked up and pointed at the rest of them. "After Pempro, you're all next. One by one. Don't you dare run."

He hadn't noticed the tension in the air. Jonathan lunged forward, but suddenly two stones hit him square in the chest causing him to wail in anguish and fall to the ground. He began to cry. Time froze, then thawed slowly. The wind whistled by and all eyes were fixed on the scene. Pemphero looked down at Jonathan who was now holding his chest and writhing in pain. Everyone was astonished at how easily he had collapsed to the floor.

Mark, the attacker who had launched the twin stones from a wooden sling, stood in a daze. Jonathan lay at Pemphero's feet. Only now did the others step forward, though timidly. What Pemphero said next was even more startling than Jonathan Gray writhing on the ground from left to right.

"Mark, shoot him again. This time at close range." He sounded heartless.

Mark hesitated, but Pemphero looked at him as though to say, "the hard part is past. Don't fail us now." It was enough to mobilize him and he stood above Jonathan who was looking up and begging to be left alone.

Smack!! Across the stomach this time causing an even louder wail.

Pemphero put his foot on Jonathan's chest and told him not to resist.

"If you ever pick on anyone of us again, each of us will be armed with slings. Instead of three stones hurled at you, there will be twenty."

Jonathan looked up and noticed that more people had congregated around him. To him, their eyes appeared menacing, as a wolf's eyes reflecting the moonlight.

"I'm sorry, I'm sorry," he said repeatedly.

Laura was rooted and hadn't moved during the whole ordeal. As Pemphero was turning he caught her eyes. Yes, those eyes he dreamt of. How lovely they were. He remembered the other day when she had half-pleaded his case, when he was told to stand at the door as she and Jonathan enjoyed each other. He had neither a look of triumph nor vindication. He had more courage facing Jonathan Gray than talking to Laura Belcoe.

"Give us back our things," Pemphero demanded. Jonathan got up obediently with no trace of defiance.

They began to reclaim their possessions, Jonathan undressing in front of everyone. Pemphero retrieved his cap, Mark his shoes, and Thomas his belt, leaving Jonathan with baggy trousers that could no longer hold around the waist.

"Let's go," Pemphero said, before Thomas struck Jonathan with his belt, buckle to flesh.

"Don't ever lay a hand on me again!" He shouted suddenly. His action triggered an avalanche. All of a sudden, everyone who was ever violated by Jonathan Gray rushed forward to avenge himself. Pemphero stood between Jonathan and the exploding mob.

"Stop!" he shouted. Jonathan looked up in terror. He had always known that he was feared. That was what he wanted. To him to be feared was to be respected. But that afternoon he realized he was more than feared. He was hated. And he couldn't quite understand how he felt about being hated. "We are finished here. Let's go."

The mob instantly cooled. Pemphero reached into his pocket for his inhaler and took deep, heavy breaths. "Let's go," he said again. The Rubicon had been crossed. The skinny asthmatic was now the undisputed commander of legions.

Pemphero hadn't stopped everyone from having a piece of Jonathan because he felt sorry for him. Far from it. He had done so because Uncle Badu had said that if he were to be beaten properly and beyond a certain point, he would be pushed too far, to an extreme, and maybe get friends or brothers outside school. This was war. One must act and not react. What needed to be done to end this war was to humiliate him. Humiliate him so that he couldn't tell anyone about what happened.

The crowd dispersed and Jonathan Gray picked himself up. He held up his trousers with one hand and walked away in his socks, which happened to have holes at the big toes. He was muttering something to himself and sniffling.

It had been a strange day. He hadn't seen a sling in years.

DONALD MOLOSI

EMMANUEL IDUMA: Is there sense in the idea that being an artist cannot mean being just one thing? That creativity transcends technique or form?

DONALD MOLOSI: Absolutely. When history's legendary *griots* told stories they did not pause to ponder whether they were dancers, singers, actors, or performance historians. They just put out the art, and that is what art is—an energy that you never know how it will manifest itself, how it will opt to be birthed. In that way, our obsession with categorizing talents is a loss of some sort.

EI: It's fascinating that your writing has a life of its own. It morphs across genres. Is this some form of textual justice, to be able to work in whatever genre befits an idea? This is considering the fact that your writing ranges from short stories to meditative essays, mostly poems.

DM: You know, I can sit here and say that my writing is separate from my acting, which is separate from my singing, and that is true on some level. But essentially these are all my instruments, and as such they play different tunes of my politics. The tune—the content—always picks its genre, its instrument. I do not decide what will become a play or a poem or a short story. Essentially, I write and perform from a mostly unconscious place and that is perhaps the reason for that lack of predictable categorization for my work.

EI: Why did you write the poem "Haiti Can Hold Me"? Do you have strong sentiments toward Haiti?

DM: My politics are global. I have strong sentiments about the world and Haiti is a part of the world. You will see in my writing and acting work that I jump from Haiti to Zimbabwe to England to Uganda; that has been my experience. I am not rooted. Sokari Ekine, a great writer and inspiration, was kind enough to publish my poem about Haiti on *BlackLooks*, and that rippled to its being published in *New Internationalist* and so forth until it reached Haiti itself, and I was absolutely humbled.

EI: And then you are, of course, not Haitian. Yet there was this feeling of being there, right in the middle of all the energy and chaos, the miraculous happenings. I guess every writer must evoke feelings, but how did you manage to do that so well in that poem?

DM: Thank you for the encouragement. My friends lost their families and possessions in the earthquake, and I was sad and angry about the losses and all the horror that the survivors endured. I wrote about Hotel Montana in the poem, and that detail is because one of my friends was frantically updating her Facebook statuses from Massachusetts begging people to rescue her aunt, who was stuck in Hotel Montana in Port de France, buried under rubble but still texting for help. It is that chaos that pushed that poem out of my heart onto paper. But I did not want to rant. Rather, I chose to remember the people who died in the earthquake in a way that honors them, but does not deny reality.

EI: Is it possible that a writer can deny reality in a work? Are you aware of that possibility?

DM: Absolutely. The African's humanity is something that is a part of reality. And its omission from narratives, propagated by Western media, is a denial of reality. I hope through my work to counter the idea of writers not being able to look past the spectacle of something like a disorganized African city or Haiti's economic helplessness to the humanity of the people. I try not to deny the reality of a shared humanity in my work.

EI: Your story "We Have Known Ironies" in *Saraba Magazine* comes off as a direct relationship with the subject that has enraged and ignited us all. This interrogation of what it means to be African, what it does not mean to be African, what must not be considered—do you assume that it must be written of consciously?

DM: It used to make me livid. The idiotic idea that African identity is a monolithic block used to anger me, let alone the condescension that comes with it. But now I just look at that mentality with pity because it is ignorance. Authenticity is such a problematic concept and probably does not exist because of the unthinkable diversity on the continent. So, yes, it is a hot issue we should address, but only by diversifying stories of what it is to be African, to endow the term "African" with multiple narratives.

EI: Do you write with a theme in mind?

DM: I do not write consciously. I usually read things I have written only to find that I do not recognize them. What I will say though is that I am conscious of the shameless damage that art and performance have done to Africa's humanity over the centuries and—more importantly—the need for work that humanizes Africa. So, although my work is not themed, I have been consciously publicizing only my Africanist work because it is an urgent call.

EI: Would rather write a poem, short story, essay, or a film?

DM: I wish I could answer that, Emmanuel. The narrative picks the format, really. Sometimes I write a one-minute song about a narrative and that works. Sometimes it needs to be performed constantly for six years and its aura comes from repetition, as is the case with one of my one-man shows. I do not write or perform from a conscious place, so I cannot answer that.

EI: Is there a bifocal range that being a writer and an actor accords you? Maybe you see from two "sides of the coin"?

DM: Maybe being an actor forces me to articulate emotional beats much more in prose, but I do not know because I do not really analyze my work. My friends who are writers comment on my protagonists in short stories as having the "actor's eye" and taking in details about surroundings in a way that pans like a camera. I suppose there is something there, but writing and acting are so separate in my conscious mind. That is why it takes me a while to learn lines (a conscious act) from scripts I wrote myself (from an unconscious place). But when I perform I go back into the unconscious world.

EI: Have you ever hoped to remain in that unconscious world?

DM: Absolutely! It is full of lovely silence and flowing thoughts. I work it into my schedule. I have to have two days a week where I turn off the lights and sit in the dark in silence and scribble freely in the dark for a couple of hours. So even though I cannot—

because of practical reasons—live in that world all the time, I visit it often.

EI: You were the first Botswanian who was off-Broadway. I recall reading about your award on Facebook and wondering if it was an award first for you or a first for Botswana. What did you think?

DM: I have worked extremely hard toward this passion for performance since I was 10 years old. I will not discredit my own tireless efforts, but I do dedicate this honor to the memory of Sir Seretse Khama, our heroic founding president. "Blue, Black, and White's" success is a first for me and for Botswana, and since the show is a love-letter to Botswana, of course it proudly flies our Botswana flag high.

EI: This suggests a line of thinking: could a map of a nation turn out to be a map of the world? And what element would make that transition from the local to the international?

DM: Whether it be in books or performances, we Africans need to tell our stories in ways that only we can tell our stories and have them be enthusiastically consumed by our own people first. Only then, once we have legitimated our work on our own terms, will others pay serious attention. The awards I have won internationally are blessings and I am humbly grateful, but they were never the goal. The goal was to create work I would be able to justify to my people and ancestors and my consciousness, even before someone puts my name on the ballot for an award in a Western country.

EI: One more bit on this: Is it good reasoning to work with the ambition to "map the world" from a locality? It could be a distraction, you know.

DM: I am not convinced we always need to "go international," as people say. We can legitimate our work ourselves if we set up the right structures and take our views seriously. This overly romantic idea of working abroad is not necessarily as good as it gets for the African artist.

EI: I recall having read Mukoma Wa Ngugi, Akin Ajayi, and Tolu Ogunlesi on the subject of structures. In all they did not mention more than ten literary journals within the continent. How can we build these structures? Do you think you're playing a role?

DM: I am reviving my theater company I founded in Botswana to give a platform for good theater in Botswana to be seen by Batswana. I am hoping for more collaboration as a structural choice in how we create work. That is one way of setting up a forum outside of the government structures we mostly rely on in Botswana.

Journals all over Africa need to actually be good. I think the problem is that although we have many journals and theaters, only a few like *Farafina, Saraba, Chimurenga, Kwani?,* and a few more are actually consistently documenting excellent writing. We need even more that are like that, so that publishing on the continent has more of a legitimating voice before we even consider being legitimated by winning the Caine Prize or something foreign like that.

EI: Does being out of Botswana feel like being in exile? I use "exile" because I am thinking of necessity, you know, political necessity. But your reason for being out surely isn't political. The point of this is to question if you ever feel cut off, shut out, too far away?

DM: Botswana is in me, wherever I go and whatever happens to me because I love my country. I was born there and went to school there. I have, however, always been an observer wherever I was. Even as a child in my grandmother's house with family all around, I was watching and observing people and goats and cats so that I could imitate them later. So I don't feel far from Botswana when I am geographically away, because I am always in my dreamland of sounds and shapes and lovely darkness.

EI: And how does this influence your creative process?

DM: I suppose that even though I still feel very connected to Botswana, I do struggle not to nostalgically romanticize it in my work. It is not a distance thing. It is a matter of turning an insult into pride. It is the instance of—this is a true story—it is the instance of someone telling me Botswana is a strange name that sounds like a disease; it is that ignorance I encounter outside Botswana that makes me defensively love Botswana even more. It shows in my work, including my one-man show on Sir Seretse Khama, in which I proudly celebrate the Father of our Nation.

EI: You said in a BBC interview that you had a "chronically colonized curriculum." We're a generation that has to continually undefine. Is this a major thrust of your preoccupations?

DM: Yes. Through my Africanist work that forces me to do research, I am constantly filling gaps for myself because I dislike that as a child I was taught about Russian Czars before I learned about Seretse Khama in just as much detail. I dislike the fact that people in Botswana still take a day off work to watch Prince William marry Kate Middleton, yet our own Botswana kings and Swati kings marry all the time and we do not even care. Do minds get more colonized than that? I mean, of course I do not regret having learned about the Czar and Rasputin and the lovely snow in Russia, but those things should never be taught in a Botswana school as substitutes for our peoples' history.

EI: I consider your work trans-African in nature, and in that sense, I readily refuse to nationalize you. Do you permit me?

DM: I do. Haha. My work is trans-African, yes. African borders are a construct after all; they were drawn to serve European greed. So, yes, my work eludes borders on purpose.

EI: You have created mostly one-man plays and short solos. There might be so many reasons for this—cost of production, flexibility, brevity, etc. Is brevity in your mind the soul of wit? What attracted you to the minimal form?

DM: I love subjectivity. I love being able to follow one character's ups and downs and present them undistracted by other characters' stories. I do other ensemble work on short films and television, but they do not get as much press as my solo performances, so that may be why it looks like I do only solo work. For example, I was touring with an ensemble cast in Tanzania for four months last year, and I filmed a movie in Kenya and Tanzania last year as well. I was on a TV show in

Vermont last summer, but none of these projects blew up in the media as much as the solo shows. But, yes, I love solo for its subjectivity and the fact that it is difficult to do!

EI: When did acting and writing become a marriageable possibility?

DM: My fiction writing is definitely not married to my acting. As they say, necessity is the mother of invention, so if no one is going to write me a script about Hubert Ogunde, I am going to write it myself. That is the attitude that made me write more solo work.

EI: Maybe what you did with Seretse Khama's life is akin to re-humanizing politics. I get these ideas about how politics must be given an interpersonal face, portrayed without the borders of public and private. Because I think that's how we are going to make sense of its art. Is that silly?

DM: You are right. It is that attempt to chronicle the humanity of the man despite politics. I want to take him from a statue to an identifiable face and voice in time and space. It is a humanized story, not hero-worship, because humans find inspiration in human stories.

EI: Who are the artists that have influenced you most? Musicians? Painters? Writers? Are there those of this generation of writers and artists who move as older ones do?

DM: My friends are tired of hearing about my endless respect for the work of Chimamanda Ngozi Adichie and Binyavanga Wainaina. I think they are the writers who showed me the possibility of artistically engaging with the 21st century through an African lens sparkling with intelligence. I obviously look up to people like John Kani and Hubert Ogunde who paved the way for my generation.

EI: How has the politics of all the places you've lived affected your writing, your creative process? And these are highly politicized places — Morocco, USA, United Kingdom, etc.

DM: Botswana is wealthy and stable, even more so in the African context. Growing up I only saw beggars when we visited South Africa because Botswana did not have any visible people who were that poor. That complacent, unperturbed mood was not good for my inspiration as an artist. I need to be ruffled by something, so all these places give me that vicarious ruffle. From Kuwait to Morocco to Zambia to Pakistan, I have found new struggles and passions of people that move me to articulate in art with certain grit.

February 20, 2012

BACK TO LOVE

Donald Molosi

"...to call someone a wayfarer is a painless way of saying he does not belong."

— from *Anowa*, a play by Ama Ata Aidoo

When she raises her face to regard Thero across the table with eyes softened by affection, Katie's eyes refuse to stay still. Zoom zoom. Up and down. They wander about the martini glass, jump up to Thero's flashing brown eyes and quickly drop to hover over the kente tablecloth, suddenly shy. Light falls on Katie's face; she favors a Vermeer painting.

She tucks her thin blonde hair smoothly behind her ear. Taking in a prefatory breath with a smile, she asks him about Botswana in that irksomely pitying way, as though his identity were a disability and thus fit for patronizing. Impotence. Pity. Limp pity. This is New York City.

"The women in Cape Verde and their rights? Just breaks my heart. But I am sure it will be fine," she pushes her hair behind her ear, strangely reassured. Zoom zoom. Up and down.

Thero's lips feel hot and heavy. He is desperately itching to tell Katie that her "scholarly" articles on Cape Verde are shit. That she abducts knowledge that already exists intact in *língua cabo-verdiana* only to proliferate it like it is new, in dispassionate English jargon.

"I mean, T, Africa has so much to offer and that's why I think you should go back and help out when you graduate or whatever."

Thero envisions his own head inflating like a balloon and then becoming a glowing-hot ball of entangled bulb filaments. He wishes he could reprimand her for having rescued a stray cat in Cape Verde last summer and then packing it in her checked luggage on the plane to smuggle it all the way here, to Manhattan. He does not tell her how poisonous that mentality is, the one-way trans-Atlantic rescue. Now his eyes are the ones zoom zooming. Up and down.

"Tell me about the big five in Botswana!" she winks with her mouth open. "I can imagine them just walking the desert sands, chilling like whatever."

Thero casually begins to speak, his words oozing like a lullaby. He talks about daily life in Botswana instead of the folktales, or whatever Katie had requested he speak about. As he guides her eager mind's eye with childish theatrics, she pictures chickens, cattle, and school children all heralding the break of dawn with a chatter, a clanging cowbell, a cuckoo cuckoo! She sees the brisk morning air tinted with a film of smoke from the morning fires as every household in Mahalapye prepares the morning sorghum porridge, the village air is enlivened with the dust kicked up by the massive Scania trucks on the road to Gaborone, the big city.

"...the man is majestic even in bad weather. I saw him one day swaggering, I say swaggering in the rain. He did not care. It was like he was daring the raindrops to fall on him," Thero characterizes Zorro, his neighbor in Mahalapye, and then shakes his head to solicit Katie's childlike mirth.   Amidst   heady laughter, Katie envisions Zorro marching past Thero's house, loudly rattling away on his cell phone in broken English. In the rain. The ground must have smelled green and wet.

"Book-oh-lah!" Katie squeals, and suddenly feels awkward.

"Bokgola," Thero repeats, congratulating her. His mind drifts off with that word— petrichor, the scent of rain on dry ground.

*

A stale odor of collective sweat that smells vaguely like freshly chopped onions has permeated the church air. It has a safe, homely quality that only a familiar odor can have, like bokgola, the smell of rain on dusty, powdery sand.

Motswagole comes in late and I cannot catch him up on Zorro's latest episodes before the sermon; he loves my stories about my regal Kalanga neighbor. Motswagole sits down in the third row next to me, saying nothing. He puts his Bible, with the thin blue hymn book lodged in its middle, on his lap. We do not acknowledge one another. For discreetness, I think.

The Praise Team stands in front, behind the glass podium. They trill into the wireless microphones, "Give and it shall come back to you." Three wide-bottomed sopranos from the Mokubatse Secondary School's Scripture Union in ankle-length black skirts and garish long-sleeved blouses of highlighter orange, lawn green, and hot pink sing with fire. Four brawny baritones, also from the Scripture Union, are draped in oversized black suits festooned with white Prayer Warrior sashes. Magdalene, a dark-skinned young woman with blonde cornrows is this week's soloist. She hurls her trembling hands into the air and weeps with eyes closed as the spirit commands her. That is when Motswagole also begins singing too fast, his voice an unintelligible rap of sorts, almost hiccupping.

*

"We in the U.S. just have no spirit. We need that deep soul, that edge..." Katie says, shoving her hair behind her ear again as she continues to state that she thinks America's blandness is "just sad."

Thero ignores her lamentation. His lips feel cooler and lighter. He swigs his red wine and tells her more about Botswana. That although Botswana was never colonized, it was once a British protectorate, which is just as awful. That there are more than twice as many cattle as people in Botswana and maybe that is why beef is the staple food.

"Just come to my village, Mahalapye, one day and see! I tell you, even a child born yesterday loves meat and probably knows how to prepare it in many different—"

"Awesome! Haha."

"You can make *seswaa*—that's pounded. You can make *segwapa*—that's dried, and you can make *serobe*, which is mixed with tripe and things," Thero says sounding like a melodramatic commercial, really only trying to cheer himself up. "The question anyone in my village would ask is, 'what can you not make with beef?'"

They share a loud laugh. Thero right then notices that Katie's piercing eyes have changed color slightly because the lighting in the restaurant is now a moody green.

Katie "adores" Thero's perfectly straight teeth. Watching his teeth twinkle in shapely whiteness, she cannot believe that he never wore braces.

"Even a child born yesterday loves meat and probably knows how to prepare it."

He can make anything sound so exciting. He comes so close to being "ideal." For instance, Katie always found it fascinating, really impressive, that Thero speaks crisp English despite his being African. At the same time though, that pathology — Africanness — makes him caring, gentle, and lovely. Watching this beautiful specimen of a man talk reminds her why she would like him to father her dream children. He is a man cut from a good stone despite his mysterious and erratic mood today. But it's only a fourth date so...

"Seems so convenient! I bet there's tons of beef jerky in umm... your country," Katie says caressing the stem of her martini glass with her right thumb. Her shapeless fingers remind Thero of Motswagole's misshapen toes.

*

Stop staring at his toes in public, I chide myself. *But who wears sandals to church anyway? Foolish boy.* I turn to look at him and realize that he still has the bite-shaped bruise on his neck.

The ushers hand out the envelopes. Almost everyone stands in the queue meandering toward the altar where they will deposit their offerings. The money thunks against the wooden base of the small, square *mmanki*. Its larger clone, the other reed basket, looms at its side expressly for those offering checks and crisp banknotes instead of worn coins. Thunk. Thunk.

At the tail of the line wait the Big Basket People, lip curl and all. Tradition dictates that their humble banknotes or checks be slotted into the thin, brown envelopes fully exposed at the altar in view of the entire congregation. As usual, the fat roll of money is wedged by the ineffective thrust of ceremonious fingers and protrudes outward. The big basket people curl their lips at the altar, seemingly bothered because the tiny envelope cannot hide it all. Wedge. Wedge.

Pastor Tibe emerges from the first row of seats swaggering to the beat of "Give and It Shall Come Back to You." He stands behind the podium. His hands are raised above his head. His mouth is bound into a tight circle because he feels inspired. "Fish Face," Motswagole and I call it. Geev and eet shall come behhk...

Pastor Tibe sports plastic spectacles to look important. They have no lenses. He does not really need them because looking light like a white man while simultaneously not being a Bushman already garners him enough respect to be chosen Pastor.

"God is good!" he says out loud, and the congregation replies,

"All the time!"

I can tell Motswagole is getting bored. He is beginning to tap his misshapen toes on the floor.

Botswana heat is at its cruelest. It curls around everyone's necks. Some of the older women are already fanning themselves with the Easter Celebration Program. Motswagole looks at me and grumbles in that restrained way of people who know that nothing can be done about the heat.

"Hei! This heat! We are almost collapsing!" Motswagole always had a penchant for straight-faced sarcasm.

"Yes, *monna*. We are almost dying," I say facing forward.

"You are funny," he says dryly.

"I thought I would have to pull your arm to get you to speak, *monna*. You just came and sat without a word." I pout and wait.

Despite the loud preaching around us, silence descends between us. Hot and heavy silence.

"You are leaving again," Motswagole whispers.

*

Katie gingerly lifts her glass from the table toward her mouth. They sit in thick silence for countless still moments. Her emerald eyes dart around the restaurant sweeping past the mahogany wine racks on the left, past the fake version of "Girl with a Pearl Earring" hanging above the entrance, past him, who is just homesick, she is sure. The silence grows old. It almost dries.

Bitter unease persists. It swirls around and within. It repeats, is born anew, froths, detonates, and subsides, only to rise again as a string pulled taut. Thero's chest is full of hot music, and so he looks down at the table. "Best African Restaurant in New York City!" is stamped on the kente in pink ink.

Light cracks like ice in front of Thero. Slowly he looks up at Katie, searching her face for understanding. Any understanding. Any warmth at all. But she too is no longer at ease.

"Ohmygod, funniest story ever!" Katie bursts forth, shattering the silence. She is already chuckling when she says, "So today my mom texts me and she's like, 'your father's pants just ripped on the subway and guess what he screamed: my butt has a hole!'" Katie is laughing so hard that her face reddens and tears pour quickly out of her eyes. Her charcoal mascara begins to smudge but it does not run; it is waterproof. She is literally crying from laughter, "Oh, Mom and Dad."

Thero only summons a weak smile, as weak as water. He bites his nails as he recalls last year's Thanksgiving dinner with Katie's obese parents in Philadelphia. They were only friends then. It had been his first Thanksgiving in the U.S. and Katie had been a gracious classmate to invite him over. Katie's parents had insisted that Thero call them by their first names.

"It makes us feel younger!" Katie's mother, Molly, had said too loudly while warming up the linen napkins in the oven before dinner. "Don't mind the napkins. It is a WASP thing."

Molly had a strikingly wide bottom for someone with a long narrow face.

Dick and Molly were both delighted to have Thero as a conversation piece; to ask him too many questions about Botswana, about his necklace being "tribal" and his name being "native" and his opinions being "cultural," leaving no room for his individuality.

Thero himself had never understood why privileged White Americans conversed in an awkward and contrived manner at meals. Even with their loved ones, Thero had observed. Is it a thing of privilege? Is it a White thing? Instead of letting the focus of conversation change more organically, privileged White Americans thrust one person at a time into the judgmental spotlight with questions like "What are you doing after graduation?" And then everyone goes silent as they judge you and periodically nod when you give them answers they want to hear like "I sent out strong applications to the best law firms in New York City and I have already booked interviews with half of them." They like happy news. It keeps them cradled from the big bad world. There is no scope for "Oh, actually I am not interested in law anymore, and I want to move back to Botswana to start over." Thero felt like the proverbial fish out of water and so he gulped a glass of water and relished the joke by himself. That Thanksgiving evening Thero played the smiling guest crippled by gratitude. When he got angry he simply stared at the delicious carcass in the middle of the table and smiled until his irritation subsided.

Music starts to play in the restaurant and it is a song by Jonathan Butler. It is sublime and jazzy, almost romantic:

Let's get back to love where we started from.

Back to love...

Thero hums along and swigs his wine. Katie liberates an airy laugh, awkwardly. She takes another sip of her vodka martini. Her red lips, shimmering with glittery gloss, softly pinch the martini glass with every tiny nip. Red lips look dark in green light. "Curious," Theo thinks, but does not share the thought.

*

"Blessed church of Mahalapye, I greet you all in de mighty name of Jesus Lawd and Savior," Pastor Tibe declaims from the pulpit, his face and mouth momentarily scrunched up so that he can slide his glasses upward over the ridge of the nose.

"Amen!" the church choruses. Motswagole and I snicker.

"We fank Lawd dat it is Good Friday. On a day like dis I want us to be finking on what it means for our Jesus to have been dying for us. Amen!" Pastor Tibe says in a voice suddenly hoarse. He pauses, also for effect, and his face sags, forming tired pouches below his eyes.

"Hallelujah!" the church says, rapt with anticipation of the special Easter sermon.

"De very son in de trinity of Fahdah, Son, and Holy Spreet. He was conceived by de Holy Spreet! Amen! Crucified. Dying! Buried, amen! Buuut on de fird day he rose again. De Bible say dat de son of Man will come again weef glory to judge de living and de dead!"

These days, Pastor Tibe seldom speaks Setswana during sermons. Apparently, Motswagole tells me, that ability eluded Tibe last November when an American preacher visited Botswana on the same day I feasted on bland turkey with Dick and Molly. Reverend Ernest Angley came to visit the Mahalapye branch of Vigorous Faith Ministries as part of his African Thanksgiving tour.

Motswagole whispers that the eerie-looking reverend had come to the Special Service bearing gifts of American blessed cloth, cotton rags drenched in anointing oil. During that special service, Pastor Tibe crowed that although he had never met his father, he was certain that he had been a white missionary from Texas.

"...sweet sweet troof dat my dear fadah spread de word, amen!"

After Pastor Tibe's speech about folktales or "Spreet," Motswagole seizes the next choral amen to grunt to me about Pastor Tibe's silly tendency to roll the English r's to make them sound like Setswana, with words like ruminate, rumble, and sacrament suddenly becoming menacing.

I feign a cough to suppress my laughter.

*

He feigns a cough to conceal his boredom. He and Katie are discussing dried Botswana meat again. He wonders why they need to.

"I used to eat much of it as a boy," Thero appeases her. "I would toss a piece of it into the fire and watch it squirm as it cooked on the coals. The Setswana word for it is *segwapa*."

"I knew that! Haha. Wait... but T, it's already dried meat! It's already ready to eat," Katie says with too much excitement.

Thero smiles. He takes yet another lingering gulp of his wine. His dark lips clasp the glass before his tongue moistly squishes against it.

"Yeah. It is just to give it a different flavor."

The perfunctorily smiling waiter briskly approaches the table this time with the food menu, "Hi, y'all. Today's special is African Sweet Potato Stew and..." He is blonde and thin, with the assertive air of a flamboyantly gay young man. Thero pretends not to notice him and continues to speak about *segwapa*. Katie listens and nods in that erratic yet confident American way that means she is paying attention, like an agama lizard on a hot day. A moment later Thero turns to the waiter and places their orders.

*

"Today is too hot," Motswagole complains.

"Sssh. Hold on. Watch his inhalation. He is about to yell out," I say to Motswagole.

Sure enough, Pastor Tibe screams, "VIGOROUS FAIF MINISTRIES! Sweet sweet Jesus want to make you a promise carrier!" Pastor Tibe continues to jump up and down like a child ill at ease. His light brown wisps of hair sprouting from the center of his outer ears remain unmoving despite his leaps. Pastor Tibe has the full cheeks of a much fatter man and they jiggle as he jumps.

"I think to be outcasts means we notice every little thing around us," Motswagole whispers to me.

"Definitely." I reply.

"Amen!" the congregation hollers, moved by Pastor Tibe's high-voltage preaching.

"Burn de weetch doctors weef de fire of the Holy Spreet, Amen? Burn de idol-worshippers, Amen? Burn de homosexuals! Burn burn weef de Holy-Holy Ghost—I FEEL SOMEFING!" he says stamping his feet on the grey tile floor like he is squashing tough cockroaches. He then bursts into song and the church immediately joins in, "Fire follow me! By de grace of my God, FIRE FOLLOW ME."

I do not command fire to follow me. Neither does Motswagole. We cannot force ourselves to join the voices in heady exuberance of the promise of the Blood of Jesus. Our thoughts are not of God but of each other.

*

Katie cannot conceal her concern, "Babe, do you really need a vodka shot after the wine?"

"I think to be the outcast means we notice everything around us."

"Tota."

Thero snaps back without taking his bleary eyes off the drinks menu, "Just leave me alone. I miss home."

Katie sighs deeply in hopes that the breath would obscure her shaky voice. "T, are you okay?"

She opens her mouth to speak, but changes her mind.

"I think to be the outcasts means we notice everything around us,"

"Tota."

Thero loudly bangs his fist on the table, "Don't tell me what to do."

The flamboyant waiter is watching with his head tilted to the side in sarcastic mock sympathy. The flamboyant one is enjoying the fight, Thero thinks. It probably always galls the waiter to see White Americans in interracial relationships. That they behave like they deserve a medal for having benevolently acquired a "diversity" lover.

"T, you've never spoken to me like this. What's going on?"

"You are funny."

"I thought I would have to pull your arm to get you to speak, *monna*. You just came and sat without a word."

"You are leaving again."

208

"I am sorry, baby. It has been a hard day and my flight from Botswana yesterday was so long. Forgive me?"

"You scared me."

Thero leans over the table and kisses her passionately before she can complete that thought.

The nosy waiter rolls his hazel eyes. His stride is deliberately measured because watching this shamelessness spices up his workshift.

"Two orders of Folusho's Fried Plantains, one order of Panyin's Pepper Soup, Magic Yams, and Bitter Leaf Soup..." the waiter says in a halfhearted singsong voice as he daintily places each item on the table.

"Thanks!" Katie smiles at the waiter, wiping the gloss from Thero's dark lips with her palm. She has that glow that is almost a mocking bashfulness, the giddy kind of someone who is happy to have been caught frolicking with her boyfriend but pretends otherwise.

Her red lips look dark in the green light.

*

"Dark, dark lips."

"Shapeless toes," I whisper back.

"Fuck you," Motswagole says looking straight ahead.

"You already did."

For that Motswagole elbows me and I almost laugh.

Pastor Tibe shouts out something prophetic. He thumps on his Bible. That snaps me out of my fit of suppressed laughter. I swallow the lump in my dry throat. Again I do a sweep of the congregation noticing many chapped lips. People must be fasting over Easter.

"Prayer!" Pastor Tibe thunders into the microphone, and on perfect cue everyone starts intoning individual prayers. Prayer items range from pleas for employment to requests for safe births. Pastor Tibe ends the prayers in a fake American accent, "Agree weeef me dat it is well weef your soul! Agree weef me!"

"We agree," the church says back more excited.

"Preach! Yes, Spirit!" Mma Selelo, a thick-lipped, light-skinned woman with a Brazilian wig, bellows from the back of the church. We know she is about to convulse. She has been moved by the Word. She is a big basket person. Motswagole and I roll our eyes.

"Sin is why we are living in the sickness realm! Amen? This Easter, I cover the demon of sickness in blood! This Easter, I stomp on the demon's head! We shall not be stress free about dis issue!" Pastor Tibe continues.

Something is different today. I, Thero Toteng, accept for the first time my endless list of fears. Monthly practices of cannibalism with bread and wine. Having to deal daily with the devil. Having to negotiate with an angry God who is insulted by the flawed nature he gives to humans.

My scalp begins to crawl. Blood. Fire. Brutal murder on a rugged cross. I never quite believed that startling talk of impending famines, earthquakes, and doom. I was always simply scared.

What is happening to me?

I look at Motswagole with no discreetness. He looks lovely: full lips and eyes deep, as though mysterious with kohl. I wonder what he is thinking. I do not, however, wonder what foolishness possesses me that I find the smell of a man's fresh sweat so beautifully raw and exciting. I can smell him next to me. Something definitely just snapped in my chest.

The bench I am sitting on is suddenly too hard. My hands tremble. The church is getting hotter and stuffier. My mouth is parched. My tongue could crumble out of my mouth. I feel every hair on my body standing out long and far from my body and painfully touching everything around me. A strange liquid anger rises in me and so I rise and walk out of the church. I walk the way I never walked before: with no guilt.

As I plod through the rusty gate of the church compound, a strange wave overwhelms me. A painful shock passes through the strands of my hair and it feels like my scalp is shrinking. I let out a suppressed sigh, which comes out sounding more like a purr.

I am about to walk past Blue Lagoon Bar on the right side of the dirty road when I hear a familiar voice, almost angelic, calling.

"Thero! Thero? Where are you going?"

I attempt to run. My legs refuse. I hear his orange sandals pah-pah against the soles of his misshapen feet. He walks toward me. His eyes are large with concern. They dart up and down.

"Thero!" He stands close to me and notices my tears. I remain silent because I am paralyzed with a kind of anger so strong that I need to cry first before I can articulate it in speech. He places his hand on my shoulder. He speaks softly, almost in a whisper,

"What is wrong?"

I begin to walk again and he follows. In a brief, whispered monologue, I detail to him that I love him. That I am angry that we have to hide. That I am quitting church. That I am angry for being different.

"I will always be with you, Motswagole," I say conclusively.

We walk together in knowing silence across the Mahalapye Railway Line, past the Mokubatse River, which has dried up. It is now choked with litter, with faded Shoprite plastic bags, rusty aluminum cans, human waste, and factory rubbish.

We finally reach Mmoko Hill, our usual spot. Sitting on a smooth rock, I look him in the eye. His face has drained of color like the skin of a tightening fist. Even without speaking, we know. I am leaving. I am angry about that, also. I am also angry about Big Basket People, chapped lips, fake eye glasses, and society. I am expected to leave for the U.S. and come back with a law degree to milk for cash in Botswana. That angers me.

Is a law degree worth it?

I let out a single tear. This tear is different from the hard tears I had known all my life. In this tear I feel a new sense of peace wash over me. I smile toothily and embrace him too tightly. A few exchanges of smiles later, he brushes his hand against my cheek to wipe my most important tear.

"You are the only one who knows me—the real me and the fake me's," I say.

"I know," Motswagole replies and it almost make us cry again.

We sit and silently watch the sun dip into the Kalahari Desert. At the foot of the hill, young, barefoot shirtless boys in dirty shorts are herding cattle back to the kraals. Two women from Motswagole's ward, Mma Dipogiso and Mma Autwetse are standing in the middle of a dusty footpath with their hands on their waists exchanging delicious Mahalapye gossip, often raising one hand to their heads to adjust their brightly colored head-wraps as they talk and giggle.

"Hei mma, I hear the Pastor's wife stole Camphor ointment from a chemist in Gaborone."

"She has become that poor? I say even a high-flying eagle has its time to come down."

"Hei! The happenings of this village, mma!"

*

"Maybe you are jetlagged," Katie suggests.

"Yes. I am tired."

It is unlike Thero to admit that he is tired. He has always been energetic. Even before they started dating last month, just before he went to Botswana for a week, Thero had always been a dream. He would send her several text messages just to wish her a good night, and even send a sweet text message during the day to say "good noon." At Thanksgiving, with her narrow face, Molly complained that Katie was getting "a little heavy in the thighs." After that, Thero had been there for Katie through it all, to squeeze lemons for her and hold her hand as she underwent three weeks of drinking only lemon juice with a pinch of cayenne pepper. But this recent trip to Botswana had shifted him.

Another saccharine number by Jonathan Butler starts. As if on cue, Thero reaches into his pocket and pulls out a diamond ring. It sparkles brighter than even the Kgalagadi sun.

"I want you to have this, Katie. I got it for you."

"What?"

"It's for you." He puts it on the table.

"Are you—"

"I am not proposing. I bought it for you, and you should take it," he says.

"This is crazy—ohmygod it's gorgeous. I am still confused, I mean—ah—I'm not sure."

"Actually there is something I want to tell you."

"Yeah?" Katie lodges her hair behind her ear, blinking too fast.

"We are good friends, Katie. Really good friends. And I have a great home and this place is not my home. I can have a good life in Botswana even without a law degree. You present me to your mind in a light that I don't want to stand in, and I want to go back to—"

"What are you saying?" she spits daggers, broken.

"I want to return home, Katie."

"T... what? You wanna go back to Africa?"

"To Botswana. It is my home and the people I love live there."

Fast tears flush her cheeks as she asks, "Like, when?"

"Tomorrow, I think. Tomorrow. I am so sorry, Katie." His mind is made up.

"What about us? Did I mean anything at all to you? I mean you are just leaving and considering only what you want. What about what I want? Does it matter how I feel about you—about us? Does it matter?"

Katie begins to sob. Guilt chokes him the same foul way that litter had choked the Mokubatse. It feels as though he is choking on his sins. Still he manages to say, "I think we should break up."

"What? Is it me?" She is red in the face and her nose is running, but he can see she is trying to take this news with a strong heart.

"You are perfect. You are intelligent and beautiful. You deserve someone better than me. I am not good enough."

"But why? Why? Do I not tell you all the time how ideal you are for me?" She is sobbing furiously, almost harshly, and she has the attention of people at the next table who are only too happy to watch the freak show that is an interracial couple in distress, with accents and colors flying all over the place.

"Katie, I cannot do this anymore."

Katie shrivels. Before his eyes she squirms and shrinks like a piece of *segwapa* in the fire. The liquid in her eyes seems to turn fiercely solid as her nostrils flare. He almost cracks and feels pity. He doesn't. He must do this.

She tucks her hair behind her ear for the last time that he will see. She speaks from low in her stomach sounding solid and resolute.

"You know what? You know what? You are right. I do NOT deserve someone as flaky as you. I thought we were going somewhere and then you just pull the rug from under us. You are right, if that is who you are, I do deserve better. Motherfucker!"

She picks up the diamond ring. She throws it between his eyes. She splashes the martini in his face.

His words are without feeling. "I am sick of this place full of fake people and you won't help because you can't and all you want to do is tell me about your illegal immigrant cat. I am tired of having to explain myself all the —"

Fire fire fire! Fire follow me.

Fire fire fire! Fire follow me.

By the grace of my God, fire follow me!

When she pulls her iPhone from her bag, he fears the weight of an iPhone against his shaved head. But she begins to type frantically instead. She slings her bag on her shoulder and flies out of the restaurant, her blonde hair heaving and her scarf flying turquoise, like a storm.

He watches her leave. She storms past the wine racks, past the fake Vermeer, and out of his life.

NOVUYO ROSA TSHUMA

EMMANUEL IDUMA: Describe your writing table. Do you keep a strict schedule, working on this table?

NOVUYO ROSA TSHUMA: My writing space is where I live, an apartment. I will write anywhere in this space—on my student's desk, on the floor, on the couch, in bed, with my laptop perched on my lap. I write in bouts—spurts, I would call them—something about that elusive thing called a muse, but really it is more about taking advantage of your free time. I have studies with which to juggle my writing, living, and getting work that needs to be done, done.

EI: Was there a point when writing became a decision, or part of a decision?

NT: Indeed there was. At the point when I discovered the contemporary African writers, I became overwhelmed by the realization that the culmination of my writing into something meaningful would require a conscious cultivation on my part. This was at the end of August 2007. I had always been writing but had never consciously thought of it. Probed by a deep, jagged sense of writing and career crisis, I dropped out of my architecture program at the National University of Science and Technology in Zimbabwe and ventured into a year of soul searching, some fumbling, as it were, in the dark.

217

EI: Did you feel at the time that dropping out of the architecture program was necessary for your writing? The conscious cultivation you refer to, does it also include sacrifice, the choosing of an alternative career?

NT: Architecture is a field that requires dedication and a great level of passion. This dedication and passion was not something I could ever sacrifice willingly to architecture. While we were learning about great and inspiring architects I was busy daydreaming about great and inspiring writers. It became evident that architecture was not for me.

A conscious cultivation is to say: I shall dedicate time to honing my craft, to nurturing writing, to seeking opportunities that foster growth in my writing. This automatically reduces time for other opportunities and informs the paths you take.

EI: To get on with his day's work, Hemingway sharpened up to seven pencils. Do you also sharpen pencils?

NT: Mine is work done on the computer. Rather, I sharpen my writing momentum.

EI: A sense of dislocation surrounds your stories, the kind that is replete with the familiarity of an itinerant's disorientation. Do you think that because you are *out* of Zimbabwe, you write *about* Zimbabwe? The kind of thing that happens to a writer in the diaspora, in exile?

NT: Hmmm. I am out of Zimbabwe, indeed, but I am so close to it—South Africa is a close neighbor—as to be *in* it without really being in it. Perhaps it is this intimate distance that allows me a perspective I may not possess were I totally immersed in Zimbabwe. The relationship between Zimbabwe and South Africa is a very interesting and complex one, you see, and here I speak of the social dynamics. Zimbabweans, like many foreigners here, have permeated the South African culture. We are, literally, everywhere. Our interaction with this environment, though— which is sometimes hostile—has something of a corrupt cadence to it. For some, there is a need to belong, to find seams of familiarity in terms of tribe and culture, in which to embed themselves and reap the many benefits of a country as advanced—in structural terms—as South Africa. For others, there is a visceral reaction against this environment. I am fascinated by the contradictions of this love-hate relationship.

Now, I believe the sense of dislocation you speak about represents a broad unplugging that plagues one when one is in foreign lands. The feeling of not really belonging is a very stark, if not disorienting, one. And one feels this no more than in the complicated landscape that is South Africa. There is ignorance within the formal halls of South Africa of the foreigner and his place here outside the cliché views of "illegal immigrant." This only serves to further alienate the foreigner, so that he skulks about as something not wanted, per se, but rather tolerated, within this space.

EI: Has the friction of South African politics affected you in any way? Do you, by studying in South Africa and by being a witness to xenophobia, Jacob Zuma, crime, etc., long for home? Perhaps a feeling of melancholic homesickness?

NT: South African politics affect me in a personal sense, insofar as they affect my quality of life as a Zimbabwean living here. I am randomly stopped on the street and asked to produce identification. I'm ever aware that I "do not belong."

Do I suffer from homesickness? No. I love home without wanting to be in it. What I am more interested in is a geography that may act as a buoy for my sense as a writer. In this sense, I may claim a melancholic homesickness in terms of my writing. Which is in itself a shadowy concept, as my writing is not purely a culmination of geography, but may lay claim to abstract homes. I can say that my coming to South Africa provided fertile soil for my roots as a writer—perhaps in a way home may never have— in terms of opportunity, in terms of "opening my eyes," in terms of crushing my naiveté. And yet, home becomes the manure which I use to fertilize these roots. So, it is all inter-connected.

Do I share a certain romanticism with South Africa? Certainly not. I am not disillusioned by my relationship with her. We are ambivalent about one another. But the social dynamics of this place are so broad and so complex as to be fascinating.

So, perhaps I may go so far as to say I do not want to necessarily commit myself to geography. It is not helpful to myself as a writer to do so. New spaces provide new, fascinating interactions; you find that geography exposes different dimensions of yourself. Is the me in Zimbabwe the same me that is in South Africa? Not entirely; the rules of each space provide different opportunities for self-illumination. What this does, though, is cultivate an internal sense of vagrancy.

EI: The literary theorist Gayatri Spivak said, "I fall into a place and I become of that place." It's like having roots in the air, so that you become familiar and okay with your disorientation. And this, as you have noted, affects your writing. More or less, your writing appears as a trans-African response to your asymmetry, so that you take up the challenge of intersecting Zimbabwe with Ghana, Uganda, Nigeria. There's the conscious attempt in your stories "The King and I" and "In Bed with Ikeji" to affirm that you are not afraid of your fluidity, that you are at home everywhere, and not at home anywhere. Is this even plausible?

NT: Intersecting ourselves with different cultures and nationalities is not at all a challenging thing in today's multicultural environment. The writing of it becomes, really, a reflection of our cross-cultural interactions. Venture the streets of Johannesburg and you will hear the laden tones of the Shona, the heavy intonations lugged about by Nigerian pidgin, the staccato English uttered by the French-speaking Congolese, the chopping up of syllables by the Chinese. India in the shops—the distinct smell of a curry. Leonard Zhakata blares from a radio on the street, across the road some Sam Mangwana. All of this in addition to the rich mesh that is South African culture. The melting pot stews.

EI: Was leaving Zimbabwe important for your writing life or did you leave only as a person and not as a writer? Or both? Do these lines even exist for you?

NT: Cognizant of the importance of education, I left Zimbabwe to attend university in South Africa. This move proved to be fertile to my growth as a writer; South Africa has a lush writing environment.

In retrospect, I may say it is important to seek opportunities that will make you a better writer, that will allow you the opportunity to hone your craft, expose you to an expansive range of reading, and so on.

Now, as to the person and the writer, hmmm. I would rather put it this way: the writer and his writing need not always converge to a personal point. There are the manipulations of fiction to consider.

EI: Speaking about reading, which African and non-African writers have moved you recently? And which books?

NT: I enjoyed how Dambudzo Marechera bullied and battered the English language in his famous *The House of Hunger*, bruising it into something unique and beautiful. The authentic characterization in Toni Morrison's *Song of Solomon*. Turkish delights in Orhan Pamuk's *The Museum of Innocence*. The eloquent depression in James Baldwin's *Another Country*. The detailed meanderings in Teju Cole's *Open City*. The disarming use of language in Binyavanga Wainaina's *One Day I Will Write About This Place*. The illumination of the mundane into something gripping in Jhumpa Lahiri's *Intepreter of Maladies*. The comic, sometimes tragic feminism in Ama Ata Aidoo's *Changes*.

EI: Both of your stories "Waiting" and "You in Paradise" convey what Rushdie, in reference to Dickens, called "a pitiless realism" and "a naturalistic exactitude." Do you seek to do this, to spark off a feeling that your reader can take hold of your scenes, your characters' souls, their bedraggled existence?

NT: Well, in retrospect I may be able to say I seek to do this. But really, the process of writing is something of a subconscious one and more intimate. To make writing exact may actually rob the tale of the natural flow of the very elements with which one seeks to imbue it. More importantly, it may take out that innate pleasure the writer derives from the process of creating his or her work.

EI: You speak, interestingly, of tales with political infusion, which raises, again, the debates on the social function of literature, as well as the question of stereotyping Africa. It is perhaps useful that your writing speaks to afro-modernity and afro-cosmopolitanism, as much as it does to matters such as xenophobia, immigration, and even Westernization. So do you think there's a foreground-background approach to handling your themes—that a family's story can serve as a foreground to an overarching tale about, say, xenophobia?

NT: I am not at all interested in stereotyping or de-stereotyping Africa. Let a story be a story first and foremost. Attempting to fight the politics of writing, such as stereotyping or de-stereotyping, may lead to didactic veins in a story, perhaps even killing the commitment to story one needs. What does this mean? It means that the political infusions that you speak about, as well as the afro-modernity you refer to, are simply products of the reality that I inhabit. My stories are set in Zimbabwe and South Africa, societies in which I have negotiated existence. I write, perhaps not what I see, in the literal sense of the word, but what I experience, in an emotional sense, an intellectual sense, a subconscious sense, what I may choose to experience for others through the page.

Zimbabwe—I will tell you now, as I have experienced it—has been a highly political society, with politics informing daily existence, particularly during the years of severe food and fuel shortages. Existence became politicized simply because of the extreme political imbalances that rocked the country, seeping into economic and social existence, remapping our interactions with one another. A neighbor was a neighbor on the street; in a *mielie-meal* queue he became an adversary.

What may help move Africa away from this "stereotype writing"? One way is reading and reading widely. That certainly has opened up the dimensions of writing for me. For example, I read Jhumpa Lahiri's two short story anthologies, *Interpreter of Maladies* and *Unaccustomed Earth*, and I was taken by her electrifying illumination of the mundane. Here, for example, one can learn that melodrama—with reference to Africa, things such as famine, war, political tension—need not necessarily fuel a story, but that mundane existence may be fueled by the emotional pull of a story, by the manipulation of language.

Now, does this mean that one cannot write about war, famine, or political tension? Certainly not. Allow the writer the freedom to write as he chooses; many are impassioned by such experiences and the rendering of such experiences cannot be dismissed as obsolete simply because so much has been written about them. They are relevant insofar as they continue to exist. As such, political tension may be a fresh angle for me, insofar as it is that it is my experience, what I choose to experience for others. The issue, I would say, is never really about the experience itself, about war or famine or hunger, but about our different comprehensions and internalizations and handling of such experience, and the differing geographies these experiences inhabit. To broadly dismiss a piece of writing as "another tale on hunger or war or famine" is to, sadly, miss the finer points of a tale, to miss the characterization, to miss the setting of a particular space, to miss the interaction of language with emotion. Let a story fail only because it misses what it aims to do. The idea of stereotyping Africa in literature may actually lie not with the writer primarily, but with those critical halls that put a beam on a particular spectrum of writing. Must the writer now suffer for this?

EI: The writer has the freedom to write as she chooses, of that everyone agrees. But the African writer often faces a different accusation, which is that the freedom she expresses is misplaced, owing to a craving for Western praise, accreditation, prizes. It is a dangerous and preposterous accusation. But the imagination, as Mũkoma wa Ngũgĩ writes, cannot be moved by ideology, otherwise it gives the ideology a different form. Can you reinforce your opinion, speaking less of freedom, but more about the compulsiveness we often face when we want to tell a story?

NT: I speak of a freedom because that is precisely what it is. In our eagerness to de-stereotype the stereotype, we risk creating new stereotypes. I have already spoken about how primary interest needs to lie with the ingredients of the story and how they come together to do what they do.

Let us not be unfair by being dishonest in our honesty. Praise is a natural human desire. Writing motives are a tricky thing. Writing for prizes must be a difficult, sad—if not disappointing—thing because literature cannot be made precise like mathematics. But prizes themselves expose a writer and may elevate his career. You yourself say this: that "the art of writing fiction thrives on validation."

But let us not be so condescending toward the writer; his creative process cannot just be a fickle thing—fickle motives alone may be cause for a fickle pen. I will say this: as a writer, I welcome the opportunity to better my craft, the opportunity to better my writing.

Let's agree that the writer cannot exist, survive, and flourish merely upon fickle motives for his writing, because writing really is hard work and writing excellence requires, primarily and above all motives, that dedication and personal commitment to the creative process in and of itself. We may then be honest about the relationship between the African writer and the West. Let us not fault the West for her excellent writing schools, her rich literary industry, her well-cultivated readership. The significance of her literary prizes, how they have the power to, literarily, like a magic wand, transform a writer's career. All of this has benefited the African writer: many of the African writers who flourish are based in the West. This is perhaps a reflection on our hostile literary industry in Africa, how it is difficult to survive as a writer in Africa. Yes?

But let us not be so sullen about the West in terms of the African writer, because opportunity is indeed a generous thing, trickling down, invariably, to the source: the African writer goes to the West, is afforded the opportunity and resources to hone his or her craft, produces some stunning work, wins some accolades, becomes a writing beacon. And then look—something like a Farafina Trust is born in Africa, something like a *Kwani?*, affording space, opportunities, and resources for the writer within Africa, remapping Africa's interactions with her own literature. Nadine Gordimer refers to it in her compilation *Telling Times*, how the writer in Africa faces the extra burden of concerning herself with the quality of education, with cultivating readership.

EI: Let's return to your earlier response on critics, and the story being a story first, before anything else. Have you received reviews you considered under-representative of what you tried to do? Do you think of those reviews? What do you suppose is a useful way to deal with this?

NT: There is no need to worry about dealing with reviews. Enjoy the positive reviews; they may well keep a young writer going in a hostile industry where rejection is the norm. You may pick up a useful element in the constructive ones. And well, the shattering ones, I don't see the point in allowing yourself to become a shattered writer. It does nothing for your writing stamina. Keep your eye on your writing and how you may improve it.

EI: And is it true for you what Hemingway said, "Read anything I write for the pleasure of reading it. Whatever else you find will be the measure of what you brought to the reading"?

NT: Well, for a writer, I would say finding pleasure in your own writing is natural. Maybe there's a dose of writer's vanity in it. Reading becomes an interactive process between the reader and the writing; hence, although the writer may judge the measure of his own work by his enjoyment of it—tricky thing as one is so close to one's own work—at some point he needs to apply ruthless honesty in the assessment of his material. We write so others may read, and if we agree on the significance of this, then we may agree on our responsibility to present our work in its best form.

EI: It is easy to suspect that when you use words like "self-examination," "self-consciousness," and "self-depiction" you give in to a pleasure symptomatic to the writing process. Do writers spend too much time trying to understand who they are, their place in the world, and how best to express that relationship?

NT: Hmmm. Perhaps. In memoir writing, indeed one undergoes a direct, intimate, introspective and retrospective view of oneself. In fiction work, perhaps it does not matter so much. It is the jagged pieces of existence that make it interesting, and not the pieces that fit together.

EI: If we agree on this, then you may also agree that it is equally necessary for a writer to be burdened with divesting herself from a work? There are bits of yourself, it is proposed, in every story you have written; that your characters are not entirely fictitious.

NT: Not necessarily. But it is an element that is ever there; one cannot run away from it. It is an unnecessary burden, for it will invariably be there, this element of "oneself" at different levels.

EI: Your constant foreground is family life—the disorientation, mostly, that surrounds it. In this you are not alone; other contemporary African writers have explored the subject. What is this attraction to family? Is this reminiscent of clichéd references to "African family life" or "African traditional life," or is there a striking modern connotation?

NT: African family life is a rich mosaic. Africanism has always rooted itself in community and has always put community above the individual; the family becomes a miniature view of community. African family life continues to flourish even in the face of modernization. The cliché lies only in the reference of the term; the experience is a relevant and fascinating phenomenon.

EI: How did you feel when you were shortlisted for the Intwasa Short Story Competition in 2009? And did you feel differently when you won the competition? And afterward did you say, "I am a writer now"? What did you say to yourself afterward?

NT: I was excited and green, clinging onto wispy strings to form something of a progression in my novice writing steps; it was super-cool. Winning was, of course, a nice thing. Afterward I looked at myself in the mirror, scratched my chin, nodded and said, "Yeah, we aren't too bad, this thing called writing and me."

EI: What difference do you strive for in your writing? Wit? Stylistic dissidence? Inventiveness? Or are you intent at striking a familiar chord in a reader's heart, making a character look familiar to lived experience?

NT: I may look for something different in different pieces of writing. The fun lies in the experimentation. Difference cannot, for me, be a conscious thing; it becomes a futile thing. Rather, I simply seek to "utilize my writing voice," that voice that is "me."

EI: You've termed your genre "realist fiction"—what hat did you mean?

NT: By realist fiction I mean fiction based on the spaces we inhabit and our interaction with our environment.

EI: Hemingway said that what amateurs call a style is usually only the unavoidable awkwardness in first trying to make

229

something that has not previously been made. Have you experienced awkwardness in any form, especially because you say you are not conscious of attempting a "difference"? Is this conception of an unavoidable awkwardness altogether misplaced?

NT: That is how we learn; like the first wobbly baby steps, we learn to trust our own feet by trying, stumbling, and at times falling. But there is that thing called writing personality.

EI: Having described writing as a "state"—even a "constant" one—will you have a lifelong career as a novelist, a storyteller? Are you often shaken by the suspicion that no one out there is listening, and that your talent will not necessarily contribute differently to an understanding of who we are?

NT: Self-doubt is a writer's inseparable companion. When you stop doubting, you stop striving, stop growing, stop learning. Do not make self-doubt your closest counsel, though; it may well cripple you with its wicked whispers, its creeping laughter. Adopt determination, even a little dose of obsession once in a while, and let them fuel your pen.

It is useful to inhabit the inner state first—the private sphere of you and your story. Then, having written something, and wishing to share it with others, you may lay it bare for public inspection. You need to be, as a writer, your greatest critic and your greatest motivator, and you need to know when to interchange these roles. Having faced rejection, you may mope at the pain of it and swear never to write again; but after a while, you find you are at it, and you are enjoying it so much that not even the possibility of more rejection can derail you. You want to take this thing called writing and master it, and do it until you "have it."

I enjoy writing. I get lost in it. Such enjoyment becomes addictive. Write; let the readers read.

EI: What do you find yourself doing when not writing? How does this affect your writing?

NT: Oh, I like to think I am a normal person. I do all those living things, those people things, those socializing things, those eating and sleeping things. Those reading things. Those must-go-to-the-grocery-store things. Those need-to-read-for-a-test things. Affect my writing? Oh, sometimes you see things and experience things as you go about these living things, and one day, boom! They are scribbled on paper. If writing is an obsession, let us at least agree that it is sweet.

January 18, 2012

TELEPRESENCE

Novuyo Rosa Tshuma

She logs onto Facebook in the evening. She knows Addae has written to her, and more than once, at that. Their routine has become predictable, perhaps a little boring. The cauldron of aromatic love has become bland from staying too long on virtual stoves. She finds herself thinking of him most when she is spooning down the limp, browning lentils in her mother's Chakalaka Sunday Special.

She is not surprised, then, to open her inbox and find five messages from him. She has been deliberately avoiding opening Facebook all weekend, hoping that when she finally did, it would be to a cavernous emptiness that would stimulate a yearning for him, instead of this bloated feeling that has begun to cause heartburn. She spent the weekend with friends, in jovial, intoxicated reverie all over Johannesburg; three cheers to finally completing her dissertation.

"Hi."

"Hello… hope ure enjoying ur wkend."

"Thinking of u."

"Ure awfully quiet. Iv bn checking my inbox all wkend, hoping 2 catch u online. I hope ure all right."

"Did u read abt the scandal of the Swedish Minister? theres a pic of her doing the rounds on the net; in it shes laughing n clapping as she cuts in2 a cake designed in the form of a black female w mutilated genitals. its meant 2 b sum sort of awareness campaign, bt Africans r screaming that its downright insulting, n ey r demanding that she apologise. i think its downright racist. u wont believe the things i ve 2 put up w here 4rm the Russians.

think w live in trees in africa n all of that. can u imagine. in this day n age. when i was walking the other day an old woman actually came up 2 m n rubbed my skin, 2 see if the colour wld come off, she said. i almost screamed my head off. just the other day some1 asked if ey cld touch my hair. i refused. i think if ey could, ey'd display me in a zoo. un-fucking-believable! hope ure ok. miss u."

She decides she doesn't want to talk to him just then, but as soon as she updates her status, he pops up in the chat window.

"Hellooo? any1 home? knock knock? pretty boy looking 4 pretty girl?"

"Hi. Sorry for the silence, been a busy weekend, working on my dissertation and all of that. Presentation with the course conveners coming up. How are you? Sorry to hear about your experiences. You know how Abaza is such an insulated little town, perhaps you can educate them about Africa a little bit. Haven't seen story about Swedish Minister, off to google it. Miss you too."

"They r very racist. i don feel like a person here. m home sick."

"Not to worry, you'll be done with your student exchange soon, and you'll be back in Ghana before you know it. Hang in there."

"Actually, think im gonna finish early. if that happens, ill b able to fly to sa b4 i go back 2 accra. wldnt u like that? 2 c ur baby?"

"That'd be super. Would love that."

"Wish i were there w u now."

"Me too."

"Do u know what id do if i were there w u now?"

"What?"

"Id hold u in my arms n kiss u."

"Ooh, your lips taste warm."

She looks up at the television, flicks through the channels.

"Im putting my tongue in ur mouth."

There's nothing interesting there. She logs onto her Twitter account, begins scrolling down.

"Ooh, that feels so good."

"My hands r moving down to ur hips. n im pressing u close. look? whatu doin 2 m?"

"Uhuh. That feels so good."

She scrunches up her face; perhaps she could have gone into a little bit more detail in her dissertation about the merits of a specific set of governing rules regarding environmental law?

"Ah ah ah. ooh ooh ooh. do u like that?"

"Darling I'm running out of data bundles, my phone will switch off any minute, let's chat later?"

"☹ Ok."

"I'll make it up to you, I promise."

"Ok. Sleep tight n dream of m. Love u."

"Love you too."

She quickly logs off, turns her attention to Twitter.

She tries to remember what it is about Addae that first attracted her to him. Long before their conversations degenerated into these exchanges that hardly veiled the anxieties of a relationship starved of physical intimacy. Judging by his Facebook pictures, he is not conventionally handsome. Was it the heated, long arguments, looping into and out of themselves like badly tied shoelaces? Until they became wispy and evaporated from the sheer weight of their abstractions, so that what was left was this ferocity that burned, strangely, at the loins?

"I'm a sapiosexual," he confessed after this first encounter.

She had googled the word and then, desperate for something witty to say, typed, "intelligence is a sophisticated foreplay. Like that delicate lace on well-adorned lingerie. Traces like art. You know a Victoria's Secret when you see one."

"Oh, that is so fucking sexy."

But, she holds back. She does not really know him, she decides. How can you really know a person you've never met? Best to proceed with caution. And yet, she cannot help the vats that blister in her chest each time she tries to imagine what he may be doing with another, faceless female. She finds herself stalking his Facebook page, friending women with whom he seems too familiar.

She goes out spontaneously one evening, at the invitation of a friend, Vincent. They met at a party in Pretoria. At the party, they danced a little, talked a lot, and ended up exchanging a kiss in a discreet corner. They traded numbers, promised to keep in touch but never did. She's pleasantly surprised by his call; it's a Saturday evening and she's been home all day, editing her dissertation.

"I'm in town," he says.

His voice is low, hesitant, and she's not sure if she detects a hint of expectation.

"There's this *braai* tonight, a friend, nothing fancy, but lots of meat, lots of booze. Do you want to come with?"

She readily agrees. The *braai* is in Sunninghill, a neighbourhood with which she's not too familiar. She's not aware of how much she's eager to see him until she gets lost a few times. She begins to worry as she squints into the darkness that descends suddenly, like a bad fall, and breathes when she finally finds the correct house. She arrives to the raucous noise of people yelling at the DJ to turn on the music. His computer has crashed.

Vincent apologizes, warms her a plate of pap and vleis, and afterward—hand in hand—they slip out.

Her skin tingles, like static material, each time he brushes his hand across her shoulder—he places it on her thigh, raises it as he speaks, gesticulating, it seems, for effect. Vincent is tall and dark, with polished skin and teeth that are a beautiful contrast. He's from Botswana and ventures into a monologue that feels stiff, about how Botswana is considered the poster boy of Africa only because it plays to the tune of the IMF and the World Bank, and has decidedly boring and unambitious politics. When he says this, he reminds her of Addae. She has this effect on men who find out she is doing her PhD and are eager to impress. They stumble into cliché recitals plagiarized from SABC or BBC or CNN, in a bid to make up for the shortcomings they suddenly feel at the lower rungs of their own education. Usually she takes great pleasure in calling them out, asking opaque questions that ensnare them in the deficiency of their knowledge. But she likes Vincent, she decides.

"You don't speak about Zimbabwe much," he comments. "How come? You don't miss home?"

"I suppose a part of me does. But well, not really, you know? I don't really believe in being too attached to place. It's the people I can say I miss. But then most of them are no longer there, sucked up by the diaspora. And so when I travel there I get this sensation that home is this gaping landscape, looted of its people and their vitality."

"Do you plan on settling in South Africa?"

She ponders this question. "Well, there's nothing tying me down here."

"No boyfriend?"

She thinks of Addae, hesitates. "No."

They find themselves at the Alexander Bar in the Montecasino, Fourways. It's her first time at the famous Montecassino, and she marvels at the ceilinged sky painted into various times of the day, so that in one place they are walking as if in daylight, beneath a blue canvas sky and fluffy puffs of cloud, and lighting which is impressively close to the impressions of daytime. At another place they find themselves strolling under a star-studded night sky.

Alexander Bar has the historic urgency of a traditionally bohemian joint—so out of place in the cultured distractions of the Montecasino—jazz music soft-pedaling, teasing laughter, bodies profiled in suggestive light, underground artists scheduled on the board by the entrance. There's something vulnerable about Vincent that etches itself in the sepia tint of the evening. They are the only black people there. She orders an Irish coffee. She does not remember the conversation, but she remembers the atmosphere well, of flirtation at play. After several glasses of Irish Coffee, she is feeling sufficiently warm and jovial, and leads him away from the bar. At each red light he leans over and plants a kiss on her lips. His lips are cold and moist, his whisky breath warm. She imagines this must be what Addae's lips feel like. He stops at a drugstore; when he emerges empty handed, she knows he has bought condoms.

By the time they reach his apartment, all pretenses have evaporated, and they undress quickly. As they caress their bodies in the darkness, she pretends he is Addae, but the deception fails; she imagines Addae would be bulkier. Vincent guides her to his bed. His languid movements irritate her. He moans in an effeminate way she has never heard a man moan. When he whispers in her ear how much he loves her, she is taken aback by the American twang his tone has suddenly acquired—a poor imitation of the sex of white people she has seen on TV. She wishes he would shut up. She is sure he must be reliving moments with another lover; this is not the fucking of strangers. She has no need for false intimacy, desires instead the physicality of sex. And so, she presses him firmly into her and pushes up against him, guiding his pace with the movements of her hips.

In the morning, as he drives to her apartment, he keeps rubbing her hand and throwing naughty glances her way. She thinks how it feels, oddly, like the familiar creases of a relationship.

As she opens the passenger door, he leans over and brushes his lips against hers, whispering, "Thanks for last night. I'd really like to do that again. I had a good time."

She nods, smiles. "Call me," she says, even though she knows she won't be doing that with him again. The fun lay in the spontaneity. Repeated encounter, she knows, will eventually turn into a complicated mesh of emotions she's not willing to deal with.

Traffic is unusually kind the day she goes to pick up Addae from O.R. Tambo airport. She drives with her windows slightly rolled down, the dance beats of Euphonik booming from her speakers. She arrives early and rides the elevator to the second floor, where she meanders about the shops, admiring the items on display and indulging the shop assistants, even though she has no intention of buying anything. She fingers a "Welcome to South Africa" scarf and wonders if Addae expects a gift. Perhaps she should have come with something wrapped and ribboned, a gesture of care, of thought? In the end, she disappears into the bathroom and spends a good ten minutes gazing at her face in the mirror, making sure her makeup is even, practicing her smile, making sure nothing is caught between her teeth. A child and her mother walk in and while the mother uses the bathroom, making a long "droo" sound as her pee splashes bulls-eye into the water, the child places her hands beneath the taps and removes them each time silvery streams gush into the basins, giggling with delight. Their eyes meet in the mirror, and she smiles. The child smiles back and continues to play with the faucets. Her eyes fall on the child's hair. A glaring, blonde weave has been sewn onto her head, and it now sits askew, with the vein along which it has been plaited beginning to come apart. The style is one she often sees on adults, and it has the effect of turning the child into a midget.

Satisfied with her appearance, she takes the escalators back down to the ground floor and settles on one of the steel benches arranged at the edges, near the glass walls, which gives her a good view of the arrivals area.

She sees Addae first. He's pushing his trolley slowly, a frown creasing his forehead, biting his lower lip. She stands up, irons out her dress.

"Lusanda!" he exclaims when their eyes finally meet. He bends over and pulls her close; his hug has the intimacy of their Facebook chats, but his kiss is light, hesitant. "You look so much lovelier in person! So beautiful."

She smiles, mumbles how he looks so much better in person too. She imagined he would be taller. She wonders if he's simply being polite and how they will pry beneath the bland social banalities to get to the depth of their true emotions. He's dressed in a black jacket that falls all the way down to his ankles, buttoned half-way up, with the collar pulled up around his neck and ears like a wind muffler. He removes it the moment they step out into the sun; the sky is a glass heated blue with cracks of cloud occasionally splintering the surface.

He sits with his body angled toward her as they careen across the freeway. She feels him studying her intently, uses the road as an excuse not to have to look at him.

He refuses to be awed by Johannesburg's immensity and metropolitan sophistication. He gazes at the wide tarmac across which they purr as if gliding on water, at the neat buildings protruding from the landscape on either side, at the well-meshed road system and says,

"But what about the poor people?"

She shrugs. "The poor people are poor."

"I've been reading up about some interesting places. I'd like to go to Soweto to see where Hector Pieterson died. And I'm told the Johannesburg Museum of History is a spectacular place."

She's mildly irritated by his presumption that she'll play the tourist guide and chauffer him wherever he needs to go. She doesn't respond. Instead she asks him about his flight, what he intends to do when he finally gets to Ghana.

"I think I'll continue with my post-graduate studies, start on my PhD."

"Already? Wouldn't you want to work awhile, perhaps?"

"Well, a PhD consists of teaching as well. It will take me five to six years, but I'm sure once I'm done I'll be the youngest professor of anthropology in my country." He grins. "And when you come, you shall be the wife of the youngest professor of anthropology. Wouldn't you like that?"

Her smile hardly veils her irritation.

Things become awkward when they reach her apartment. They lie beneath the covers for a while, facing each other in the darkness.

"So," he whispers.

"So."

She warms up to him, thinking this is what she has wanted, to remember the map of her lover's lips, to relive his scent. But when it's time, his penis hangs half-stiff, half-flaccid and, try as he might, he cannot slide it in.

"I'm sorry. This has never happened to me before. Perhaps it's these condoms, not used to the brand. I think they're too tight."

"It's okay," she says, even though it's not okay.

They settle for cuddling. She thinks of Vincent, suddenly yearns for him, purses her lips in the darkness. But the next morning, as they get ready to leave for Soweto, the air is light again and they're chatting about books. Addae is delighted to discover that she has some Ghanaian literature on her shelf, takes it to mean that she acquired it upon the inspiration of knowing him. She chooses not to correct him. They don't discuss the events of the night.

He's surprised to learn that she's never visited the Hector Pieterson site before. Or any other historical site or museum in Johannesburg, for that matter.

"What do you spend your time doing?"

She shrugs. There's a bus ride arranged every year by Wits University primarily for first year students, which takes them on a day trip to some historical sites of note. She feels no obligation to South Africa or a burning interest in investing herself in the folds of its history.

In Soweto, he stands for a long time by the picture of Mbuyisa Makhubo carrying Hector Pieterson, caressing it. His lips tremble; he looks like he's about to cry.

"So beautiful," he murmurs.

She thinks he's behaving like a white tourist and wants to chide him for what to her are manufactured emotions. She finds his gesture shallow; how disappointing, to find that he too, plays out preconceived notions of a Western type of sophistication. She wonders if she's being too critical. She turns to the picture, tries to think of something kind to say. She finds the famous photograph grotesque, a capitalist commodification of grief. Instead she says, "What I find actually ironic is that this boy who is carrying the Hector boy, this Mbuyisa Makhubo, is famous for just that, carrying Hector Pieterson after he was shot. It was because of this very picture that he was harassed by the authorities and had to flee South Africa."

"But it's this triumph, captured in this moment, that has become the hope of so many."

"The hope that the many need is that they will get out of their slum houses soon and into the housing promised them for so long by the government. This," and she sweeps her hand across the picture, "is an intellectual type of hope, connected to issues of classism and a Western form of narcissism."

The sparring does not contain the animated electricity of their Facebook debates. If anything, he seems irritated. She remains quiet throughout the remainder of the tour, smiles politely and grunts occasionally. She thinks how easy it is to criticize South Africa, a country that is not her own, how safe it is to draw hard lines like one who is assured of being an outsider. In her head, she runs a quick check through her dissertation, wonders once again if she's fit to tackle the topic of the possible criminalization of environmental violations. She opens her mouth to say something to Addae about it, hesitates. She lacks his generous emotions, finds her clinical approach to life stunted by his gushing passions. She is suddenly afraid of being misunderstood, is surprised by how desperately she wants him to like her.

In the evening, when she picks through the papers on her desk for a Debonairs menu and asks Addae what his favorite pizza is, he makes a face and says, "I'd like to taste the food that comes from my wife's hand."

"I'm not your wife."

She doesn't mean to sound so sharp and they both look away, embarrassed. She frowns at the brochure and mutters how she's tired, what a long day. Perhaps she'll cook something tomorrow? In her mind she's always had this wildly romantic idea of being with a man who has a flair for the kitchen.

"Then marry a Western man," her friends said. "A French man or an Italiano. Even the American men are well domesticated these days."

"These fast foods are not healthy," Addae says, softly this time. "It's why South Africa, like America, has a serious obesity problem. This unhealthy lifestyle."

She has always found his strong character attractive, but now she just finds him opinionated. She suddenly feels tired, yearns for her space. She dials Debonairs and orders the meaty deluxe. When it arrives, Addae eats only a slice, nibbling at the edges. She switches on the television to drown out the awkwardness.

She takes an unnecessarily long time in the bathroom. She flushes the toilet repeatedly, squats on the seat with her palms pressed firmly together. She hopes he's asleep by the time she comes out, but he's awake, blinking into the darkness, watching her movements as she undresses. As she listens to his uneven breathing, she thinks how, actually, they are strangers after all, and this—him visiting—feels like they're only beginning to really know one another. It would be different if they were just friends. She would not feel this weight pressing down on her chest, squeezing her lungs, her heart, so that she feels as though, try as she might, she cannot make herself small enough to fit into the preconceived notions he seems to have of her as his lover. She's relieved when he doesn't try to fondle her. And then she's offended. Doesn't he find her attractive? She replays the events of the previous night. Perhaps he has an erectile problem? She is certain she's not the one with the problem; she thinks of Vincent and smiles, smug. But there's an unpleasant taste in her mouth. She lies awake for almost an hour, listening to Addae's breathing. The yearning is sudden; she turns around, so that she's facing him. She begins to kiss him, slowly at first, and then urgently. It's this way that he wakes up, and this time, he slides into her easily. He is silent, his hands balled into fists pressing down on the bed, his body elevated. This, she knows, is what fucking really is; there is none of the intimacy for which she so desperately yearns from him. Afterward, she turns her back to him, hugs herself, and tries not to cry.

The ride to the airport is quiet, strained. Although she has been feeling crowded, she is taken aback when he announces that he has switched to an earlier flight.

"Something has come up back home," he mumbles, looking away.

She is too proud to press him.

The traffic on the freeway is horrendous and she curses it silently. Words hover in the car, begging to be said, swelling into capital letters in the heat. She keeps her lips pursed. He does not sit facing her but instead keeps his eyes on the road, his arms curled over his duffel bag. He is humming a tune she cannot place, something not quite Ghanaian, but rather with inflections that remind her of Richard Wagner and Hitler. She wants to say, "Russia really got under your skin after all, didn't it?" But she says nothing.

He hugs her for a long time in the departure lounge. She leans into him, enjoying the sentiment of it; a little whiff of regret?

"I'll call you," he says.

"Okay." She tries to sound casual, the disinterest carefully measured in her voice.

It's all for the best, really. They don't know enough about each other. Distance and all of that. But as she watches him amble away, his buttocks bouncing with each step, she's overwhelmed by a sudden deluge of regret. They could have at least been friends, and now, perhaps they may not be able to manage even that.

The disappointment each time she opens Facebook to find a cavernous space next to his name sinks deeper with each passing day. She blames it on the marketing gimmicks of Facebook—the flash of the red dot each time one receives a notification must have links to some psychological machinations. The color works as some sort of trigger, like Pavlov's dog and bell experiment, trains the brain to anticipate. And thus her inexplicable addiction to Facebook, to him. Her own fabricated explanation fails to satisfy her. She finds herself scrolling through his Facebook wall, noting the times he updates his status but omits to write to her.

Finally, she cannot hold it any longer, and types long, furious paragraphs, which she deletes and instead writes, "What went wrong?"

She can imagine him rubbing his lips in the way he is prone to do when lost in thought. She wants to go into a drawn out introspection about the self pity this question evokes, what she hopes is a collective self pity. She cannot say outright, I miss you.

"I really like u, i do," he replies. 'But...u rnt... i thought u... u feel so much older than m n yet... what i mean is that u... u just have too much *experience...*"

It takes a while for the meaning to sink in, but when it finally does, she feels the fire rising to her throat.

She wants to write, how dumb, thinks how inadequate this is, googles for a synonym and types, "how banal. So terribly trite. So bromidic."

"I'm sorry."

"You are so disappointingly ordinary."

When fifteen minutes pass and there is no reply: "You are such a cliché."

After another ten minutes: "So *blah*."

"In my culture, it matters that the woman is… whole."

"Oh, so now you're a cultural man, is that it? How convenient. That's so very sapiosexual right there."

She does not wait for his reply, but quickly logs off. She rubs her eyes, does not understand why she's so upset. She's supposed to be holding back, couldn't wait for him to leave. All the right reasons are there. They are too different. Don't know each other well enough. Distance and all of that.

She picks up her phone, dials Vincent. She knows he'll agree to see her and that when she's with him, she'll wish he were Addae.

SUZANNE USHIE

EMMANUEL IDUMA: What fascinates you about the writing process?

SUZANNE USHIE: The inexplicable thrill that comes with finding a potential good story. I go about with a notebook where I write down ideas as they come. It helps me assemble my thoughts. Writing itself, the actual act of filling a blank Microsoft Word page, doesn't really fascinate me.

EI: I get the sense from your story "Dissembling" that history is happening now; history is not past. What we see every day in Lagos is what will be collated eventually. Aren't we tired of all the class stratification?

SU: "Dissembling" wasn't born out of a need to establish a link between the past and the present. I didn't think of it in terms of history. I wanted to write a story about a wedding, but then again, whoever first said that fiction bears a multiplicity of meaning had a good reason for saying so.

I find human stratification alluring—the amusing arrogance with which people often dictate roles they have no business dictating and the sometimes-unconscious acceptance of those roles by other people. There are traces of this allure in my stories "Dissembling" and "Aunty Rose."

EI: With stratification comes dangerous complicity. In "Dissembling," using the story of Faith and Nenka, you seem to agree with this. This complicity, I believe, arises when those less fortunate agree to be made inferior by those better placed—a constant form of needfulness that surpasses self-esteem.

SU: When "Dissembling" was published in *Sentinel Nigeria* a lot of people had opinions—they hated Nenka, Faith was a wimp, Faith had an inferiority complex, etc. There were some demands for a sequel. Alternative endings were offered. I became forced to provide intelligent answers to all kinds of questions. I hope no one recorded those conversations because I can't defend those answers. I think Faith is a much more difficult character to understand than Nenka. Her motives aren't entirely driven by low self-esteem. It just never strikes her that she can say "no" to Nenka and survive. Faith gives, Nenka takes. It's an imbalance of roles. But those are the only roles they've played, or even understood.

EI: I first got published online in *African Writer*, yet I can't bear to reread those early stories. What effect do you suppose this will have on the emerging writer, given the absence of a proper editorial process? We need these platforms, yes, but what must we sacrifice? Of course, this is not to undermine the efforts of *African Writer*, *Naija Stories*, etc.

SU: The Internet has made life easier for me and tons of other emerging writers. Good editing is still a challenge, but some of these online publications are cash-strapped and short staffed. They may not have money to pay contributors or staff, who works part-time and pro bono, even if they wanted. The first time I received an acceptance, I was pleased that I was going to be published. Editing was the last thing on my mind in that joyous moment. I know some writers who pay close attention to technique in the absence of good editors. I hear stories of writers who, after achieving some success, attempt to have their early stories taken off the Internet. However, some publications try to adhere to certain standards. That being said, no matter how reputable a publication is, I never read any of my stories after they publish them.

EI: While working on your story "The Ghost of Joy," did you play with the idea of working on a story from Ayomide's perspective? I wonder if this is something you could try out next. Benjy, Faulkner's protagonist in *The Sound and the Fury*, is a good example. Just wondering.

SU: The "Ghost of Joy" came to me in the second person. I didn't consider the possibility of telling the story any other way. It's a complete story, so there won't be a sequel.

EI: My idea is that writers can play with alternative approaches to the same story. Maybe this doesn't work for you?

SU: Sometimes it works. Most times it doesn't. The first approach I use usually ends up in the final draft.

EI: Do you suppose that as a newer generation of Nigerian writers we have the task of Nigerianizing the English language? We are aware of how important Soyinka is in this regard, maybe Saro-Wiwa with *Sozaboy* and, Uzodinma Iweala with *Beasts of No Nation*. And of course, Roy's *God of Small Things* set a useful postcolonial antecedent for the indigenization of the English language. In Nigeria, we have a rich tapestry of accents, Pidgin English, ethnocentric mannerisms, etc., we could work with.

251

SU: My characters sometimes say sha, now, sé/shey, na wa, or abeg—common Nigerian speak. But that's as far as it goes. Pidgin isn't my forte. Neither are ethnocentric mannerisms. I leave that to those who do it well.

EI: Have you considered that your stories could prepare you for motherhood, child-raising? I thought of this while reading "The Ghost of Joy," recalling something John Irving said about writing stories because he didn't want to experience the tragedy he described. And I know, being a writer of fiction myself, that often we try to purge ourselves of our nightmares.

SU: I doubt that my stories can prepare me for anything. I wrote a story about a mother raising a son with Down syndrome because I had never read a story like that in a Nigerian setting. Toni Morrison's quote about writing the book you've always wanted to read is an old favorite of mine, which is ironic seeing as I won't read the book after writing it. A friend said she couldn't read "The Ghost of Joy" to the end because it was sad. Later, she admitted to being frightened that an incident in the story could happen to her.

EI: The emerging writer could become carried away by the possibility of renown. If you consider this problematic, can we argue that the need to speak to one's times, the need to emphasize scholarship and not fame, transcends every other aspiration?

SU: At some point every writer reflects on the possibility of success. It's important for writers to be published and read. A wide readership may give way to validation. With validation comes fame. This is not to say that scholarship isn't important.

MFA programs and writing workshops abound for those who choose the formal route. A less structured way for any writer to improve is to keep reading and writing. You learn without even knowing that way.

EI: Which books of the 21st century have influenced your writing most? How?

SU: From Chimamanda Adichie's *Purple Hibiscus* I learned that humanity thrives even in villainy. Eugene made me develop a love-hate relationship with flawed characters. I hope it has influenced my writing.

EI: Do you suppose more writers of fiction should pay attention to creative nonfiction? Are there possible advantages? Possible dangers?

SU: Some writers write fiction and creative nonfiction with equal grace and proficiency. Not every writer is able to achieve this balance, though. A writer friend said she stopped writing creative nonfiction because it had damaged her ability to write fiction. I respect *One Day I Will Write About This Place* for its inventiveness of language and lush prose. It's so beautifully written that I forgot it was nonfiction while reading it.

EI: Joan Didion likens working on fiction to working on a painting, and nonfiction to sculpting. Her thinking revolved around what I consider the difference between static details and malleable ones; in fiction we use details that we mold to suit our characterization, but in nonfiction we essentially work our writing into inflexible details. Is this similar to your creative process?

SU: I don't really write nonfiction. There are times when I feel a story isn't going anywhere, so I back away, read a novel or a Jhumpa Lahiri short story—I love all the stories in *Unaccustomed Earth*—in hopes that I'll find my way back to my own story. I may write non-fiction to help me clear my head in those moments. I don't have a defined creative process for each genre. I just write, or pretend to.

EI: I return to "The Ghost of Joy." I return to your fine story because it reminds me so much of struggles I have experienced, witnessed. For instance, the complexities surrounding an inter-tribal union. Yet you're also aware that there are ramifications of intra-tribal unions. Often, we might consider ourselves progressives to argue for the nullification of such borders, but have you considered the case for tribal pride? That *intra*-tribal unions could perpetuate indigenous languages?

SU: I suppose questions about inter-ethnic unions and culture and language will always come up when people read "The Ghost of Joy." Ayomide's mother, like me, is from Obudu in Cross River state. I like the name Lekan—I'm a bit obsessed with names—so I named Ayomide's father Lekan, and of course he had to be Yoruba for the story to work. There are complexities in every union, be it inter-ethnic or intra-ethnic. My fiction is either set in Calabar, where I grew up, or Lagos, where I live. I've never tried to make a case for ethnic pride. The characters come and I tell their stories.

To my undiscerning writer's eyes, "The Ghost of Joy" is a simple story about a mother's love for her mentally challenged son. I've been told that that love is a reluctant one, borne more out of an absence of alternatives than free will. But I leave critics to do their job and readers, hopefully, to read and find meaning.

EI: Who is closer to your heart, the reader or the critic? Whose opinion weighs more?

SU: The reader.

EI: There's a sense of non-finality in your stories, more or less like you are presenting a showcase of endless possibilities. Is this deliberate?

SU: I've been told that my endings are too abrupt, that I leave stories hanging, that it's frustrating. I wish I could provide one of those profound literary reasons for doing so—endless possibilities and all, like you say. But it isn't deliberate. The story just ends there.

EI: Ama Ata Aidoo makes the point that no one has conveniently defined what it means to be Third World, and I argue that equally no one has sufficiently defined what it means to be second class. Your work suggests that classes exist within the same space, and it sparks the contemplation that the world belongs to all of us, after all. Not the one percent. Not even the 99 percent.

SU: Classes do exist within the same space. I see that every day in Lagos. The world is large enough for everyone to find their place. But what that place is, and how to own it, that's where the challenge lies.

EI: Is there an element of your creative process you are afraid of losing?

SU: I don't have a defined creative process, but I love researching. Making character notes, asking question after question gleefully because the people I pester are too polite to tell me to get lost. My sister christens my characters with beautiful, unusual names. Last year, I harassed her for yet another name so intensely that she finally went, "Okay, okay just name her after me." That story, "From an Empty Place," is in *Fiction Fix*. I'm quite the pest when I get hold of an idea. I wouldn't want to lose that zeal.

EI: The question that comes to me after reading your essay "The Serious Guide to Becoming a Seriously Unfashionable Writer" is whether pop culture conflicts with literary life. Should we escape glamour for the sake of retaining our creative sanity?

SU: I won't offer a decisive solution. It's possible to exist in both worlds. It piques me, though, that female writers of African descent are often stereotyped: angry feminist, Ankara-loving, hair weave despising, and all that jazz. I wrote that piece as a reminder to never take myself seriously, no matter what.

EI: Do you make a distinction, then, between taking yourself seriously and taking your work seriously? I know the answer might be obvious, but in my thinking, the person is never disjointed from the work.

SU: The perception that every writer leaves a piece of themselves in their work has always been there. I'm not sure if it's true—or always true. I take my writing seriously anyway. But myself? That's a story for another day.

EI: Could you describe your living quarters? How does being there every day expand your capacities as a writer?

SU: I live in a one-bedroom apartment. My bedroom has the most soothing pastel green walls. I imagine that the ambience calms me while I write, preferably at night into the early hours of the morning, or at dawn into noon. I write on the couch in my living room, too. I don't know if my small apartment has improved my writing, but I enjoy the solitude it brings. If a sentence looks odd, I read it aloud to know for sure. I laugh when a character amuses me. I frown when a character upsets me. People might be alarmed by this, which is why I prefer to write when I'm alone.

EI: If you ask me, we should call this character-intrusion, this possibility of being enraged by a character. I am always concerned that reality is trivialized as fiction. Do you share this concern?

SU: Not exactly. Perhaps because fiction that closely mirrors reality resonates with me more than any other kind of fiction. I find it very profound. That being said, I love a good book so when I stumble on one, I read and enjoy without trying to analyze its depth or lack of depth. And if the story is particularly haunting, it stays with me for days, months even, afterward. I felt that way after reading *The Color Purple* and *A Thousand Splendid Suns*.

EI: What event or experience do you consider most prominent and most useful in your writing career?

SU: Enid Blyton was the idol of my childhood—an all too familiar tale. I grew up longing to taste ginger beer, dreading to make a face in case the wind suddenly changed, and hoping the dining chair would develop wings and whisk me away to a faraway land. I also read Achebe's *Chike and the River*, Saro-Wiwa's *Tambari*, L. Solaru's *Time for Adventure*, and many other books, but none of them held the magical allure of Blyton's world.

So one morning, during general assembly in my primary school, I read a story called "The Bird Egg Adventure," which I had written for an English assignment. Like my previous stories and the novel I was writing then, it was very Blytonish, with a secret garden, a kind fairy, a mischievous elf, a bird egg that didn't want to be found, and a precocious bird egg hunter that looked suspiciously like me. The students oohed and aahed as I read. Naturally this pleased me. Then the principal looked at me sternly and said that I didn't write the story, that I must have stolen it from a book. We argued back and forth until I was asked to leave the stage. Now that I'm older, I understand why she found it implausible that a seven-year-old girl in Calabar could write about a foreign world with such sureness. After a few horrific attempts to write about unfamiliar worlds, I've now learned to write about what I really know.

EI: How do you juggle your writing with money-making? As I guess you are not full-time. I like when the writer Novuyo Tshuma refers to something of this sort as the nuisance of living. Is anything a nuisance for you when it has no bearing on your artistic work?

SU: Because I love writing fiction, I always make time for it no matter how hectic my full-time job as a copywriter gets. I don't try to compartmentalize or equalize my experiences as a fiction writer and a copywriter, even though my experiences as an ad woman occasionally show in my work. "Above the Line and Unforced Errors," an early unpublished story, is set in advertising agencies. It's a fun, laidback, half-glamorous world, and I've met the most intriguing and talented people there. Unsurprisingly, they inspire some characters in my fiction.

EI: Will you be famous for long fiction or for shorter work?

SU: I don't know if I'll be famous for anything. Nonetheless, I hope my long fiction will be read someday.

February 29, 2012

FINE RED DUST

Suzanne Ushie

The Fasten Seatbelt sign goes off. My heartbeat slows and flattens my fear. I stretch my legs as far as economy allows, willing myself not to grip the armrest like I did when we left Lagos. Two flight attendants—a boy who looks as nervous as me and a girl wearing bright red lipstick—push a trolley laden with pastries, cashews nuts, Nescafé and Chivita juice down the aisle. When they stop at my seat, I go for coffee and a packet of cashew nuts. The girl pours a thin stream of condensed milk into a disposable cup, those red lips twisted sideways. Her lipstick is well confined to the bow that borders her lips. It isn't a color I would wear. It is more vermilion than red, somewhat unusual and rather earthy, almost like the clay in Aunty Adidi's house.

Aunty Adidi's street in Federal Housing was narrow with speed bumps in sequential strips, too elaborate for the quiet estate with red brick bungalows hemmed in by neat ixora hedges. I jumped each time Papa's black Volvo went over them. "Unnecessary things," he would say to me in the rearview mirror, as though they could possibly stop him from driving to her place straight from the tennis club every Saturday. With the windows down and Bob Marley on the stereo, the humid Calabar air mingled with his sweat and cologne, he laughed and said Aunty Adidi was right: Marley was a genius.

I liked her compound. It was big and green and clean. There was a mountain of clay in the backyard that I first mistook for an anthill, a few paces away from fraying twine from which a row of identical yellow pegs clasped her clothes. They swayed and danced in the wind, stretching from an almond tree to a coconut tree with the thickest trunk I had ever seen. In the warm shade of

261

those trees, I sank my hands into gluey red clay and molded teacups and saucers, which she displayed on the sideboard in her living room, as though they were priceless artifacts.

"Dirt does not kill children," she would say when Papa tried to stop me from rubbing my dirty hands in my hair. Her eyebrows were thick, unlike the trim arc of Mama's, and they twitched when she told me that the carpet grass in her garden wasn't prickly because elves had trimmed their sharp tips. I was nine, too old to believe things like that, but it didn't stop her. Her garage was cluttered with old tins of Dulux paint in exotic colors like Venetian Crystal and Martian Skies. The walls of her house often went from one color to another in expert strokes that made it difficult to spot the holes left by long removed nails.

Papa acted different, erratic even, when he was with her. He scolded me the time I removed her stethoscope from an unfriendly-looking black bag on her dining table. He laughed when I pressed its metallic coolness to his hairy chest, his heartbeat a steady dum dum dum in my ear. He frowned when Aunty Adidi told him to dish *afang* from the pot. But the next minute he declared—a stringy green leaf caught in the gap between his front teeth—that it was the best soup he had ever tasted.

They were a secret between Papa and me, those visits. He didn't have to say I shouldn't tell Mama. I just knew not to; so I said nothing when he told her that we already had lunch at the tennis club, or when she asked me why there was sand in my hair. I saw her mouth tighten whenever Papa came home late, eavesdropped at the living room door when Aunty Kate told her that Aunty Adidi was Papa's girlfriend. "That harlot has sold her shame in the market. My dear, don't worry. At least you have your boutique on Marian Road." She hissed and stared at the tusk-shaped gold pendant resting on Mama's floral blouse. Mama looked small.

It wasn't long before that blouse, like Mama's other clothes, grew tight around her stomach. Her caramel skin lightened and she complained that Papa's cologne made her nauseous. Papa's regular trips to Abuja for government contracts stopped. Everything he said either began or ended with, "When the baby comes." Then those men who told Papa things like, "Your people want you to contest for governor," started coming with their slippery smiles. One night they drank bottle after bottle of Remy Martin, and then staggered out of our house, leaving dark patches of spirit on the milk-colored couch. Mama grabbed Papa's shirt and said it was bad enough he was an adulterer but did he want to add alcoholism to his résumé too? Their voices were so loud that it seemed our house had no walls. I turned over in my bed and squeezed the bed sheet, one with tiny drawings of Disney characters that Papa had bought in America, and imagined I was molding castles of clay in Aunty Adidi's backyard.

*

The Fasten Seatbelt sign comes on. "Mild turbulence," the pilot announces. The tall man in 14B turns and asks if someone is waiting for me in Calabar. When I say nothing, he shrugs and continues reading the in-flight magazine. Outside the window, the clouds look like wisps of smoke frozen in time. The wings of the plane slice through them easily, like they aren't there. It reminds me of the way I feel when Wale's friends at the country club tease him for dating me just so my blood will keep him baby-faced. I always defeat the urge to say there is nothing babyish about his features. His cheekbones are unusually high and sharp, as though they were Photoshopped on a computer and then attached to his face. Sometimes I'm convinced that Wale and his friends are bound only by their pedigrees—the UK university degrees, the Victoria Island streets named after their fathers. Other irrational times, though, I'm certain it's the ludicrousness of their marriages—the fact that all of their wives live in America—that binds them. It gives me a delicious and wicked pleasure, the thought of Wale's wife moaning about the Lagos sun during visits. I struggle to open the packet of cashews. It is so stiff that I begin to think it wasn't made for humans. I give up and tuck it inside my bag.

I hadn't known what the structured purple bag was when Wale gave it to me on my birthday. Not until my colleague Munachiso checked the seams and said it was an *original* Birkin. She giggled like it was normal for me to own a bag slightly cheaper than my Honda Accord. Her hands and head moved when she laughed and the child-like effect thrilled me. One day, I told her about Aunty Adidi. She listened without fidgeting once, her lips slightly apart, and then took me in her arms. Munachiso could be dramatic like that. But she didn't have the look I saw in Aunty Kate's eyes, that of someone who listened to your problems just so they could deride you. So I didn't mind that she often peered over the white square separating our cubicles in the PR firm and asked about Mama. Once, I told her that Mama's voice sounded phlegmy on the phone, that I knew Mama was ill although she denied it. Munachiso said I was lucky to have Mama. Her own mother lit a circle of candles in their living room and, in a disturbingly pleasant tone, told her to step inside and pray for the arrow of God to locate her future husband. Shortly after, Munachiso moved out.

*

Papa and Aunty Adidi's voices drifted into the backyard through the open French windows. "Give me one good reason why I should believe in your Catholic saints," I heard her say. A gust of hot wind drowned Papa's heated reply. Of course I had heard their faith-driven arguments before, her idea that Catholics were idol worshippers, his idea that Protestants were misguided fanatics—ideas I was too young to grasp—so I should have been content to eavesdrop from my usual spot under the trees. But I wasn't. When I fell, the cut on my knee wasn't that big. It was the surprising color of my blood—more thick black than bright red—that made it seem horrific. I screamed when Aunty Adidi dabbed iodine on it. I wailed when Papa consoled me. I continued screaming until Aunty Adidi said, "Leave her alone. When she's tired she'll stop." Her mocking indifference silenced my sobs. Just before the afternoon air turned chilly, Papa and I went to High Quality and bought vanilla ice cream. As the cone melted into goo in my palm, I became more certain that Papa was rewarding me for being brave. It was so easy to tell Mama I had slipped on the stairs at the tennis club.

The first time I slept with Wale, he bit the scar, a light brown crescent on my knee, and laughed at how pliable it was. He said he liked all my flaws in a way that made flaws sound enchanting. He teased me, saying the moment he saw me in the queue at Shoprite, something in my cart told him I was a woman who wasn't ashamed to be cared for. "You're not one of those girls who say they're independent when they really want a man." I knew his wife's spirit was too far away to stir; yet I tiptoed around his Ikoyi mansion that night. And as the black marble cooled my toes, I thought of Aunty Adidi, and wondered if she ever tiptoed too.

*

The headrest is too hard, the coffee too bitter, the ache in my lower back too strong. I move in my seat and wonder if Mama felt a similar pain when the cramps came and took the baby. Papa started going to Abuja again. There was a new democratic government, which meant there was a new set of people to suck up to. Mama refused to move to Abuja when he was appointed to head a quasi-governmental organization. Tourism was booming in Calabar; she wanted to convert her boutique to a travel agency. Aunty Kate said she should go and fight for her marriage; otherwise, Aunty Adidi would win. But there was no Aunty Adidi when I went to visit Papa in Abuja; even though sometimes when I came back from Grand Square the house smelled like her, even though his bedroom walls were a brilliant azure I knew he couldn't possibly have chosen. Back in Calabar Mama asked me if I had seen anything. I told myself that a lie by omission wasn't really a lie, and said no.

*

My bladder is full, but I'm wary of brushing against 14B to get to the lavatory. I find myself longing for the generous legroom in business class, for the freedom to strut past the elegant people with the ease of someone who knows they are elegant too. I remember how, with a dull plunk, my pearl earring fell into the toilet on a flight to Abuja three months ago. And how, in a surging frenzy, I took off the one I still had on and flung it in, and then watched the two cream studs drown in the swirl of blue water. In the cabin I told Wale I had lost my earrings. He shrugged off the story and said he could buy me a hundred more. I had expected his anger, had even prepared for it, but it was the implied meaning that things could easily be replaced I couldn't handle. I ate a sponge cake with a tremor in my hands, and when the plane took a sudden dip, I wished I could open a window and float away on a cloud.

The trembling was gone the next morning. Wale was gone, too, attending the economic summit somewhere. A single red rose lay on his pillow. I plucked the wilting petals and felt him sliding down my thigh. Later, I drew the taupe drapes apart and flecks of sunlight, the color of the insides of an orange, sparkled on my face. As I rode the elevator down, I said our Hilton suite number—one thousand and three—and the floor it was on—eleven—over and over again so I wouldn't lose my way. An Indian couple walked into the elevator hand-in-hand as I stepped out. I liked that they held each other freely. I smiled at the brown-skinned woman and was pleased when she smiled back. In the overpriced souvenir shop on the ground floor, I strolled around admiring abstract paintings and handmade beads. I was stunned to see Aunty Adidi standing beside a dour-faced shop assistant.

"Andameye, is that you?" she asked.

At first I fooled around with the idea of pretending I didn't know her. Finally, I said, "Yes, Aunty."

I shouldn't have called her that. She wasn't my *aunty* was she? But I had never considered the possibility that we would meet again, or that she would recognize me if we did, so the "aunty" came effortlessly.

"I knew it. There aren't too many people in the world with that forehead."

I might have believed that she was happy to see me if she wasn't so slow to smile.

She picked up a wooden carving of an elephant from a glass shelf. "Hmm. I saw something like this in Sudan. And I still don't understand the thinking behind it."

I found it odd, the way she switched topics like that, as though she were resuming a conversation. I wanted to ask where she had been, what she had been up to. Instead I asked if she lived in Abuja. She shook her head. She was visiting. She used to work with the Technical Aid Corps just outside Khartoum. It suited her. I could just see her telling swollen-bellied children that hunger doesn't kill. She placed the carving back on the shelf. I stared at her dried-up hands pressed against the poorly carved tusks, and wished they could smooth the lines on her face, even out the past.

"How is your father?" she asked, her head tilted haughtily. I wondered if she had heard about his latest girlfriend, the barely-twenty undergraduate whom his cook and driver called madam.

"He's fine."

The silence that followed was unbearable.

"How long were you in Sudan?" I asked, because it seemed fair, polite, to ask.

"Six years. I'm already beginning to wish I hadn't come back. Up until now they haven't given me my severance pay. In fact I came to Abuja to try and sort things out."

It must have been the downward curve of her mouth that made me say I would help. After all, Wale knew the right people. An alien sensation gripped my stomach as I stored her number. Munachiso called this feeling "purpose" when I described it. She had a name for everything.

*

I reach up and close the overhead air vent. "Cold?" 14B asks with a slanted smile. Again I say nothing and he mutters, "Ahn ahn. is it a crime to talk to someone?" Red Lips goes about raising tray tables, collecting soiled napkins, telling passengers to fasten their seatbelts. As we begin our descent into Calabar, I look out the window at the foliage spread out like a giant green carpet below.

The plane bumps on to the runway and the wind chases us into this small town where everybody knows everybody's story.

Outside the plane I inhale deeply. The air is so fresh, so still that I wish I can trap it in my bag and take it back to Lagos with me. In the airport restroom I read the writings on the door—*Capo 4 life, Jesus is coming repent now*—with amusement while I urinate. Afterward I switch on my BlackBerry; Wale's messages demand to be read in the blinking red glow of the indicator light. I ignore them. At the taxi stand I am too tired to argue over the fare. Besides, there is something endearing about the driver's insistence on opening the door for me. I see a huge Destination Cross River billboard in the distance and remember the day it went up, how Papa said the pretty blue and white text reminded him of a warm sky in August, how Aunty Adidi laughed and said he should just wait and see that it was all a charade.

The driver is rather chatty. He says the government has banned *alalok*. I am confused for a while, but then it dawns on me: *alalok* and *okada* are the same—commercial motorbikes. I shift uneasily on the see-through factory wrapper on the seat. Mama doesn't know I am coming.

*

When Wale said the head accountant at the Foreign Affairs Ministry had disappeared, I held back from slamming my fist on the table. We were at a breakfast buffet in the Protea Hotel. I pushed a tasteless vegetable salad around a side plate. His eyes darkened when he saw my clenched fist and he called for a Chapman cocktail, an unusually watery one I couldn't drink. I stirred it distractedly with my straw, the ice cubes clinking against one another, while he stroked a spot on my forefinger and asked who Aunty Adidi was, then added, with a wink, "I don't mind if she's your lover, you know." On the table next to ours, two women glared at our entwined hands, their blouses shapeless and identical, their faces clouded with righteous judgment.

"Don't mind them," he said when I pulled away. "They're just jealous because you're my girlfriend."

The word "girlfriend" had a radiant irreverence that irritated me. He reached out to caress my thigh under the stiff table linen. I swatted his hand away. He leaned close enough for me to smell the wine on his breath, saying, "Stop being difficult."

The phone calls to Aunty Adidi began. At first I was careful, then I became unrestrained, unafraid. I made up the kind of boyfriend I wanted her to think I had: a man who didn't delete my BlackBerry messages immediately after he read them, a man who knew why the tremor in my hand was back, because I didn't know why and nothing made sense anymore. She listened and said, "Aww," then said the clay in her backyard had hardened since there was no one to play with it. I laughed with the heady thrill of nostalgia. And when I remembered the clay teacups and saucers on her sideboard, something tight and heavy coiled inside me, so I said my contact in the ministry was doing everything to make sure she got paid. But she was getting by. Her salary as a visiting consultant at the University of Calabar Teaching Hospital wasn't bad, she told me over lunch at Yellow Chili when she came to visit. In the sunlit interior where she sucked her breath because the fresh fish pepper soup was too spicy, I tried not to stare at the seamless skin on her ring finger, or wonder why she looked so small. It was a different smallness, the kind that comes with aging, nothing like the way Mama had looked when Aunty Kate told her about Papa and Aunty Adidi. Soon the mojito mellowed me, left a minty buzz inside me, and I was laughing a little too loudly when she asked about my "young man," when the bald waiter who cleared our table joked that madam wasn't as used to pepper as her daughter.

*

"This yoke must be broken, O'," Munachiso said one afternoon.

I glanced up from the press release I was typing. "Ehn?"

"That weird thing you have with that woman. It isn't normal. It's sick."

Sick. I couldn't believe she had used such a vapid word. I glared at the fair skin I envied, the dove-gray pencil skirt that fell above her spotless knees. I didn't speak to her for the rest of the day.

*

We are now at the traffic light on IBB Way. The scenery is bleak and uncluttered, then I realize what is missing: no hawkers selling phone cards and gala sausage rolls and fizzy drinks, no beggars thrusting cancerous sores at me, no *okadas* slicing through lanes of traffic. Lagos has coated its chaotic sheen on my skin. The green light appears. We circle the roundabout and go up Marian Hill, past the bronze Mary Slessor statue, down the tree-lined road where the zoo once sat. Our street is the same: unpaved and dotted with small puddles. When we stop at the gate it looks old and rusty; or perhaps it just seems so because I haven't seen it in three years. I press four brittle, five hundred naira notes into the driver's hands and he says, "God bless you. You'll marry a good man." His gratitude over money that rightly belongs to him embarrasses me.

The compound is larger than I remember, the fence now a disturbing shade of green. I feel silly as I knock. This is my real home after all; not my Lekki apartment with sliding windows that let in hot air even on cold days. The door opens and Mama is there. She doesn't seem surprised to see me. We hug, a brief press of our bodies, and when she steps back I see that her hair is a mass of silver streaks, her front teeth are yellowing. The foyer is stuffy, almost as if she never opens the front door. I can tell, from the stain in the beige carpet, that she rarely withdraws the money I pay into her bank account every month.

I keep my suitcase on my bed, marvel at the sameness of my room. Grainy pictures with photographers' signatures chronicle my university odyssey. Rocks of various shapes and sizes, collected during geology fieldtrips across the country, clutter the reading table. I pick up a translucent pink quartz and squeeze it, foolishly imagining that something, a teardrop, will ooze out. I laugh when nothing happens. At the dining table the *eba* is hard, just how I like it. When I praise Mama her smile soothes me.

"How is work?" she asks when my soup is almost finished.

"Fine."

She picks up a glass of water. "You should talk to your father. He can help you get a job in Shell or Mobil," she says after a long drink.

I don't tell her that I don't want to work in Shell or Mobil, that the last time I phoned Papa he said hello, all breathy and giggly, and I hung up when I heard his girlfriend fretting in the background.

Now Mama's eyes hold mine. "So you heard that she's dead."

The silence stretches.

"Yes, Mama," I say at last.

"I know that your father used to take you to her house. I'm not stupid." She pulls a basin of water close, washes her hands and dries them on a gingham towel. The *eba* on my plate suddenly looks lumpy, ugly.

272

"So that's why you came home." She gets up. I long for her to shake me, hit me, do something. Instead she says, quietly, "Do whatever you have to do," and walks away. I listen to the measured music of her feet, and wish I could patch her broken strings.

As the taxi speeds along the expressway that evening, I think of the way things might have played out if Aunty Adidi's sister hadn't answered her phone two weeks ago and said, with the calmness that disguises grief, that she was dead. A ruptured appendix. "You need closure," were Munachiso's matter-of-fact words when I told her that after I heard the news, I scrubbed all my pots with an iron sponge and their restored sheen made me feel stained, so I scrubbed my shaky palms until they turned a sore, blubbery pink and I stopped when they began to bleed.

My bag vibrates. I open it and read a text from Wale: *Why aren't you picking up your phone? Call me back.* I press delete.

A large banner dangles from a tangle of electric wires at the entrance to Aunty Adidi's street. IN MEMORIEM, the misspelled headline above a black and white picture of her says. I settle the taxi fare and enter her compound, a landscape of cars and people in clothes made of the same black and yellow patterned ankara fabric. They look like a swarm of honeybees perched on white plastic chairs, on short stools, the fence, and any other place where the foil packets of *jollof* rice and fried beef will reach them easily, some of them swaying to music from the gospel band on the podium. The coconut tree looms above in the backyard. The mountain of clay is now a hard hill of earth—just like Aunty Adidi had said. I scratch at it until some clay settles in my palm.

A condolence register is spread on a table by the front door: *Rest in peace. You'll be missed.* I think of writing something that isn't contrived. Because the words don't come, I go inside. The living room is dimly lit, the walls awash with fresh turquoise paint, the air charged with memories unforgotten. An open coffin sits on the dining table. A woman rolls on the floor scratching her shrunken virgin hair, screaming "Chei! Adidi you have finished me, O!" The guests look at her, then at each other, the way people do when a genuine show of grief reminds them of their own mortality. Anyone can guess, from her wild eyebrows and the fierce set of her jaw, that she is Aunty Adidi's sister. I look inside the coffin, half-fearing someone will stop me. Her skin is withered, as black as coffee with no milk. I'm not sure, but I think I see a small smile on her face. Maybe I'm just hoping she is amused that the sharp pain she felt turned out to be no ordinary stomach ache. I want to pull her close and ask why she is so still, why she is wearing this ridiculously showy ivory dress. I imagine her body weakening, emptying, as life left and a swift serenity took over. I back away.

I am almost at the door when a timid voice calls out. But I keep walking even though the fiery knot in my chest tells me I am the person being called. A warm palm touches my arm. I turn around and see a teenage girl whom I recognize from the living room. She holds out a familiar purple shape and says I forgot my bag. I hope my voice doesn't betray my relief as I collect it and thank her. As I make my way through used plates on the floor and people slouched sluggishly in their seats outside, I wonder if she thinks I'm crazy or forgetful. Then I wonder why I even care what a stranger thinks of me. The thought quickens my step and for a giddy moment I feel as though I'm walking on new limbs. I like the warmth of the wind on my skin. It is a night of starless skies, yet I go down the street without stumbling once. I will break up with Wale. I say it again and again in my head until it sounds plausible. What will Munachiso call this? Courage, perhaps. Or victory. I raise my left hand to do a mock salute and find my fist clenched. I open it; a lump of red earth unfurls. The clay from the backyard. I must have carried it around unknowingly. I leave it in my moist palm for a little while, and then I let it go.

CONTRIBUTORS

ABDUL ADAN was born in Somalia and grew up in Kenya. His work has appeared in *African Writing, Jungle Jim, Arab World Books, StoryTime, Kwani?, SCARF,* and the *African Roar* anthology. He studies literature at Washington University in St. Louis. Adan is currently working on a collection of stories and a screenplay for a Somali feature film (in collaboration with Hot Sun Films).

AYOBAMI ADEBAYO was born in 1988. Her short stories have appeared in *The Weaverbird Collection, Farafina Magazine, Saraba Magazine, East Jasmine Review,* and *African Writing Online.* Her work was highly commended in the 2009 Commonwealth short story competition. In 2012, she was a writer in residence at Writers Omi International (Ledig House), New York. In 2013, she participated in the 5th Femrite residency in Uganda. Her first novel, *Stay With Me,* was shortlisted for the *Kwani?* Manuscript Prize and is forthcoming. She holds B.A. and M.A. degrees in English literature from Obafemi Awolowo University, Ile Ife. She is currently pursuing her M.A. in prose fiction at the University of East Anglia.

DAMI AJAYI is a medical doctor, poet, short story writer, occasional essayist, former blogger, book reviewer, and fiction editor for *Saraba Magazine.* His works have appeared in several journals in the United States, Canada, Cameroon, Europe, India, and of course, his home country, Nigeria. He lives in Lagos.

RICHARD ALI, a Nigerian lawyer, was born in Kano and grew up in the resort town of Jos. Author of the warmly received 2012 novel *City of Memories*, Ali was a runner-up in the 2008 John la Rose Short Story Competition. In March 2008, he was selected among 50 other emerging Nigerian writers to participate in the British Council's Radiophonics Workshop. He is a co-owner of Parresia Publishers Ltd, home to award winning authors, including Helon Habila, Abubakar Adam Ibrahim, and Chika Unigwe.

Ali is presently on the Board of the Pan-African Transcultural Academy, chaired by Beverly Nambozo Nsengiyunva, which is at the forefront of redefining African literature and its study. Ali has attended several residencies, including the Chimamanda Adichie-led Farafina workshop in 2012 and the 2013 Granta-British Council New Writing workshop in Nairobi.

ABUBAKAR ADAM IBRAHIM's debut short story collection, *The Whispering Trees*, has received wide and critical acclaim since its publication in 2012 by Parresia Publishers (Lagos). The title story was shortlisted for the prestigious Caine Prize for African Writing in 2013 and the collection was long-listed for the inaugural Etisalat Prize for Fiction.

Ibrahim, who was born in Jos, Nigeria, is also a 2013 Gabriel Garcia Marquez Fellow and winner of the 2007 BBC Africa Performance Prize, as well as the 2008 Amatu Braide Prize for Prose. He also won the International Short Story Day Chain Gang Challenge as part of the 2012 Sextet Pen. His short fiction has appeared in *Sentinel Nigeria* and on Africanwriter.com, African-writing.com, and Hackwriter.com, among others.

EMMANUEL IDUMA, born in 1989, is the author of the novel *Farad* (Parresia, 2012). He has worked as editor of 3bute.com, co-publisher of *Saraba Magazine*, and Director of Research and

Concept Development for Invisible Borders. In 2013, his novel *Becoming God* was long-listed for the *Kwani?* Manuscript Prize.

A lawyer by training, he works as a writer and art critic. He is studying for his M.F.A. in art criticism and writing at the School of Visual Arts, New York.

DANGO MKANDAWIRE stumbled on the pen by accident and after musing over the curious obstacle, found it to be sometimes an anchor, other times a beacon, and always a beautiful mirror. He spends his days doing business intelligence and sometimes fancies that magically, one day, the numbers in the spreadsheets will morph into fluttering colors and swallow him whole into a better world. He lives in Blantyre, Malawi and every morning upon waking, faces the direction of the Lake of Stars.

DONALD MOLOSI is a U.S.-based, Botswana-born actor-writer. He has written and performed a number of one-man shows that have appeared off-Broadway, including the noted *Today It's Me* (2010) about Philly Lutaaya, the first African to publicly declare he had AIDS, and *Blue, Black, and White* (2011), which earned him both a Best Actor Award at the Dialogue One Festival and a Best Solo Award for an off-Broadway performance. He writes afrocentric poetry and fiction and is currently working on a poetry collection that articulates African identity within the continent as well in the Western context.

SHAUN RANDOL, an essayist, critic, and interviewer, is the founder and editor in chief of *The Mantle,* an online forum for emerging critical voices from around the world. Randol is an Associate Fellow at the World Policy Institute and a member of PEN American Center and the National Book Critics Circle. He lives in Queens, New York.

NOVUYO ROSA TSHUMA, from Zimbabwe, is the author of *Shadows* (Kwela, 2013). Her short fiction has won the Yvonne Vera Award and has been shortlisted for the Zimbabwe Achievers Literature Award. She has been a participant in both the Caine Prize and Farafina Trust Writing workshops and is a fellow at the Iowa Writers' Workshop.

SUZANNE USHIE has a B.A. in English and literary studies from the University of Calabar and an M.A. in creative writing (prose fiction) from the University of East Anglia, where she awarded the African Bursary for Creative Writing. Her stories have appeared in several publications, including *Open Wide Magazine, Fiction Fix, Overtime,* and *23 Small Good Things.* She lives in Lagos.